Advanced
Turbo Prolog®
Programming

Howard W. Sams & Company
Hayden Books

Related Titles

Understanding Artificial Intelligence
Henry C. Mishkoff

**Crash Course in Artificial Intelligence
and Expert Systems**
Louis E. Frenzel, Jr.

**Mastering Expert Systems
with Turbo Prolog**
Carl Townsend

Expert Systems in AI
Thomas C. Bartee, Editor-in-Chief
(forthcoming)

Advanced C Primer++
Stephen Prata, The Waite Group

**C with Excellence:
Programming Proverbs**
Henry F. Ledgard with John Tauer

**C Programmer's Guide
to Serial Communications**
Joe Campbell

**C Primer Plus,
Revised Edition**
*Mitchell Waite, Stephen Prata,
and Donald Martin, The Waite Group*

Turbo C Programming for the IBM
Robert Lafore, The Waite Group
(forthcoming)

Quick C Programming
Carl Townsend
(forthcoming)

MS-DOS® Bible
Steven Simrin, The Waite Group

Discovering MS-DOS®
Kate O'Day, The Waite Group

MS-DOS® Developer's Guide
*John Angermeyer and Kevin Jaeger,
The Waite Group*

Tricks of the MS-DOS® Masters
*John Angermeyer, Rich Fahringer,
Kevin Jaeger, and Dan Shafer, The Waite Group*

*For the retailer nearest you, or to order directly from the publisher,
call 800-428-SAMS. In Indiana, Alaska, and Hawaii call 317-298-5699.*

Advanced
Turbo Prolog®
Programming

Dan Shafer

HOWARD W. SAMS & COMPANY

A Division of Macmillan, Inc.
4300 West 62nd Street
Indianapolis, Indiana 46268 USA

International Standard Book Number: 0-672-22573-5
Library of Congress Catalog Card Number: 87-81110

Acquisitions Editor: *James S. Hill*
Manuscript Editor: *Susan Pink Bussiere, Techright*
Designer: *T. R. Emrick*
Illustrator: *Ralph E. Lund*
Cover Art: *Visual Graphic Services, Indianapolis*
　　　　　Keith J. Hampton, Designer
　　　　　Debi Stewart, Illustrator
Indexer: *Sandi Schroeder, Schroeder Editorial Services*
Compositor: *Shepard Poorman Communications, Indianapolis*

Printed in the United States of America

Trademark Acknowledgments

*To the memory of Sean Daniel. Your time with us was so short,
but where you are now is so much better.*

Contents

Preface

Prolog is an exciting and powerful language. Turbo Prolog from Borland International has not only popularized this language, but also presented the world with a high-speed implementation.

Many Prolog purists insist that Turbo Prolog lacks too many features of "Standard Prolog" for it to be considered a "true Prolog." They have described Turbo Prolog as a cross between Pascal and Prolog, or a "toy Prolog." I wrote this book in part to dispel the notion that Turbo Prolog is anything less than a serious and powerful language. It does lack some of the features you might expect in a more traditional implementation of the language. And it requires variable typing and predicate declaration, two programming disciplines that have been anathema to Prolog programmers everywhere.

But like all tradeoffs, these omissions have positive aspects as well. They impose discipline on the programmer, requiring him or her to think through the programming process and the logic of the code in advance.

Turbo Prolog cannot do everything that more full-bodied versions of the language can do. But it can do a lot. This book is proof of its power.

Advanced Turbo Prolog Programming addresses design considerations and issues that are often omitted from other books about this AI language. Some of the highlights are:

- a thorough discussion of modular programming using Turbo Prolog's project approach
- detailed explanations of how to interface programs written in Turbo Prolog to code written in other languages as well as to the operating system
- a solid introduction to natural language processing in Turbo Prolog, including context-free grammars and augmented transition networks (ATNs) and a full ATN parser

- more than a dozen helpful list manipulation routines not included in Turbo Prolog that will make your Prolog programming life much easier

- an analysis of several helpful and entertaining programs written in Turbo Prolog, including two that demonstrate how to simulate the ability to call predicates within Turbo Prolog

- a discussion of how to use the Turbo Prolog Toolbox routines to access data contained in Lotus 1-2-3 and dBASE III files

Acknowledgments

I have many people to thank for this book's appearance. Foremost are my agent, Bill Gladstone, and the people at Howard W. Sams & Co. who believed and persevered even when I kept changing the book's contents and scope. Jim Hill, Jim Rounds, Greg Michael, and their colleagues and staff are due a big vote of thanks.

Dr. Michael A. Covington at the University of Georgia performed the technical review. His contribution to the quality of the finished product is difficult to overstate, though any mistakes remain my responsibility. How he fit this project into his busy schedule of writing his own Prolog book, lectures, seminars, and classes is beyond me.

The programming is largely not my own. I chose, rather than reinventing the wheel, to search out interesting and well-written Turbo Prolog programs to present and explain. In some ways, this is similar to the "old school" of learning to program. It works best for me, and I hope you find it helpful as well. For the most part, these programs appear in part 4 and part 5, where the authors are acknowledged.

A very special note of thanks goes to Tom Emerson of Lynrick Acres, VT. Tom contacted me on CompuServe early in the development of this book and offered to do an ATN parser in Turbo Prolog. His work is sound and imaginative, and it says something about the future of this country that he is in high school and already so capable a programmer. Nice work, Tom!

Dr. Fernando C. N. Pereira is a luminary in the world of natural language processing and Prolog. He has worked in the field nearly as long as anyone. The many hours I spent with him on a related project enlightened me considerably on the subject of language and Prolog. He shared a prepublication copy of his compiled lecture notes on Prolog and natural language—a major contribution to my understanding of the subject.

Dan, Mike, and Kelly at Borland International's Turbo Prolog technical support desk were incredibly helpful in clarifying issues and answering questions. Neil Rubenking, a CompuServe regular, and Jeff Gordon, another

CompuServe friend and fellow Prolog programmer, made frequent good suggestions that led to ideas presented in this book.

During the pressures of book production, Kathy Ewing of Howard W. Sams and Susan Bussiere, my editor in Mattapoisett, MA, were very patient as I kept finding more to add and rummaged about for answers to their questions.

Finally, of course, my wife, Carolyn, and our daughters showed infinite patience while I wrote this book. I cannot express the contribution they make to whatever success my work and career enjoy, now or in the future.

Introduction

Who the Book Is For

Advanced Turbo Prolog Programming is not for beginning Prolog programmers. It does not explain Prolog programming concepts except as new, advanced ideas are introduced. It presumes that the reader knows Prolog and has at least a nodding acquaintance with Turbo Prolog. If you are new to this language, consider starting with my *Turbo Prolog Primer,* also published by Howard W. Sams & Co.

If you have some experience programming small applications in Turbo Prolog and are anxious to extend your knowledge of its capabilities and your facility with some of its intricacies, you'll find this book exactly right for you.

What You'll Need

To use this book most effectively, you should have access to Turbo Prolog and an IBM PC, XT, or AT, or a compatible computer system. For a few exercises, access to the Turbo Prolog Toolbox from Borland International is also useful.

What Is in This Book?

This book is divided into five parts. Part 1 (chapters 1-6) discusses modular programming and the use of Turbo Prolog's powerful project concept. Part 2 (chapters 7-11) explains how to program Turbo Prolog so it can interact with programs written in other languages and access DOS routines. Part 3 (chapters 12-14) covers natural language processing, an exciting AI application for which Prolog is well-suited.

The programs in part 4 and 5 serve two purposes. First, they solve real problems or provide interesting applications. Second, they can offer a fascinating learning experience if you take time to run, analyze, change, and study them. Part 4 (chapters 15-20) collects a number of Turbo Prolog problem-solving applications. Finally, part 5 presents (in chapters 21 and 22) some useful Turbo Prolog utilities that extend the language's power considerably.

Program Listings

All the programs can be typed from the text. Programs in chapters 16-22 can also be obtained by accessing CompuServe Information Service (CIS). If you have a computer and a modem, you can join CompuServe. The programs are then free except for phone and computer charges, which are minimal for the time it takes to download these programs. They are stored in data libraries in two forums: the AI/Expert Magazine forum (named AIE) and the Borland Programming Forum (named BORPRO). I am not supplying the program names and data library locations because they are subject to change.

If you have access to CIS, just log into the proper forum, go to the data library area, find the Prolog areas, and then use the BROwse command to find the file(s). Every program stored in a CIS data library is stored with a set of associated keywords. For example, to find the mortgage calculator covered in chapter 17, go to the appropriate data library and type

```
BRO /KEY:MORTGAGE
```

and the program's name will appear. After you know the program's name, use the DOWnload command to retrieve the file from CIS and store it on your computer. (If you have problems downloading files from CIS, leave a note in the forum and you'll get plenty of help. If you like, you can send your note to me by EasyPlex electronic mail at my address, 71246,402.)

If you are not a CIS subscriber and don't want to become one, I can send you a PC-compatible disk of the programs in chapters 16-22. Please send your request with a check or money order for $10.00 to:

Dan Shafer

277 Hillview Ave.

Redwood City, CA 94062

Note that this is *not* a charge for the programs; the authors have contributed them either to the public domain or for this book. The fee simply compensates me for the time and supplies to copy, package, and mail the programs.

Let's Talk Prolog

If you have any comments, I'd enjoy hearing from you. You can reach me on CompuServe (by EasyPlex electronic mail at my address, 71246,402) and at the address listed in the previous section. I'm always interested in talking about Prolog, AI, and expert systems. It's how I learn. I hope to impart some of that knowledge in these pages.

Part **1**

Modular Programming
and Turbo Prolog
Projects

Overview of Modular Programming

The designers of Turbo Prolog evidently decided that the language could and would be used for large-scale, real-world applications. Why else would they give Turbo Prolog the power of modular programming?

In this chapter, you take a brief look at modular programming: what it is, why it's important, and what to take into account when undertaking a programming assignment using this approach. The rest of part 1 develops a small application program using the modular programming techniques introduced here.

What Is Modular Programming?

Modular programming is the process of breaking a project—generally but not necessarily a large project—into components and developing each component separately. In Turbo Prolog parlance, the total product that is designed and built is a *project*. Each component is a Turbo Prolog program file that may be an executable program or a file containing information used by the entire project. Each component program is developed and tested individually. After all the modules have been constructed and checked, they are linked into a single executable project file.

Why Program in Modules?

To the end user, a project built modularly and then linked is no different from a project written as one large program. If there's no difference to the end user, why program modularly and add more steps to the already cumbersome process of constructing real-world applications? Modular programming has a number of advantages, all of which are important to the designer and developer.

Multiple Programmers

If a project requires delivery on a tight deadline (and what doesn't these days), modular programming enables the project manager to assign pieces of the project to different programmers. The work can proceed in parallel; functional components are programmed, tested, and finalized in isolation from other components.

Although modular programming using multiple programmers is not always more efficient than a single-programmer approach, it generally is more efficient on larger projects.

Problem Isolation

If a bug arises during the testing of the final project, a programmer can isolate and correct it more easily when the project is developed modularly for two primary reasons.

First, if individual modules are tested and debugged, any problems that occur in the final project are usually the result of interaction among the modules. This means the person debugging the project can look for bugs at their most likely lurking place: where the modules connect (where they pass data back and forth or call each other). Second, if the bug is confined to a specific part of processing, the single programmer of that module can be assigned to solve the problem. Finger pointing is held to a minimum while efficiency of coding is increased.

Ease of Maintenance

The reasoning that makes the discovery and correction of bugs easier in a modular project than in a large-scale single program also applies to program maintenance. Because programs are used by people who did not design them, new features and "fixes" are usually added. Often, the person responsible for making these changes is not the same person who coded the original program.

If the product is built as a modular project and a fix is needed in one area, the maintenance programmer can quickly determine what portion of the code needs to be modified. After that is known and the fixes have been made, all the arguments in favor of modular programming—particularly the ease of debugging—apply to the maintenance programmer.

Steps in Modular Programming

In general, the steps in modular programming are the same regardless of the language or development environment. But Prolog is knowledge-based, unlike other languages, so you have to consider one additional step that is not usually part of modular programming. The basic steps to modular programming are outlined in the remainder of this section.

Step 1: Decide What's Global

Programs that are linked into some type of modular project usually must share information, call each other into execution, and interact with the same data files. Data—variables, constants, and data files—that needs to be accessible to more than one module is called *global* data.

Information that can be confined to a specific module is *local* data to that module.

Early in the design of a modular program, the designer must decide what data will be global and what will be local. The criteria for making these decisions are the subject of chapter 2.

Step 2: Designing the Modules

The next step in modular programming is the design of the individual modules. This step has two phases. First you determine how to break the total project into modules. Then you design how each individual module will work.

For example, the system designer and project manager might decide how to divide the project. The programmer responsible for coding the individual modules might also design them. How to decide where to divide a modular project is the subject of chapter 3.

Step 3: Writing and Testing the Modules

Next, the programs that make up the project must be written and debugged. Essentially, the processes in this step are the same as those you use for a standalone Turbo Prolog program. Chapter 4 discusses this topic in some depth.

Step 4: Preparing the Modules for Implementation

During the process of testing and debugging individual modules in isolation from the rest of the project, you often have to make allowances for the absence of other modules. For example, you might have to create test data that is local to your program at one stage, but in a disk database in the final project.

Because of these necessary changes, some modules require modification when they are linked into the final project. This and other considerations in preparing individual modules to become part of the integrated project are discussed in chapter 6.

Step 5: Compiling and Linking the Modules

In most programming languages and environments, particularly on microcomputers, the programmer must learn another language to compile and link the modules. This other language is a compiler or linker-compiler, which has its own peculiarities and syntax.

When Borland International first shipped Turbo Prolog, such an approach was necessary. But with the shipment of Version 1.1, the company included an integrated linker-compiler that makes this step easy. What was one of the most error-prone, confusing steps in Turbo Prolog is now a single command.

But understanding how this step works, what can go wrong, and how to make corrections are still important for the person who designs substantial projects in Turbo Prolog. This process is described in chapter 7.

The Missing Step: A Prolog Peculiarity

You may have noticed that chapter 5 was skipped in the description of the order of the topics covered in part 1. Often, the designer must add an intermediate step between steps 3 and 4 in a Prolog application. The missing step is adding a *consultable database* to the project.

A consultable database usually resides on disk. Turbo Prolog uses it as a source of information to assist the project in carrying out its assignment. For example, this external database could store employee data for a Turbo Prolog expert system that helps personnel managers make promotion recommendations.

Although this step can take place earlier in the process, it is easier to work with memory-based data until you are sure that the underlying database design is sound. Changing whole disk files of information to accommodate a change that emerges during the assembly of the finished project can become quite time-consuming and expensive.

Turbo Prolog and Modular Programming

As mentioned at the beginning of this chapter, modular programming is an easier task in Turbo Prolog than in many conventional computer programming languages. Turbo Prolog's superb development environment includes two features designed primarily to facilitate modular programming.

Module Lists

Turbo Prolog includes a definition of a specific type of file called a *module list*. As you can see in figure 1-1, the Files menu option offers a choice called Module list. Figure 1-2 shows what happens when you select this option and press the RETURN key: Turbo Prolog displays a list of all files on the current directory with a .PRJ (for project) extension.

A module list contains the names of all modules in a project. The project takes its name from the name of the module list. A file called GENEALOG.PRJ, for example, denotes a project called GENEALOG.

The format for a module list file follows the pattern shown in figure 1-3. Each file in the project is listed without its file extension (which must be .PRO), and all are connected by a plus sign. The plus sign at the end of the module list is required.

Menu-Driven Compilation and Linkage

After you define a project's module list file and complete the modules for the construction of the final project, the Options menu alternatives come into play (see figure 1-4). One of the choices is of particular interest.

Before you compile the project, select the Project (all modules) option from this menu. When you do, nothing happens until you use the C option to order Turbo Prolog to compile the project.

At that point, the project's module list is called into memory and used as a map to tell Turbo Prolog what files to compile. If the compilation proceeds without errors, an executable file with the .EXE extension

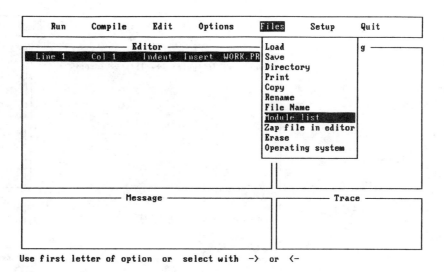

Figure 1-1
Module list menu option

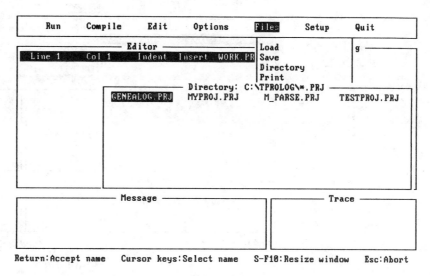

Figure 1-2
Sample module list file directory

is created. Linkage of the modules along with any external files explicitly included in the programs is automatic.

Note: To work correctly, the module list for the project must have a .PRJ extension and must reside in the directory defined as the .OBJ directory. The other modules must be located in the .PRO directory. Use the Setup menu option to change these directories if necessary before compiling.

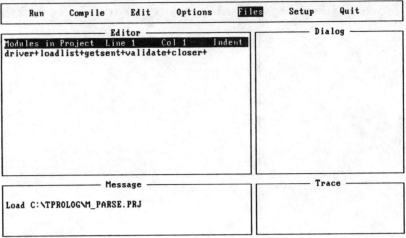

Figure 1-3
Module list format

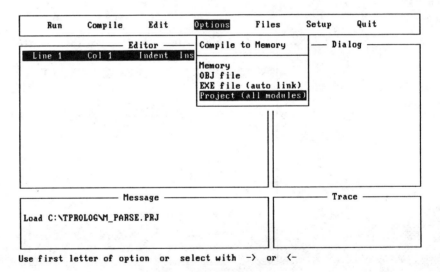

Figure 1-4
Options menu

Summary

In this chapter, you learned the advantages of modular programming. You looked at the main steps in designing and executing a modular programming project. Finally, you saw how Turbo Prolog facilitates such programming by making it possible to have special module list files, which serve as maps to the system during the automatic compilation and linkage of projects into executable files.

Domains and Predicates: Global versus Local

This chapter examines how Turbo Prolog differs from other programming languages in its use of variables. It also examines the implications of those differences for modular programming in Turbo Prolog. Finally, it explains and demonstrates the steps necessary to design and build a working, executable Turbo Prolog project.

Turbo Prolog Variables

In most computer programming languages, a variable's role is to retain information throughout its "scope." By default, the scope of most variables is the entire program. In other words, a variable's value is accessible to any portion of the program that needs to use or modify it. In BASIC, the earliest microcomputer language, there were no other options: all variables were global in scope.

When Pascal and other structured languages for microcomputers emerged, the concept of local variables became significant. A local variable is one whose value is known only within a certain portion of the program. Generally, this portion is a procedure, which is equivalent in most respects to a Turbo Prolog predicate.

Local variables are important in programming. A programmer can use the same variable name in several places in a large program without being concerned about conflicting with a variable of the same name elsewhere in the program. In Pascal (and other languages as well), variables are global by default. If you want a variable to be local in scope, you must explicitly define it as such.

In Turbo Prolog, variables are entirely different kinds of objects. Furthermore, they are handled differently than variables in other languages. As a refresher on this subject, look at the following interchange taking place in the Turbo Prolog Dialog window, with an empty Editor window so that interaction with the program is immediate:

```
Goal: X=9.
X=9
1 Solution
Goal: X=X+4.
Error 2201 Free variable in expression
```

Clearly, when you first assign a value (9) to the variable X, Turbo Prolog does not remember that value after it has been reported to the user. When you try to *use* that variable in the next goal statement, you are told that you have attempted to use a free variable (X with no associated value) in an expression. Because Turbo Prolog does not permit this usage, it generates an error message.

Even if you try to use two variables—the classic case of adding two variables rather than incrementing one variable—there is a problem:

```
Goal: X=9.
X=9
1 Solution
Goal: Y=4.
Y=4
1 Solution
Goal: A=X+Y.
Error 2201 Free variable in expression
```

The only way to add two values in Turbo Prolog is to ensure that they fall within the same predicate or goal statement:

```
Goal: X=9,Y=4,A=X+Y.
X=9, Y=4, A=13
1 Solution
Goal:
```

Finally, Turbo Prolog "remembers" the values of X and Y long enough to perform the calculation you want. This demonstrates that the scope of a variable in Turbo Prolog is *always* local to the goal statement or the predicate in which it appears.

How Prolog Programs Share

This localization of variables means that one part of a program does not have direct access to variables generated or used by other parts of the program. Therefore, the question of how various segments of a Turbo Prolog program share information must be addressed. The answer lies in two places.

First, Turbo Prolog programs don't have segments or procedures that need to share information. This is because Turbo Prolog is a descriptive language rather than a procedural one. Second, the means by which information is exchanged between predicates is in the parameters explicitly passed to predicates when they are called.

When one predicate needs to call on the services of another predicate in the same program or module, it calls that predicate with the arguments—instantiated and uninstantiated—required by the predicate being called. (A variable is free, or uninstantiated, when it has no value assigned to it.) A small example will clarify what is meant by this predicate-level sharing, which is critical to our understanding of Turbo Prolog's modular programming techniques.

Predicate Sharing

Look at the following listing. This is a complete program and may be typed into Turbo Prolog. Run it as you read the following section.

```
domains
  person=symbol.
predicates
  parents(person,person,person).
  parent(person,person).
  ancestor_of(person,person).
clauses
parent(A, B) :- parents(A, B, _).
parent(A, B) :- parents(A, _, B).

ancestor_of(X, Y) :- parent(X, Y).
ancestor_of(X, Y) :-
  parent(X, Z),
  ancestor_of(Z, Y).

parents(ellen, ed, dianne).
parents(tom, joe, vera).
parents(anna, mel, corinne).
parents(ed, don, eleanor).
parents(dianne, brian, kathy).
parents(ted, steve, susan).
parents(steve, tom, anna).
```

In this classic Prolog genealogy example, the `ancestor_of` predicate must determine whether a relationship called `parent` exists between two people before it can succeed or fail. So it passes the variables X and Y to the `parent` predicate by simply calling the `parent` predicate with uninstantiated variables in the slots the `ancestor_of` predicate is attempting to fill. Note, however, that the `parent` predicate need not use the same variable names. In fact, good Prolog programming practice usually dictates that they be different.

Similarly, the `parent` predicate passes these same two variables as arguments to the `parents` predicate as it attempts to satisfy its own goal.

Variable Sharing

This unusual use of variables—which, as you will see, makes modular programming much easier in Turbo Prolog than in many more conventional languages—is possible because of the concept of variable sharing. If two variables are matched with each other during a program run, when one is instantiated, the other is also instantiated. In our genealogy example, when the `ancestor_of` predicate calls the `parent` predicate with the values X and Y as variables, one of the variables is typically (though not necessarily) instantiated. When the `parent` predicate is called, it has two variable names associated with it and two values that have been passed to it by the `ancestor_of` predicate. These variables share, as shown in figure 2-1.

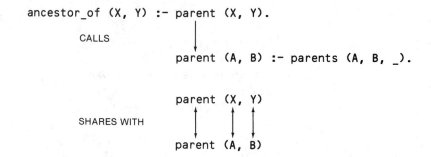

X SHARES WITH A; Y SHARES WITH B

Figure 2-1
Variable sharing

When X is instantiated, A is instantiated. Note that this is true regardless of *when* the instantiation takes place. If X is already instantiated when `ancestor_of` calls the `parent` predicate, then A is instantiated when the `parent` predicate attempts to satisfy its own goals and subgoals. Thus, if the call to `parent` is made as follows:

`Goal: ancestor_of(steve,Who).`

the `parent` predicate has its first variable, A, instantiated to the value `steve` and its second variable, B, uninstantiated. The `parent` predicate, in turn, passes these variables to the `parents_of` predicate, as shown in the listing.

Passing the contents of variables between portions of a program is not done in the traditional programming way, by passing the same variable *name* from one routine to another. Rather, it is done by calling the appropriate predicate with the appropriate variable positions containing uninstantiated variables or variables already instantiated to values. (Actually, "traditional" variable passing is a bit more complex than passing variable names, or references, between routines. But for this discussion, such distinctions are not important.)

Global Definitions

Within a single Turbo Prolog program, the predicate-level sharing just described takes place smoothly and easily, without any effort on the programmer's part. If you use different variable names in each predicate, the program works. If you use the same variable names throughout the program, it will still work because it is not the *name* of the variable that is significant to Prolog but rather its *position* within a predicate call.

> **Note:** The significance of a variable's position in a predicate call is part of Turbo Prolog's powerful pattern-matching nature. This characteristic leads to the ability to efficiently code complex applications with multiple levels of predicate interaction.

The problem that remains to be solved is how to share this information across program lines. In a modular project, how do you pass information from one program to another? You know from the arithmetic example that you can't share variables across `goal` statements. The same is true of programs: they don't pass information back and forth as a matter of course.

To force Turbo Prolog program modules within a single project to transfer information through predicate calls, you must declare these predicates as global. And because domains must be defined in Turbo Prolog before corresponding predicates will work, you must also declare appropriate domains as global.

Let's break our genealogy example into two program segments for purposes of illustration.

Global Domains

We'll divide the program so that the `ancestor_of` predicate definitions are in one module and the rest of the program is in a second module. But first you must determine what information will be passed between the program portions when they are physically separated.

Examine these two program segments, and you will find that they only need to pass information back and forth through the `parent` predicate. It is the only predicate they have in common. Making a list of predicates that appear in both (or all) segments of a Turbo Prolog program is an easy and efficient way of determining which predicates must be declared as global. Now look at the `parent` predicate in the predicates section of the program. Notice that its arguments are both `person`, which is not one of Turbo Prolog's standard domains. Therefore, it must have been declared in the domains section of the program. As you can see, it is. The `person` data type is defined to have the domain `symbol` associated with it.

Open a new file in the Turbo Prolog Editor window so you can set up your global definitions. First, define the global domain `person`:

```
global domains
  person=symbol.
```

As you can see, declaring a global domain is identical to declaring a local domain except you add the key word global to the definition. Before proceeding, save this file under the name GLOBALS.PRO, but leave it in the Editor window.

Global Predicates

Now all program segments in your Turbo Prolog project will recognize the term person as being a symbol. But you need to ensure that the parent predicate is also known to all program segments.

To accomplish this, you must define the predicate as global. In the same file in which you just defined the global domain person, add the following two lines:

```
global predicates
parent(person,person) - (i,o), (o,i), (i,i), (o,o).
```

As you can see, declaring a global predicate is similar to declaring a predicate in a single Turbo Prolog program, with two exceptions. First, the word global appears in the line where the section begins. Second, the definition of the predicate is followed by some strange-looking combinations of the letters i and o.

These combinations of i and o represent Turbo Prolog *flow patterns*. For the moment, all you need to understand can be summarized in a few paragraphs.

Flow Pattern Basics

A flow pattern is a description of how parameters of a Turbo Prolog predicate can be used. In a single program, the declaration of a flow pattern is unnecessary—no information is passed outside the program so Turbo Prolog does not need to keep track of it. But in a modular project, each program segment or module must be able to determine how parameters in predicates outside its normal scope are used and how to convey information to the calling module. That is the purpose of the flow pattern description.

Each parameter in a global predicate definition must be connected to an i or an o in at least one flow pattern description. If there is only one argument and there is only one way it can be used, then only one flow pattern needs to be provided.

You can think of each i in a flow pattern description as standing for an input parameter, and each o as standing for an output parameter. If a parameter is defined as having a flow pattern value of i, Turbo Prolog expects any value in that position to be instantiated when it is passed. If a parameter is defined as having an o value, it is expected to be uninstantiated when it is passed. See figure 2-2 for a graphic representation of flow patterns.

Most predicates in multiprogram Turbo Prolog projects are associated with multiple flow patterns. In our example, there are four flow patterns, which means that any combination of input and output parameter values is permitted. Figure 2-3 shows how each flow pattern corresponds to a possible way of calling the `parent` predicate.

If you wanted to make it impossible to call the `parent` predicate with both parameters unknown (in other words, uninstantiated), you could simply eliminate the last flow pattern of (o,o). If you did that, the call:

```
parent(Who,Whom).
```

would produce a run-time error condition.

As you use more complex predicates, with more than two parameters, the use of flow patterns becomes more complicated and more important in ensuring that your programs work correctly.

> **Note:** In your Turbo Prolog *user manual,* the descriptions of all built-in predicates use flow patterns to describe how they are expected to work. These descriptions might help you better understand the concept of flow patterns.

Be sure to save the GLOBALS.PRO file before moving on to the next section.

The Project Concept

You now know how to declare global domains and predicates in a modular Turbo Prolog programming assignment. As you saw in chapter 1, this is one step in creating such programs in Turbo Prolog. The other steps involve an understanding of how Turbo Prolog views modular programs.

PREDICATE NAME   (PARAMETER 1,   PARAMETER 2,   PARAMETER 3).
```
   test          (  i,            i,             o   ).
```

Acceptable:
```
   test   (one,two,Variable).
```

Unacceptable:
```
   test(X,two,three).
   test(X,Y,Z).
```

Figure 2-2
Flow pattern example

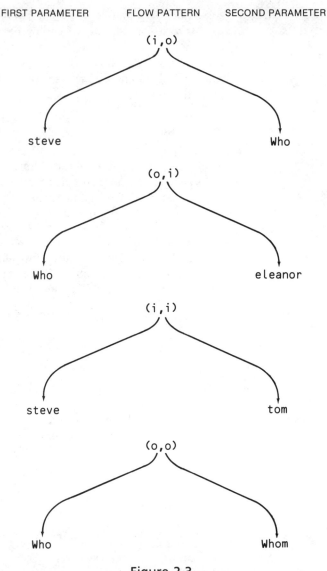

Figure 2-3
Matching sample flow patterns

Projects and Modules

A Turbo Prolog modular program is referred to as a project, made up of two or more modules. Figure 2-4 depicts a modular Turbo Prolog project and its components.

The first element of a Turbo Prolog project is the project file. This file contains the names of all modules that make up the project. We will call the two modules of our sample project ANCESTOR.PRO and PARENT.PRO. To set up a project called GENEALOG.PRJ containing references to these two modules, follow these steps:

1. Select the Module list option from the Files pull-down menu.

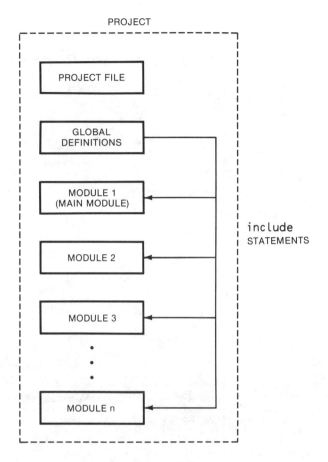

Figure 2-4
Components of a project

2. Type GENEALOG when Turbo Prolog asks for the name. (No need for the .PRJ extension; the program adds it automatically.)

3. The Editor window will be displayed with a new top prompt line: *Modules in Project*. See figure 2-5.

4. Type the names of the project modules, connecting them with plus signs, as shown in figure 2-6. Be sure to type a plus sign after the last module name.

5. When all modules are listed, press the F10 key to save the file.

Caution: If you use the ESC key to go to the Files menu to save this file, as you do with all other files you work with in the Editor window, your module list is deleted instead of saved. Be sure to use the F10 key.

The other components of a project as shown in figure 2-4 are self-explanatory. The global definitions are contained in a separate file. In

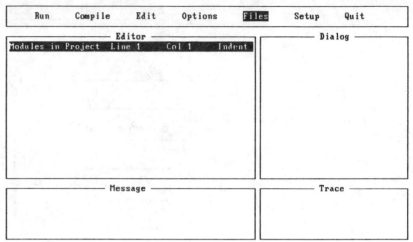

Figure 2-5
Module list Editor window

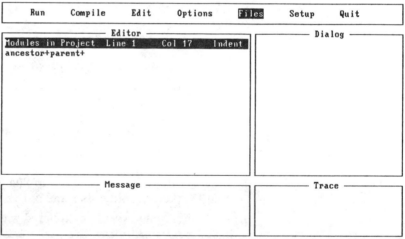

Figure 2-6
Module list for sample project

the family tree example, this file is called GLOBALS.PRO. It is created like any other Turbo Prolog program.

Each module in the project contains an include statement (discussed in greater detail in the following section) that identifies the file containing the global definitions.

Notice in figure 2-4 that the first module is also labeled Main Module. There is one sense in which one of the modules becomes the main module in a compiled and running Turbo Prolog project. Because interaction with the finished program is not within Turbo Prolog but in an executable file generated by Turbo Prolog, the program cannot generate the `goal:` prompt.

Because of this feature, it is essential that one—and only one—`goal` statement appear within a Turbo Prolog project when it is compiled. Most often, this goal is a predicate in the main module that requests some response from the user as an indication of what to do. But when the program has a singular purpose (e.g., performing a fixed calculation on fixed values or values obtained from program files in other languages, as discussed in part 2), the goal in the main module may not be interactive.

Creating the Modules

Usually, you will be typing in the new modules that make up your Turbo Prolog project. In this example, though, you are using an existing program and dividing it into two modules.

Use the Turbo Prolog editor to separate the `ancestor_of` predicates from the rest of the sample genealogy program. Store the `ancestor_of` predicates in a file called ANCESTOR.PRO. Now use the editor to delete these lines from the main program file, and save the file as PARENT.PRO.

Edit the ANCESTOR.PRO and PARENT.PRO files to add two identical lines to the beginning of each:

```
project "GENEALOG"
include "GLOBALS.PRO"
```

(Note that you must supply the .PRO extension in the name of the included global definition file, but you do not supply the .PRJ extension in the project file name.)

Remove the domains section from both files. From the new ANCESTOR.PRO file, remove the predicate declarations for the `parent` and `parents` predicates. Save this file. Open the PARENT.PRO file and remove the `ancestor_of` and `parent` predicates, then save this file. (Note that in modular program development, you would not remove the `parent` predicate from the PARENT.PRO file until *after* it had been thoroughly tested as a standalone program.)

Now open the ANCESTOR.PRO file and insert, just before the clauses declaration, the following goal:

```
goal
    ancestor_of(steve,Who),
    write(Who," is an ancestor of Steve."),nl.
```

This `goal` statement results in a single-purpose genealogy program; it will always look for Steve's ancestors. This goal will suffice because our purpose is not to produce a useful modular project, but to show how the process of creating such a project works. To design a more general or interactive goal, you would simply write a predicate that calls for some user input. Such predicates are common in Prolog programs, so we won't take time to discuss them here.

The genealogy project is now ready to be compiled and tested as a unit. Doing so is a simple two-step process:

1. Pull down the Options menu and select the Project (all modules) option.
2. Press ESC-C to order a compilation.

If all goes as expected, you will see a series of messages in the Message window in the lower left corner of the standard Turbo Prolog display. When compilation and linkage are successful, a new program called GENEALOG.EXE exists on your disk. Turbo Prolog asks if you wish to execute the program right away. When testing, you normally respond to this question with a *y*, but for now, answer *n*. This program can then be run like any other DOS program, simply by typing its name. Quit Turbo Prolog and type GENEALOG at the DOS prompt. (For the moment, ignore the fact that there is only one answer of the six that should be present. You deal with goal definition inside Turbo Prolog programs in the next chapter.) You have just created your first modular, standalone Turbo Prolog program.

Summary

In this chapter, you learned about Turbo Prolog variables and how they differ from variables in other programming languages. In the process, you learned how to transfer information between programs by variable sharing through predicate calls. You also learned the essential components of a Turbo Prolog modular programming project. Using a small sample program, you constructed your first project and experienced the steps required to design and build such a system. Chapter 3 begins the process of designing and constructing a more meaningful example of a Turbo Prolog project. You'll learn about top-down design, how to carry through the design of the goal statement, and how to predict program behavior.

Chapter **3**

Designing the Modules

In any modular project, careful design of the contents of the various modules is an essential step. Modules must be designed taking into account their function, size, and ability to be tested and debugged independently from the rest of the system. There must also be a master program that pulls all the independent modules into a whole when the testing phase is complete.

This chapter describes how to modularize a project and how to design the main program, which drives the other modules in a system. It does so by considering a project that forms the basis of the remainder of part 1. First, you examine the project's design and the process of deciding how and where to divide this project into modules. Then you create the module list, which Turbo Prolog uses to guide its ultimate linkage of the project. Finally, you write the main driver routine to hold the whole project together when it is complete.

The Sample Project

For the rest of part 1, you'll be working with a sample project that involves a small-scale natural language processing (NLP) program. Although this program is not a full NLP system, it could form the basis for more sophisticated implementations of NLP in Turbo Prolog. (We have much more to say about Prolog and NLP in part 3.)

If this program were your entire assignment, it is unlikely that you would implement it as a multimodule project. Its overall size would not justify the additional effort. However, for the purpose of instruction, we will treat it as if it were a project of more significant size.

> **Note:** Thanks to Turbo Prolog's speed and ability to deal with large programs, you may never find it necessary to design a modular project. But the other advantages of modular

21

programming, outlined in chapter 1, are still important. A
full-scale NLP project and an expert system with a significant
knowledge base are good examples of the types of Turbo
Prolog tasks that benefit from modular programming.

What the Project Will Do

Figure 3-1 is a schematic representation of what the sample program,
called Micro_Parse, is designed to do. It serves as the basis not only for
this functional description but also for the modularization decisions
you'll make in the next few paragraphs.

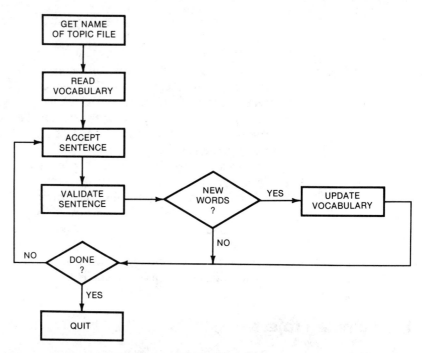

Figure 3-1
Micro_Parse schematic

The purpose of the Micro_Parse project is to permit the user to
select a subject and enter sentences about the subject that the program
analyzes. (You store a small word list about the subject in a disk file.) The
analysis is fairly trivial, consisting of identifying the parts of speech in the
sentence pattern if possible, asking about the part of speech if it is
unknown, and maintaining the disk file of words relevant to the topic.

To make the program manageable, the kinds of patterns in
sentences recognized by the program as valid sentences are restricted.
You may want to expand on this limitation. Doing so is relatively easy,
though it may involve a substantial amount of Turbo Prolog code.

Module Division

The finished program has five modules:

- main or driver module
- topic file management module
- sentence input module
- sentence validation module
- quit module

Figure 3-2 shows how these module divisions relate to the flow diagram in figure 3-1.

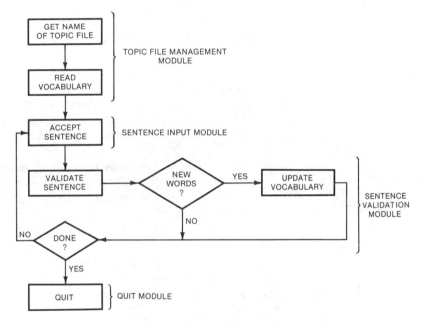

Figure 3-2
Micro_Parse schematic and module connections

Because the first two steps in the process are determining which file of words to load from the disk and then loading that module, it makes sense to view them as a functional unit. You can handle all of the error conditions associated with structuring the disk file improperly, entering an invalid file name, or entering nonexistent disk drives. Note the key characteristic: this module can be tested independently of the rest of the project. You can create some small sample files for testing only, and you can reproduce or anticipate many of the mistakes people will make in entering information to ensure that this module handles such situations correctly.

Similarly, the second module—the sentence input module—accepts input from the user and ensures that it meets certain minimal conditions. It is possible to write this as a standalone module.

The third module checks the validity of a sentence that has been accepted from the user and adds words to the dynamic database as appropriate. It may seem that this module—the "heart" of the project and the largest program—should be divided or, alternatively, made part of the sentence input module. Let's briefly examine the reasons for dividing things this way.

Separation from Sentence Input

First, why do you separate validation from input? After all, wouldn't it be better to enter the sentence to be tested as part of the validation routine's debugging? And isn't the sentence input routine going to be very small? Even more important, couldn't you simply hard code sentences during testing so that debugging requires no new input?

In a larger system, such considerations might hold sway. In this project, though, there are some sound reasons for the modularization chosen.

As you will see, you test the validation routine by supplying it with sentences as goal statements in the form of a list. You use list representation for sentences inside the program because it is the most effective and efficient data structure for dealing with their formats and content. But you don't want to ask the user to enter a list because you want the user to enter a sentence that is as English-like as possible. So the sentence input routine does more than simply accept the user's input.

Second, by separating the validation function, you can isolate the cause of the system declaring a sentence invalid when it appears that it should be acceptable. You won't have to wonder whether the input processing worked correctly, because it is not involved.

Finally, notice the interaction among the validation, input, and quit modules. The validation module can call the quit module, which in turn can call the input module. If the validation and input modules were one, this interaction would be more cumbersome and less clear.

Integration with Vocabulary Update

Another question about the approach used to modularize Micro_Parse is why we did not choose to make the validation and file updating routines (in the validation module) two separate modules.

Part of the reason for this decision won't be clear until you examine the code, but it centers on the large amount of interaction between validating the user's input and determining if the word entered by the user is a new word to add to the vocabulary. This interaction is so close-knit that the functions are virtually identical. Therefore, it makes sense to combine these functions into one module.

If you did combine these two functional elements, you would be left with just the routine to add words to the disk file. This routine is far too small and simplistic to justify creating a standalone module, so it is arbitrarily tied into the validation processing.

Vocabulary Update and Topic Management

There is one other logical place for the routine that adds words to the disk file. It could be put with the first module, which obtains the topic from the user and loads the appropriate word list. It is less functionally related there, but there is a reason why this would make sense. When testing the topic file management module, you will need to load disk files containing information. This means you must put some files containing data on the disk. So why not use the module you have to write anyway to store the word lists on the disk?

The decision is a bit arbitrary. There isn't a good reason not to put the modules together, but we chose not to do so. If you were designing a project and chose to put the modules together, there would be nothing wrong with that approach. It would simply be different.

General Principles of Modularization

From this specific example, you can draw some conclusions about the modularization decisions to make when designing Turbo Prolog projects. These general principles should be viewed not as iron-clad rules but as guidelines.

1. There are no absolutely right and wrong ways to modularize a project.
2. Group functions together in modules if they are closely related operationally, in terms of input and output or by their interaction with other modules.
3. Take into account the size of the finished module. Very small modules should be considered candidates for integration into other, related modules. Very large modules should be evaluated to see if they can be divided.
4. The key criterion to use in making modularization decisions is independence. If the module's functions can be tested and evaluated largely or completely separately from other operations in the project, then it is a good choice. If testing requires input from another module and that input is hard to duplicate or "fake," then the two modules might be more effective if combined.
5. Any module (like the quit module) that interacts with more than one other module is probably a good candidate to be made into a separate module, even if that module will be very small.

Remember, too, that modularization is significant only during the development phase. After the program is written, tested, debugged, and finalized, it is all converted into one project. Make modularization decisions based on what best facilitates development of the program.

The Module List

With the modularization decision behind you, you are ready to design the project itself. You begin by creating the module list. Although this routine does not need to be created first, you'll do so for two reasons.

First, this routine shows the overall structure of the project. Because you define each module to be included in the final project, this routine is a kind of road map to the project.

Second, some of the considerations in the use of this module list make it easier to follow and understand the process of development presented in the next few chapters.

What's in a Module List?

A Turbo Prolog module list contains the names of the programs that make up the project. Each program name appears either on a line of its own or adjacent to other module names. No file extensions are given and each program name, including the last on the list, ends with a plus sign.

In the sample project, you create a module list containing five file names. Although the names are arbitrary, like all DOS file names, they are made as descriptive as possible. Also included are comments indicating what each module does. Here is what the module list looks like in the sample project.

```
driver+  /* main driver routine */
loadlist+  /* get user input for word list to be loaded
     and load it */
getsent+  /* get user's sentence to be validated */
validate+  /* validate and update vocabulary as
     appropriate */
closer+  /* user finished processing--close out if he
     wants to quit */
```

Alternatively, you may want to compress your file by placing all module names on one line:

```
driver+loadlist+getsent+validate+closer+
```

Note that there are no spaces between the module names and a plus sign follows even the last module name.

Creating the Module List

To create this module list in Turbo Prolog, use the Files menu's Module list option. The first thing you are asked for is the name of the module list. Call the list M_PARSE, a valid DOS file name that will remind you of the project's name, Micro_Parse.

Turbo Prolog immediately displays the Editor window. Now type in the five module names. When you are finished, press the F10 key. Turbo Prolog saves the file as M_PARSE.PRJ, furnishing the extension .PRJ automatically. That's all there is to it.

How Turbo Prolog Uses the Module List

The primary way that a project differs from a single Turbo Prolog program is that a project must be compiled and linked into a finished, executable program composed of individual modules before it can be used. The module list file provides information to the compilation and linkage processes so that these steps can be carried out without intervention by the programmer.

In Turbo Prolog Version 1.1 and later, Borland includes a linker that uses the contents of the module list file to determine which files need to be linked to form the project. With the first release of Turbo Prolog, users had to supply their own linking program. As part of invoking the external linker, the programmer supplied the name of the .PRJ file containing the module list.

When the link is executed, Turbo Prolog simply loads the contents of the module list file and then links each file in the module list in the given order.

The module list file name is also used during the compilation step of project development. At that stage, it identifies a symbol table shared by all of the project's modules. This table is automatically generated by Turbo Prolog and stored as a file with the same name as the module list file but with the .SYM extension. The sample project generates a file called M_PARSE.SYM that contains this symbol list.

A symbol list is an important part of any program compilation. It holds the names of objects in memory during the program's execution.

A Word about Order

The order in which the modules appear in the module list is unimportant. Because Turbo Prolog does not follow a sequence from top to bottom when trying to satisfy goal statements, the order is arbitrary.

To make the module list more helpful—particularly in a large project involving a few dozen modules—organize it in the order in which you expect the modules to be used in most circumstances. (This is not always possible or useful because of Prolog's inherent nonlinear execution.)

The Driver Routine

You create the bulk of the project in chapter 4 as you write and test each module. But to get things started and to gain an appreciation for the overall structure of the project, let's write the main driver routine, which governs the project's execution.

Note that a driver routine is not appropriate for a project this small. You do, however, need a "main" module containing the goal statement, and this driver routine is as good a place as any for that code. For instruction and illustration, you will create such a routine even though it is really unnecessary.

Structure?
In Prolog?

To some extent, creating this driver routine represents an attempt to bring some structure to a Prolog program. Structure is something most Prolog programs lack by their very nature. The fact that Turbo Prolog requires all clauses with the same name to be grouped together is one major reason why a structure representing program flow is difficult, if not impossible, to impose on a Turbo Prolog program.

Many types of programs for which Turbo Prolog is an appropriate language do not lend themselves to the creation of a main driver routine. In such cases, do not feel that you must design one. The sample project lends itself to such a design and its inclusion permits you to see more clearly the structure and flow of processing.

Designing the
Routine

Each project in Turbo Prolog must have one and only one internally supplied goal statement. The satisfaction of this one goal then becomes the project's "reason for being." If you design a project so that it includes a main driver routine, this is the most logical place to provide the goal.

The goal is then defined as being satisfied by interaction with the user, disk files, or other devices external to the program. That process is generally defined by naming the project modules. Many main driver routines consist of just the goal clause.

Programming
the Routine

One way of programming the main driver routine for the sample project follows:

```
project "m_parse"  /* Turbo Prolog requires this line
     (see text) */
include "globals.pro"  /* File containing global
     predicates (see ch. 2) */
predicates
  go
goal
  go.
clauses
  go :-
    set_up_topic,
    get_sentence,
    check_sentence(Sentence),
    time_to_stop.
```

There is not much to study here, but we should point out a few things.

The first line of the module refers to the .PRJ file you have just created using the Files Module list option. This same line must be included in every module in the project. It is used during compilation to ensure the correct production of the symbol table. We have already discussed global predicates and their inclusion in a project. Any modules that use globally defined predicates must contain the second line in this listing.

> **Note:** It's a good idea to write the include statement into each module even if a particular module does not need the global definition file in its first design. Then if you add a routine that does require the global predicates, you won't run into compilation and execution errors because of its omission.

Finally, notice that the goal called go is made up of four clauses whose names do not appear in the predicates section of this routine. Each of these appears in a different module of the project, as you can tell from their names. Because these predicates appear in this main driver routine and must also appear in individual modules, they are clearly global and must be defined in a file called GLOBALS.PRO. This file can be built as you design the system.

Note that the inclusion of these clauses implies that each of the submodules of the project has a main clause that is the first one invoked when the predicates contained in that module are executed. In other words, each module must be designed so that its processing is initiated by calling the clause whose name appears in the main driver routine.

Summary

In this chapter, you examined the issue of modular project design in Turbo Prolog. You looked at the purpose of modularization and the five general principles for deciding when to modularize a program. You have also begun to design a small sample project that enables a user to select a topic, enter sentences about that topic, and have them validated as legitimate sentences within the definition of legitimacy contained in a module program of the project.

Finally, you looked at the top-level structure of a modular Turbo Prolog project. You have written the module list and the main driver routine. In chapter 4, you construct and test two of the other modules of the project.

Writing and Testing the Modules

In this chapter, you design and test the GETSENT and VALIDATE modules. Neither of these modules uses the `database` declaration, a subject that significantly complicates Turbo Prolog modular program design. You turn your attention to database issues in chapter 5, where you design and test the other functional modules.

You'll construct and test the VALIDATE module first. After you deal with the VALIDATE module, it will be easier to understand the GETSENT module's operation and design. As usual, there is no absolutely correct way of ordering these tasks; we have chosen the best method for instruction.

The VALIDATE Module

The VALIDATE module has two main purposes. First, it looks at a sentence to determine if it is valid. Second, and as part of the first task in most cases, it allows the user to add unknown words to the vocabulary if the user wishes to do so. These new words are added to the database file on disk when processing is ended and the time_to_stop module is invoked.

What's a Valid Sentence?

Before you can write the VALIDATE module, you must decide what constitutes a valid sentence. We are intentionally limiting the scope of sentence input that the Micro_Parse program accepts as valid. At first, you define a sentence as valid if it consists of an article (*a, an,* or *the*) followed by a noun and a verb. Figure 4-1 depicts this rule.

```
SENTENCE:: =
<ARTICLE> <NOUN> <VERB>
```

Figure 4-1
Minimal sentence rule for Micro_Parse

Using this definition, all of the following are legitimate sentences:

the boy cries

the ball bounces

the car drives

a balloon floats

an airplane flies

However, the following valid English sentences are rejected for the reasons shown:

our dog barks	Does not start with an article
a blue airplane landed	Too many words; third word is not a verb
the ball bounces away	Too many words

Later, after this structure is working correctly, you add a second valid sentence pattern consisting of an article followed by a noun, a verb, and an adverb.

VALIDATE Module, Part 1

In its first form, the VALIDATE module in Micro_Parse simply looks at a list passed to it in a `goal` statement and determines if the list has three elements. If so, it checks the elements to see if they are an article, followed by a noun, followed by a verb. In the main driver routine, we have already decided to call the key predicate in VALIDATE `check_sentence`. Its argument is a list. This domain is declared in the GLOBALS file because it is used both in DRIVER and in VALIDATE. Thus, the GLOBALS file starts out like this:

```
global domains
   sentence=symbol*
```

You add more declarations to this file as the project is constructed.

You want the word list you are working with in VALIDATE to be subject to dynamic additions, so it must be declared as a database. (As you will see in chapters 5 and 6, databases require special consideration as you move from individual module testing to project compilation and linkage.) And you need to include the GLOBALS file to ensure that the global domain for `sentence` is passed to the module.

As a result of these considerations, the VALIDATE module in its first form looks like this:

```
project "m_parse"
database
  article(symbol)
  noun(symbol)
  verb(symbol)
include "globals.pro"
predicates
  verbtest(symbol)
  nountest(symbol)
/*
no need for an articletest predicate because articles
    are not subject to dynamic additions
*/
clauses
  verbtest(Word) :- verb(Word).
  verbtest(Word) :-
    write("Is ",Word," a verb? "),
    readln(Answer),
    Answer=yes,
    assertz(verb(Word)).
  nountest(Word) :- noun(Word).
  nountest(Word) :-
    write("Is ",Word," a noun? "),
    readln(Answer),
    Answer=yes,
    assertz(noun(Word)).
  check_sentence([First,Second,Third]) :-
    article(First),
    nountest(Second),
    verbtest(Third).
article(a).
article(an).
article(the).
```

Notice that articles are supplied explicitly in the module as facts, but nouns and verbs are supplied by the user. This program will exhibit a semblance of intelligence as it deals with you interactively.

The database portion of the program is normally included in the GLOBALS.PRO file. But you have not yet studied dynamic databases and their relation to Turbo Prolog projects, so the declaration is explicitly included here. In chapter 5, you learn about dynamic databases, and in chapter 6 you modify the VALIDATE routine to fit into the project where the database is globally declared.

Also, notice that you use `assertz`, rather than the more usual `asserta`, to add words to the database file. Thus, the most recently added words are examined last when the program is validating input. This is consistent with the fact that, over time, more and more unusual words will be added, while commonly used words will probably become part of the vocabulary early.

After you have typed this program and it runs successfully, pose the following goal statement:

```
Goal:check_sentence([the,boy,cries]).
Is boy a noun? yes
Is cries a verb? yes
True
Goal:
```

The VALIDATE module simply determines that the list has three elements and then tries to satisfy the first goal, article(First), with the variable First bound to the. The fact article(the) is explicitly part of the module, so this subgoal succeeds. The next subgoal to be attempted is noun(boy). At the moment, the program has no knowledge of any nouns, so it asks whether the word supplied in the Second position of the list is a noun. If you answer yes, the goal succeeds; if your answer is anything else, the goal fails and Turbo Prolog's response is False. The same sequence of events takes place with respect to the Third word in the list.

Because you told the program that boy is a noun and cries is a verb, the VALIDATE module not only accepts your sentence but also puts both words into its RAM resident database. It now "knows" those words. To prove that, try this goal:

```
Goal:check_sentence([a,boy,climbs]).
Is climbs a verb? yes
True
Goal:
```

VALIDATE does not ask you about the word boy. It already knows that word is a noun, so the nountest clause succeeds by matching its first statement:

```
nountest(Word) :- noun(Word)
```

and not by asking the user as a result of the second statement.

Similarly, you can now use the verb climbs:

```
Goal:check_sentence([an,elephant,climbs]).
Is elephant a noun? yes
True
Goal:
```

If you ask the VALIDATE module to check a sentence with more or less than three elements in the list, it fails immediately without asking about the words in the sentence.

Note that it is not legal to call the `check_sentence` predicate with any of its parameters unbound. That's because in the second clause of each of the test predicates (`nountest` and `verbtest`), the variable `Word` appears in a `write` predicate. If you try to pass that argument as a free variable, you cause an error. (You could program the module in such a way that this use is permitted, but it isn't worthwhile to do so in this application.)

VALIDATE Module, Part 2

After the VALIDATE module is working correctly with a three-word sentence, you are ready to expand its horizons to accept the second sentence pattern. This sentence has the form: article, noun, verb, adverb. Simply create a new `check_sentence` predicate with four arguments and add an `adverbtest` clause group and an appropriate predicate declaration to the program. These additions follow.

In the predicates section of the program, add:

```
adverbtest(symbol)
```

In the database declaration, add:

```
adverb(symbol)
```

In the clauses section, following the last `nountest` predicate, add these clauses. (Although they could be put anywhere in the section, this placement retains the structure of the module.)

```
adverbtest(Word) :- adverb(Word).
  adverbtest(Word) :-
    write("Is ",Word," an adverb? "),
    readln(Answer),
    Answer=yes,
    asserta(adverb(Word)).
```

In the clauses section, right after the present `check_sentence` predicate, add these clauses:

```
check_sentence([First,Second,Third,Fourth]) :-
  article(First),
  nountest(Second),
  verbtest(Third),
  adverbtest(Fourth).
```

With these modifications, the VALIDATE module can accept sentence input like the following goals:

```
Goal:check_sentence([the,ball,bounced,wildly]).
Is ball a noun? yes
```

```
Is bounced a verb? yes
Is wildly an adverb? yes
True
Goal:check_sentence([a,ball,rolled,away]).
Is rolled a verb? yes
Is away an adverb? yes
True
Goal:check_sentence([the,boy,rolled,wildly]).
Is boy a noun? yes
True
Goal:check_sentence([the,ball,bounces]).
True
Goal:
```

The GETSENT Module

The purpose of the GETSENT module is to ask the user to supply a sentence, and to convert the sentence into a list to be checked, in the finished project, by the VALIDATE module you have just written. Because the VALIDATE module uses list representation, you must pass a list as an argument to that module. But typing the check_sentence predicate followed by a list is not as clear and understandable as simply typing in a sentence and letting Turbo Prolog change your words into the correct form for the VALIDATE module.

Adding to the GLOBALS File

The first thing you should do is update the GLOBALS file so that get_sentence is declared a global predicate. It has no argument, so it is easy to add. Simply create a global predicates section in the GLOBALS file and insert the predicate's name:

```
global predicates
  get_sentence
```

The only other global value needed in the GETSENT module is the domain sentence, which has already been declared.

> **Note:** Usually, you build the GLOBALS file as you construct the modules. You can construct the GLOBALS file at the beginning of the project or after you finish each module. The only requirement is that the GLOBALS file be up-to-date for each module before that module is tested.

Writing the GETSENT Module

Now that the GLOBALS file is updated, you are ready to write the module that obtains a sentence from the user and converts that sentence into a list for the VALIDATE module to examine.

The GETSENT module is straightforward:

```
project "m_parse"
include "globals.pro"
predicates
  make_list(string,sentence)
clauses
  get_sentence :-
    clearwindow,
    write("Type in a sentence for me to check:"),nl,
    readln(Input),
    make_list(Input,Wordlist),
    write(Wordlist).  /* for testing only */
  make_list(Input,[H¦T]) :-
    fronttoken(Input,H,Rest),!,
    make_list(Rest,T).
  make_list(_,[]).
```

This module clears the Dialog window and prompts the user to enter a sentence. It then prints that sentence after converting it to a list.

This module introduces the concept of a "throwaway" clause, which is inserted into a module only for testing. In the finished project, you don't want the program to print the list it creates from the user's sentence. But the only easy way to determine if the module is doing the correct conversion is to have it print the result.

In chapter 6, you learn how to deal with these and other design issues that are necessary during testing but unnecessary, undesirable, or simply errors in the final project.

Testing the GETSENT Module

To test the GETSENT module, simply run it and provide several sentences to convert to lists. Along the way, you will learn something about how list conversion deals with special characters and punctuation. Each test is run the same way. In response to the goal prompt, type get_sentence.

First, enter a programmer's favorite sentence into the program; respond to the prompt by typing *This is a test*. The computer's response is:

```
["This","is","a","test","."]
```

Notice that the period is treated as if it is a word. What do you think VALIDATE does with a sentence ending in a period? It rejects it as a valid sentence because the sentence has one too many elements, even if everything else is acceptable. If you were developing a commercial NLP program, you would want to correct this problem. For example, you might write a predicate that strips the last element in the list before passing the sentence to the VALIDATE module if the element is a period, question mark, exclamation point, or quotation mark.

But for our limited purposes, leave the processing as it is and

37

simply make a note not to include end punctuation in any sentence you want to analyze.

Let's try a sentence that is more like those you expect to analyze in Micro_Parse. This time, type:

```
A boy bounces
```

in response to the program's prompt. (You'll have to type `get_sentence` in response to the `goal` prompt again; the program does not yet loop until you tell it to stop.) The program's response is as expected:

```
["A","boy","bounces"]
```

Two things about this list are different from the list you entered when you tested VALIDATE. First, individual words are enclosed in quotation marks and appear to be strings rather than symbols. The words are strings. But because of the way Turbo Prolog is designed, it does not affect the program in this situation. For most purposes, strings and symbols are interchangeable in Turbo Prolog.

Second, the article *A* is capitalized. The sentence *A boy cries* will be rejected because the program does not recognize *A* as an article. You could solve this problem by adding the capitalized articles *A, An,* and *The* to the VALIDATE module (and in other places where the articles must be defined, as described in chapter 5). You could also use the Turbo Prolog built-in predicate `upper_lower` to convert the string to all lowercase letters after it is entered. Or you can simply decide to enter sentences in lowercase letters only.

The purpose here is instructional, not commercial, and you are by now accustomed to entering most input in Turbo Prolog in lowercase because of Prolog's case sensitivity. So adopt the convention of lowercase input and leave the VALIDATE module unchanged. If you are uncomfortable with this, the modification to accept initial uppercase letters in sentences or to convert them to lowercase letters is trivial.

There is one more problem to be checked before you finish testing the GETSENT module. What happens to a sentence containing internal punctuation? You can probably guess that Turbo Prolog treats such punctuation as a separate word, but let's confirm this suspicion.

Get to the module's prompt and enter the sentence:

```
the answer's no
```

The module's response is:

```
["the","answer","'","s","no"]
```

This sentence will not be accepted by the program even if you are willing to "fudge" the truth a bit and tell it that *answer's* is a noun and *no* is a verb. The sentence has too many elements and *answer's* will be recognized as three words, not one.

Summary

You have entered, tested, and debugged two of the main modules in the project. You could now stop to compile and link them to ensure that they work together. If these were large or complex modules, it might be a good idea. But you haven't learned yet how to compile and link modules, and there is little value in doing so with these two small modules.

The project now consists of a main module called DRIVER, a partially completed GLOBALS file, and the GETSENT and VALIDATE modules. In chapter 5, you design and test the LOADLIST and CLOSER modules, which work with dynamic databases.

Chapter **5**

Adding a Consultable Database

 One of the most powerful features of Turbo Prolog is its ability to manage dynamic databases that can be stored on and retrieved from a disk. But programming a Turbo Prolog modular project that uses these databases poses some special problems.

This chapter describes what a dynamic database is and how it is declared and used in Turbo Prolog. It then presents the method of programming such a database in the Micro_Parse project. In chapter 6, you focus your attention on how the inclusion of a dynamic database affects the compilation and linkage processes.

Dynamic Databases in Turbo Prolog

Our concern is how dynamic databases are declared and used in Turbo Prolog rather than database design and usage in a broader sense. (If you want to explore Turbo Prolog's capabilities as a database design tool, my previous book, *Turbo Prolog Primer,* also published by Howard W. Sams & Co., contains an extensive discussion of the subject. Many other database design books are also available.)

The databases in the Micro_Parse project consist of lists of words along with their parts of speech. Typical entries look like this:

```
noun(boy)
noun(elephant)
verb(runs)
verb(cries)
```

Databases will undoubtedly have larger vocabularies than this but the form is the same. This is not a complex data structure, so you don't need to spend time designing the database. It is already designed by virtue of its minimal contents.

41

Declaring a Database

A dynamic database in Turbo Prolog is any fact or collection of facts that can be altered during program execution. If you want to add to, delete, or change the contents of the factual part of the knowledge base in a Turbo Prolog program, you must use a dynamic database.

You declare a dynamic database in Turbo Prolog with the keyword `database`, followed by a list of the predicate forms that can appear in that database.

A database's declaration must come *after* the domain declarations and *before* the definition of any nondatabase predicates. If you don't follow this rule, an Error 233 is generated when you attempt to compile or run the program.

In practice, this means that a database declaration must come before any `include` files are read in if those included files—in our project, the GLOBALS file—contain any predicate definitions. Because that is usually the reason for calling a file with the `include` predicate, it's a good idea to adopt the rule that you will always declare databases before any `include` statements are encountered.

It is not legal to define a predicate in both a database declaration and a predicate statement. If you do, an Error 211 is generated.

Only one database statement is allowed per program or module, so it is important to distinguish between a project and a module. A single project may contain as many database declarations as there are modules in the program, provided no single module contains more than one database definition. If you attempt to define more than one database in a module or program, you generate an Error 210.

Creating a Database File

A Turbo Prolog database file must consist of facts that match the pattern of a valid database declaration. It can be created using the Turbo Prolog editor or any other word processor or text editor capable of producing a flat ASCII file (i.e., one with no control characters or high-order bits set. If you're a WordStar user, this means the file must be created, like most program files, in non-document mode).

Three rules about the format and content of a database file are not well documented in the Turbo Prolog manual. If overlooked, they can cause some difficulty. These rules follow.

1. A fact must not end with a period, even though a fact must end with a period in the program itself.

2. An argument defined as a symbol must be placed in double quotation marks, even though this is not required if it is used inside the program.

3. Embedded blanks and blank lines are prohibited and will cause an attempt to load a database to fail. A special case of this problem has tripped up many a Turbo Prolog programmer. The last line in the file must *not* end with a carriage return. Doing so creates a blank line at the end of the database file, which causes Turbo Prolog to fail in its attempt to read the database.

If you are using a dynamic database in a Turbo Prolog program and an attempt to read it into memory (as described in the next section) results in a `False` reply from the program, check these syntactical areas first.

Note, too, that within a database file, all predicates with the same name must be grouped together. You can define some database predicates in the program itself and others in the database. However, doing so is probably not useful if you save the results of any modifications to the disk file. The reasons for this become apparent when the process of saving the database file is discussed later in this chapter.

What a Database Looks Like

Before we continue the discussion of Turbo Prolog databases, let's look at what a database for the Micro_Parse project might look like. This sample file is small, but it serves the purpose of illustration.

```
noun("boy")   ←————————No period; symbol in quotation marks
noun("elephant")
noun("baby")
noun("girl")
noun("programmer")
verb("runs")
verb("cries")
verb("climbs")
verb("codes")
adverb("fast")
adverb("loudly")
adverb("obscurely")
adverb("high")
```

There are three things you can do with a disk-based consultable database in Turbo Prolog: load it, modify it, and save it.

Loading a Database

If the database is stored as a disk-based text file, it is opened and read into the computer's memory with the `consult` predicate. This predicate takes a single argument, the DOS name of the file to be consulted. A variable previously instantiated to the file name may be used with the `consult` predicate.

The file name must be enclosed in quotation marks if it is explicitly supplied, but the name of a variable instantiated to the file name must not be enclosed in quotation marks.

A text file to be consulted by Turbo Prolog must consist of facts that match the pattern of a valid database declaration predicate. If any fact stored in the database does not match a valid pattern, an attempt to consult it fails, resulting in a Turbo Prolog response of `False` when the consultation is attempted.

For example, to consult a database file called WORDS.LST, simply write a clause like this:

```
consult("words.lst")
```

Note that the file name can be all uppercase, all lowercase, or any mixture. Turbo Prolog converts the name to all uppercase before attempting to open the file because DOS file names are all uppercase.

The `consult` predicate must appear in a clause, unlike the `include` statement, which is a compiler directive and need not be included in a predicate. In other words, a consultation of a database takes place as the result of the execution of a rule.

Modifying a Database

The basic technique in modifying the information contained in a Turbo Prolog dynamic database is the standard Prolog method of asserting new facts and retracting old ones. Facts are added by assertion, deleted by retraction, and modified by a combination of the two steps.

Any additions, deletions, or changes to a dynamic database in Turbo Prolog are made only in RAM. Unless the modified database is stored on the disk (using the `save` predicate as described later), its contents are unchanged the next time it is consulted.

Asserting New Facts

The `assert` built-in predicates take a single argument in the form of a Prolog fact. The fact must match a database predicate in the program. Like most built-in predicates, `assert` predicates can be invoked at a `Goal:` prompt during program execution or by a clause in the program itself.

There are three forms of the `assert` predicate: `assert`, `asserta`, and `assertz`. The first, `assert`, is not documented in the Turbo Prolog manual. It is identical to the `assertz` predicate. The `asserta` predicate inserts the new fact at the beginning of the collection of related facts, and `assert` and `assertz` insert it at the end of that collection. For all practical purposes, the three predicates are functionally equivalent. If for some technical reason you need a new fact statement stored at the beginning or end of the list, you can use the appropriate built-in Turbo Prolog predicate. We will consistently use the `assertz` predicate rather than the undocumented `assert` predicate.

A quick example illustrates the use of `asserta` and `assertz`. If you begin with a database containing these facts:

```
article("a")
article("an")
article("the")
noun("boy")
noun("ball")
verb("cries")
verb("bounces")
```

and execute this predicate:

```
asserta(noun(girl)).
```

the database will look like this:

```
article(a)
article(an)
article(the)
noun(girl)
noun(boy)
noun(ball)
verb(cries)
verb(bounces)
```

If you execute yet another predicate or goal statement like this:

```
assertz(verb(runs)).
```

the new database is identical to the previous one, but the fact verb(runs) is added to the end of the database after the last verb fact.

Retracting Facts

You may want to remove a fact from a database for several reasons. These include the following:

- an erroneous fact has been entered into the system, found invalid, and now must be discarded
- you are ready to save the database, and one or more of the facts now stored in the RAM-based database are temporary values that you do not want to save
- the fact is about to be modified

To retract a fact, simply supply the fact or fact pattern as an argument to the retract predicate. For example, if a person using Micro_Parse inadvertently answered yes when asked whether elephant is a verb, you could retract that fact from the database by this command:

```
Goal:retract(verb(elephant)).
```

You can retract all the facts of a particular pattern by using uninstantiated variables in the retract predicate. To retract all verb definitions in a dynamic database, for example, simply type the following goal:

```
Goal:retract(verb(X)).
```

Modifying Facts

If you want to modify an existing fact, rather than remove it completely from the dynamic database, there are two steps. You must first retract the statement as it stands and then use one of the forms of the `assert` predicate to add a replacement fact that corrects the retracted fact. For example, in a natural language processing system, you might find a correctly stated fact with a misspelling in the word:

```
verb(atacks).
```

You can correct the misspelling in the dynamic database by the following sequence of `goal` statements:

```
Goal:retract(verb(atacks)).
True
Goal:assertz(verb(attacks)).
True
Goal:
```

In Turbo Prolog, there is no efficient way to retract a fact and replace it with a corrected fact in the same position in the knowledge base.

Storing a Dynamic Database

The Turbo Prolog built-in `save` predicate stores the current dynamic database contents to a disk file. It takes one argument: the name of the DOS file to which the database's contents should be saved. Alternatively, you can supply a variable instantiated to the file name.

In the WORDS.LST file, you can save the now modified file with the statement:

```
save("words.lst").
```

As with the `consult` predicate, this predicate can be used as a `goal` statement or in a predicate within the Turbo Prolog program. The DOS file name must be enclosed in quotation marks if it is explicitly supplied. Case is not significant.

When Turbo Prolog encounters a `save` predicate, it writes to the named disk file all current facts that match the patterns in the declared database predicates. There is no way to save only certain database facts. Remember, too, that you can only have one database file per module, but each such file can contain an arbitrarily large number of assertable predicates.

Databases and Projects

When using a dynamic database in a modular Turbo Prolog project, you must be aware of certain factors so you can avoid confusion and corrupted database files. Most of these considerations are not spelled out in the Turbo Prolog documentation.

Local versus Global Databases

A Turbo Prolog dynamic database is by nature local in scope. That is, it is confined to the module in which it is declared. But you can declare a dynamic database in the file containing the global definitions for the project, and the database will be known to all modules of the project even during testing.

Suppose you are designing a Turbo Prolog project in which multiple databases are used at various points. You can have multiple database declarations in the project, as long as no more than one database is declared within any single module. This may seem to violate the rule that Turbo Prolog permits only one dynamic database to be defined per program, but remember that a program is for all practical purposes the same as a module.

In most cases, however, you will probably define the dynamic database in the global definition file and then use it throughout the project's modules. A single database design is the simplest approach to the use of dynamic databases. Because there is no theoretical limit to the size of a dynamic database or the variety of facts it can store, it is generally better programming practice to define one database even when some modules of the project only need some of the facts stored in it.

Predicate Definition and Database Declaration

One problem that often arises in the use of dynamic databases in modular project design is the confusion of predicate definitions. You must keep in mind the following Turbo Prolog rule.

> **Rule:** A predicate defined in a database declaration may not be subsequently defined in the predicates section of any project module.

During testing, you might define a predicate as a nondatabase predicate in one module and then decide to make it a dynamic predicate in another module. When you compile and link the project, you will encounter errors as a result of this duplicate declaration. We'll have more to say about this subject in chapter 6.

Dynamic Databases in Micro_Parse

In the sample project, three of the four modules make direct use of the dynamic vocabulary database. LOADLIST must handle the "consult" of the database, VALIDATE must compare words to the dynamic database's list of valid vocabulary, and CLOSER must save the modified database to the disk. (In this chapter, you will deal with LOADLIST and CLOSER. Modifications to the VALIDATE module are covered in chapter 6.) Clearly, this is a case where you should use a global declaration of the database.

Declaring a Database

This database declaration is straightforward because only a few simple fact patterns are defined as dynamic. All of them represent parts of speech.

Add the following to the GLOBALS file so that it looks like this (new material is indicated):

```
global domains
   Sentence=symbol*
database  ←————————New
   noun(symbol)  ←———New
   verb(symbol)  ←———New
article(symbol)  ←———New
global predicates
   get_sentence
   set_up_topic  ←———New
```

After you modify your GLOBALS file, save it. You will use it in the LOADLIST and CLOSER modules when you create and test them in the rest of this chapter.

LOADLIST Module

As you might recall, the purpose of LOADLIST is to have the user identify a vocabulary list and load it into memory so that the other modules have access to those words.

This routine is quite straightforward. Here is the entire module:

```
project "m_parse"
include "globals.pro"
clauses
   set_up_topic if
      clearwindow,
      write("What topic do you wish to use?"),
      readln(Topic),
      concat(Topic,".LST",Filename),
      consult(Filename).
```

Enter this module into Turbo Prolog and save it.

Notice that you use the Turbo Prolog built-in concat predicate to create a new file name from that given by the user. In this way, you provide an automatic .LST extension to every vocabulary list stored as a dynamic database on disk. The user supplies only the first part of the file name, without the extension.

> **Note:** In a commercial program, you would want to check that the user didn't enter an .LST extension (or some other extension) before adding .LST to the user's input. But because you are in control of user interaction (you are the only user at the moment), you can ignore such niceties.

Building a Sample Database

If you were building a database application, rather than a program that uses a database, you would have to write a routine to create the database file in the first place. But because you do not need that capability in the Micro_Parse project, simply use a text editor to create a small dynamic database for testing. Follow this same approach to build and use any vocabulary lists for actual program use as well.

You can use Turbo Prolog's built-in text editor or your favorite word processor to generate the test file. If you use another word processor, however, be sure to save the file as a flat ASCII file. This may require you to use a Text Out feature in WordPerfect, the N mode (edit a non-document) in WordStar, or some other similar function on your word processor. If you use Turbo Prolog's editor, you are assured of generating a readable file.

Here is the small vocabulary file you will work with during the testing of the LOADLIST module:

```
noun("boy")
noun("girl")
noun("ball")
noun("dog")
verb("bounces")
verb("runs")
verb("cries")
article("a")
article("an")
article("the")   ←—Don't insert a carriage return here!
```

Create this file and save it as TESTFILE.LST.

Testing LOADLIST

Now let's test the LOADLIST module with the newly created vocabulary called TESTFILE.LST. Load and run the LOADLIST module. Your interaction with the program should look like this:

```
Goal: set_up_topic
True  ←————————————————————————————Dialog window clears
                                        here
What topic do you wish to use?TESTFILE  ←User response is
                                        underlined
True  ←————————————————————————————If False appears
                                        here, stop and read
Goal:noun(X).                           the following section
X=boy
X=girl
X=ball
X=dog
```

```
4 Solutions
Goal:verb(X).
X=bounces
X=runs
X=cries
3 Solutions
Goal:article(X).
X=a
X=an
X=the
3 Solutions
Goal:
```

You have now proved that the TESTFILE.LST file has been properly consulted by the LOADLIST module.

If you get a **False** response when you try to consult TESTFILE.LST, there's probably something wrong with the format of that file. Check to be sure you don't have any extra blanks (including a carriage return after the last entry), and that no periods appear at the end of any facts. Edit the file if necessary and save it.

CLOSER Module

The CLOSER module updates the proper vocabulary file when the user indicates that he or she has finished processing sentences. (How the user provides this indication is discussed in chapter 6.)

There is nothing complex about the module itself.

```
project "m_parse"
include "globals.pro"
clauses
  time_to_stop if
    save("STOPTEST.LST")
    clearwindow,
    write("Done!"),nl.
```

Type this program into Turbo Prolog and save it as CLOSER.PRO. Add a predicate declaration to the GLOBALS file for the new `time_to_stop` predicate.

Notice that the name of the file is programmed into the module. For the finished program, you want the file name to be the same as that chosen by the user in the LOADLIST module. But the CLOSER module is being tested independently of the LOADLIST module, so you need to supply an arbitrary file name. This is often a necessary trick in testing modules that must ultimately work together.

Testing CLOSER

It may not be obvious how to test the CLOSER module. After all, there isn't anything in the file called STOPTEST.LST, so if you run the program now it should create an empty file. That will tell you something, but unless you understand a good deal about DOS it might not tell you enough.

This is a problem you will frequently encounter when testing independent modules of a Turbo Prolog project. When you finalize all the modules and get them ready to work together (the subject of the next chapter), you will see how all of this comes together. But for the moment, you need to test the CLOSER module.

You can take advantage of the fact that Turbo Prolog lets you supply goals that are not defined in the program but are universal to the language. In this case, you'll use the `assertz` built-in predicate to add a few words to the vocabulary, and then save the file with the `time_to_stop` predicate. Let's see how this works.

Load the CLOSER routine if it isn't already in your Editor window. Now run it. Try the following interaction:

```
Goal:assertz(noun(elephant)).
True
Goal:assertz(noun(tiger)).
True
Goal:assertz(verb(growls)).
True
Goal:assertz(verb(roars)).
True
Goal:time_to_stop
True
Goal:
```

If all has worked as planned, a file called STOPTEST.LST now exists on the current drive and directory. (If you are using a hard disk and store your .PRO files on a different directory or subdirectory from other files, the STOPTEST.LST file is on the same directory as the .PRO files.) Its contents look like this:

```
noun("elephant")
noun("tiger")
verb("growls")
verb("roars")
```

There are two ways to confirm the accuracy of this description. You can use the Operating system option in the Files menu, and then use TYPE (or some equivalent command) to display the contents of the file on your screen. Or you can run LOADLIST and use the debugging techniques described for that routine.

Using LOADLIST to Test CLOSER

To test CLOSER using the tested and debugged version of LOADLIST, follow these instructions:

1. Load the LOADLIST file.
2. Run it.
3. When asked *Which topic do you wish to use?* answer *STOPTEST*.
4. Use the noun(X), verb(X), and article(X) goal statements to confirm that the nouns elephant and tiger and the verbs growls and roars are stored in the file, but that no articles are stored there.

Summary

You have entered and tested each of the four independent modules of the Micro_Parse project. In this chapter, you learned how to define and use dynamic databases in Turbo Prolog and some of the things to watch for when using such structures in a modular project. You have also designed, written, and tested the two main modules in the project that use the dynamic database.

In chapter 6, you turn your attention to the steps needed to get these modules to work together as a project.

Chapter **6**

Preparing the Modules
for Implementation

 This chapter describes, in general and in relation to the Micro_Parse project, modifications you must make to independent modules created during a program's construction so that those modules work together in a Turbo Prolog project.

First, you look at general considerations regarding problems that often arise when converting from standalone modules to an integrated project. Then you examine the main driver routine in the Micro_Parse project. Next, you determine what, if anything, must be changed in each of the project modules. All of this work prepares you for compiling and linking the Micro_Parse project. Finally, you compile, link, and execute the Micro_Parse project.

General Considerations

After you have implemented all modules in a Turbo Prolog project and the time comes to pull the independently tested pieces together, you will probably need to make changes to the modules. The need to make such modifications is not a reflection on your programming or design skills. Some aspects of project design in Turbo Prolog conflict with other things you must do to develop and test individual modules.

For example, in the Micro_Parse project, you tested the GET-SENT module with database declarations in place. You could have tested it after declaring the global database in the GLOBALS file. In a real-life design situation, you almost certainly would do just that. But you were not introduced to the idea of a dynamic database, so the database statements were included in the module. Now, as you will soon see, you have to modify GETSENT to eliminate these references.

In real-world applications, you often need to include some code segment in a module for testing. But when the project is assembled, not only is the code unnecessary, it may also cause an error.

53

Another type of change you will see as you progress from independent modules toward a fully integrated and operational project is in main driver routines. For example, you might define the driver routine to include a predicate that requires a list as an argument. Later, as you debug the routine, you find that you want to pass the list argument not at the time the routine is invoked, but later. You would have to change the main driver routine so it does not create an error either during compilation or at run time.

The primary problems when you prepare modules for project compilation and linkage are conflicts and duplication. It is important to remember that a finished Turbo Prolog project is in some ways a single program and in other ways a collection of independent programs. Learning when and how to use the project in the appropriate way is something that comes only with experience.

The Driver Module

Turn your attention to the main driver routine in the Micro_Parse project. At the same time, we will make some general observations about the role of such driver routines in projects.

Goal Statement

In chapter 3, when we discussed the methods for dividing a project into modules, we mentioned that each project requires one and only one `goal` statement. Generally, this statement is placed in the main driver module if one exists.

It is impossible to overemphasize the importance of including a single `goal` statement. Because the main driver module doesn't generally do anything, it is difficult or impossible to test during the testing phase of a modular Turbo Prolog project. As a result, the `goal` statement makes its first executable appearance during the final phase of a project's implementation. But if it is omitted from the final module, an attempt to compile and link the project's modules will most likely result in a large number of seemingly meaningless errors.

The `goal` statement is the first predicate executed when the module is run. In general, the form for a `goal` statement in a modular project is a single-word goal, such as `go` or `start`, that is then defined as a predicate in the main driver routine. The modular predicates make up the `goal` statement and appear in the order in which they are executed.

Main Driver in Micro_Parse

In the Micro_Parse project, the main driver routine now looks like this (as you may recall from chapter 3):

```
project "m_parse"
include "globals.pro"
predicates
    go
```

```
goal
  go.
clauses
  go :-
    set_up_topic,
    get_sentence,
    check_sentence(Sentence),
    time_to_stop.
```

The `set_up_topic` predicate appears in the LOADLIST module, the `get_sentence` predicate is in the GETSENT module, the `check_sentence` predicate is in the VALIDATE module, and the `time_to_stop` predicate is in the CLOSER module. This is the order in which the modules are normally executed.

Testing and the Main Driver Module

Because the main driver module "knows" about the global predicates but does not explicitly load individual modules, you cannot test it as a standalone module. In effect, it is not a standalone module. If you try to load and run it like any other module, you will encounter an Error 401: no clauses for this predicate. This is because the first predicate in the definition of your goal clause `go` is `set_up_topic` and the main driver module does not have access to the LOADLIST module in which that predicate's clause appears.

If you have a large main driver routine and testing is important, you have to "hard code" clauses for each global predicate into the driver routine. But better programming practice is to keep the driver routine small so that testing it independently is unnecessary.

Modifying the Modules

Now turn your attention to the remaining modules in the Micro_Parse project. As you examine each module, you will discover what changes must be made before each can be integrated into the project and compiled. Compiling, linking, and using the project are described later.

Project File

Assuming that you have included the names of all five modules in the M_PARSE.PRJ file, no further modification of that file is needed. Until compilation and linkage take place, this file is not used.

However, sometimes you might test portions of a project while leaving other portions out of the compile-and-link process. In such an event, you will have omitted from the .PRJ file the file names of the modules not involved in the test. If you do that with a project, be sure to add the names of the previously omitted modules back into the .PRJ file before compiling and linking the project.

GLOBALS File Quite often as you move from individual modules to a finished project, you will find that you can declare additional global predicates in the file containing global definitions. See if a predicate definition appears in more than one of the individual modules. If you find such duplicate definition, you should probably remove the individual declarations and replace them with one global predicate declaration.

Remember, too, that when you declare any predicate that includes arguments in the GLOBALS.PRO file, you must provide one or more flow patterns for the parameters.

In this example, you do not need to make any changes in the GLOBALS.PRO file because you have been building the global definitions as you progressed through the design.

LOADLIST Module In developing the LOADLIST module, as you might recall, you included the definition of the dynamic database. Later, you included that dynamic database declaration within the GLOBALS.PRO file. Not only is it redundant to declare the database twice, but doing so will generate an error indicating that there are unresolved externals in your project.

Delete the database declaration section of the LOADLIST module. No other changes are required.

GETSENT Module In the GETSENT module, you included a line that was only needed during testing. Now that you have finished testing, you need to remove that line so that the final project runs as expected.

In the `get_sentence` clause, remove the last line, which is:

```
write(Wordlist).
```

Be sure to change the comma to a period at the end of the preceding line because it has now become the last line in this clause.

No other changes are required for this module to compile and link correctly. Save it and move on to the next module.

VALIDATE Module You will not make any modifications to the VALIDATE module. But one potential change that is rejected illustrates a lesson about project design.

Notice that the VALIDATE module is the only one that declares simple Prolog facts. Specifically, it defines an article to be either *a, an,* or *the.* As previously noted, you do not need a predicate to add articles to the knowledge base (similar to the `nountest` predicate in this module) because you have defined articles to be a fixed number of facts.

It is possible, however, to remove these facts from the VALIDATE module and require that each vocabulary file contain a definition of the articles used in it. Such a decision is not wise because it results in virtually every vocabulary database file containing, in all likelihood, three additional facts it does not need. If you have a dozen such databases, you increase the disk storage requirement for the natural language system by thirty-six such facts.

But sometimes facts—included in a module during testing and not subject to dynamic database modification during program execution—should be removed from the module and placed in the database on disk. If, for example, you defined twenty such facts and in any one database file only a few are needed, you might make your project run faster and more efficiently by placing in each database only those fixed facts it needs.

Remember that if you do make such a modification, you must modify the database declaration section(s) of your project to include proper definitions for the new fact patterns.

CLOSER Module

In the Micro_Parse project, the CLOSER file requires the most modification, though the changes are not difficult.

Recall that during testing, you arbitrarily assigned a hard-coded file name to the save predicate. You used STOPTEST.LST as that file name to prove that the module correctly saved a file for later retrieval. Now, however, you must generalize this module. After all, you don't want to save each modified vocabulary knowledge base in a file called STOPTEST.LST. You want users to know where the files are saved so that they can use them again.

There are two approaches to this. One is to have the program remember the name of the vocabulary file the user specified in the LOAD-LIST module and save the vocabulary into that same file as the user exits the program. The other is to ask the user for the name of the file in which to save the possibly revised vocabulary, and then save it there.

We use the second method for a number of reasons:

- It is easier to program. The first method, because of the local scope of variables in Prolog, would be handled best by designing the program so that it writes the name of the consulted file into a text file using the Turbo Prolog built-in predicates writedevice and write. Then when processing is complete, the name of the file could be retrieved using readdevice and read.

- It is more flexible and gives the user better control. It is entirely possible that after updating a vocabulary, the user may want to retain the original file's contents for later use (perhaps by other users). This method permits the user to provide a different name from the one used to consult the file. If, on the other hand, users want to update the original file, they only have to type the same file name and Turbo Prolog obligingly overwrites the old file's contents with the updated vocabulary.

- This approach lends itself better to modular program design. If you were really interested in using the first approach, you would probably rethink your modularization decisions so that all file access—consulting and saving—is handled in one module.

Essentially, you must rewrite the entire `time_to_stop` clause in the CLOSER module. When you have finished rewriting, it should look similar to this:

```
project "m_parse"
include "globals.pro"
time_to_stop if
  clearwindow,
  write("Under what topic should I store this word list?
    "),
  readln(Topic),
  concat(Topic,".LST",Filename),
  save(Filename),
  clearwindow,
  write("Thanks for using this program!").
```

The only thing this new program has in common with the old is the `save` predicate. Note, though, that the first four lines are a virtual duplicate of the LOADLIST module's lines, so you can be fairly sure they work. The last two lines are simply gratuitous user interface items that could be omitted.

Should You Retest CLOSER?

When a module undergoes this kind of extensive revision, the question of whether it can and should be retested arises. There is no universal reliable answer to that question.

In general, if the revised module can be tested, you should test it. Sometimes, though, the modifications made at this stage make the module untestable.

In the CLOSER module, it could be argued that the modification is relatively slight, even though virtually the entire module was revised. You can tell by inspection that these new lines are almost certainly going to perform as expected.

Testing CLOSER

If you do want to test the new CLOSER module, use the technique described in chapter 5. Load and run the file, and then use `assert` clauses as goals to add noun, verb, and adverb facts to the dynamic database. When you have enough facts to be satisfied with the test, simply type:

```
Goal: time_to_stop
```

and the program asks for the file name, saves the file, and ends processing.

Whether you actually carry out this testing or not is up to you. You'll undoubtedly make the decision on a project-by-project basis.

Stopping the Program

There is one remaining flaw in the program. If you compile it now, it asks for one topic file name, accepts one input sentence for validation, updates the vocabulary, and exits the program. If you want to make substantial vocabulary additions to a file, the program has to be run repeatedly. This is because we have not provided a "trigger," or means to notify the program when to stop. As a result, Turbo Prolog quite logically executes each of the clauses in the driver module in turn.

Because the `check_sentence` predicate only goes through the process of checking a sentence one time, you must find a way to force that predicate to continue to execute until the user signals that he or she is ready to stop.

There are a number of ways to do this. One is to put in a new predicate that provides only the trigger action. In a complex program that calls a number of predicates, this might be the most efficient way of handling the task. But in this situation, you only need to add a single line to the `check_sentence` predicate, which checks for a specific input from the user. If this input is encountered, the predicate fails and the `time_to_stop` predicate executes. A second added line in the `check_sentence` module calls the `get_sentence` module after the `check_sentence` predicate has succeeded.

You can use whatever trigger you like to stop the program. Keep in mind, though, that it is useful to select a word that is unlikely to be included in the vocabulary. We'll use *halt* because alternatives like *quit* and *exit* are more commonly used in natural language vocabulary.

Here's how this line will look:

```
check_sentence([First,Second,Third]) :-
First<>"halt",  ←————————————————————This is the new
                                        line
/* the rest of the predicate is unchanged */
```

The second added line comes at the end of the predicate. It simply calls `get_sentence`.

```
/*  except for the new last line, the predicate is
      unchanged  */
getsent(L).
```

Compiling and Linking the Modules

With all of the modifications to the modules in the Micro_Parse project, you are ready to convert the project into a standalone program that is executable from the DOS prompt level. This process is simple.

First, select the Project (all modules) option from the Options menu. When asked for the name of the project file, type *m_parse*.

Next, type *C* to instruct Turbo Prolog to compile your project. There is a considerable amount of disk activity, much of it reflected in displays in the Message window. When the program has finished compiling and linking, you will see the question *Execute (y/n)?* in the Message window. If you want to run the program now, type *y*. If you want to save the program for later execution, type *n*.

To run this program later, just get to the DOS prompt with the proper path specified and type *M_PARSE*.

Summary

In this chapter, you saw the kinds of modifications that are often necessary in designing and constructing modular projects. You made a number of corrections to the Micro_Parse project that illustrate both the types of changes and their significance. Finally, you saw how easy it is to compile and link these modules into an executable file.

This chapter concludes the discussion of modular programming in Turbo Prolog. In part 2, you learn how to make Turbo Prolog programs interact with code written in other languages and with the outside world.

Turbo Prolog and the Outside World

Chapter 7

Overview of the Turbo Prolog Interface

 This chapter presents an overview of the ways Turbo Prolog interacts with programs and routines written in other languages, with the PC's operating system, and with commercial application programs.

Why an Outside World?

Although Turbo Prolog is a powerful and flexible language, it is not ideally suited to all programming tasks. For example, its arithmetic skills are rudimentary. To take advantage of the superior "number-crunching" capabilities of other programming languages, you might want to design a system in which some of the processing is handled outside Turbo Prolog, with the results available to your Turbo Prolog program.

You might also want to devise an interaction between Turbo Prolog and other programs when existing data and programs are more usable. For example, if you have set up a spreadsheet that calculates your cash flow position, you would not want to require that the user print a report of the results of that analysis and enter the answers into Turbo Prolog as a separate step. You would want to get those results from (quite probably) the same disk where Turbo Prolog and your program are stored.

Finally, you may want to undertake some actions in your Turbo Prolog programs that require more direct access to DOS and the internals of the PC than is permitted by Turbo Prolog's high-level language design. This "bit fiddling" might involve real-time data collection, communications port management, direct memory management, or other activities that take place at a far lower level than that on which Turbo Prolog operates.

There might be other reasons for wanting to connect Turbo Prolog to the "outside world." In any case, if you are to construct truly useful programs, you will probably want to design such interactions.

There are essentially two ways an interaction can take place between Turbo Prolog and another language or program. These are summarized in table 7-1 and discussed in greater detail in the following sections.

Table 7-1
Two Basic Methods of Interaction

Type	Interaction Through	Comments
Intermediate File	A file accessed by both programs	Less than automatic. Not efficient.
Direct Call	Predeclared Turbo Prolog external predicates	Difficult to program. Both programs need special care.

Intermediate File Approach

Using an intermediate file approach, Turbo Prolog and the outside world program "agree" on an intermediate file through which to exchange information. This requires the designer to have control of both the Turbo Prolog program and the external program. Figure 7-1 depicts how the basic exchange takes place. In essence, one program executes up to a certain point. It then stores some result in the agreed upon intermediate file. The other program then runs, opens the agreed upon file, extracts the results, and uses them.

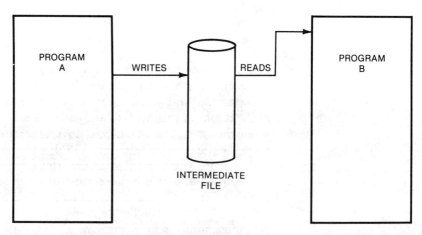

Figure 7-1
Simple intermediate file interaction

As you can see in figure 7-2, this interaction can become quite complex and involve multiple passes of variables, intermediate results, and final answers through the intermediate file.

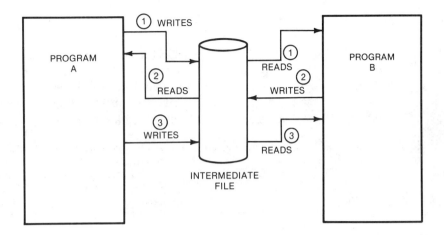

Figure 7-2
Complex intermediate file interaction

However, the interaction between the Turbo Prolog program and the external program is less than automatic. Unless the external program creates an executable object file that Turbo Prolog can call directly, the user will probably be involved to some extent in this interaction.

If you wanted, for example, to calculate the mean and standard deviation of a series of data points entered by the user into Turbo Prolog, you might set up a sequence of events like the following:

1. The Turbo Prolog program accepts the data points into a defined dynamic database and, using the **save** predicate, stores these values as a series of numbers in a file called STDEV.DTA.

2. The user exits Turbo Prolog and calls a Pascal program called STANDEV.PAS that reads the data points stored in the STDEV.DTA file. (By using loops and counters in both programs, the number of data points can easily vary from one call to the next.)

3. The Pascal program performs its calculation and stores two values—the mean and the standard deviation—in a new file called RESULT1.

4. As the Pascal program completes its execution, it notifies the user that the Prolog program should be run again.

5. The Turbo Prolog program checks to see if there are any values in a file called RESULT1. If so, it uses them to finish its processing. If not, it assumes the user is ready to enter new data points, and it executes that routine.

There is nothing very complicated about this method of interaction between Turbo Prolog and an external program. The two programs must share a common understanding about which files are used for what purposes, and the user must intervene at a few points.

Direct Call Method

Turbo Prolog includes built-in predicates and declarations that permit a program to call directly a routine written in Pascal, C, FORTRAN, or assembly language. This method is much more direct and automatic than the intermediate file approach. Figure 7-3 depicts a typical direct call sequence involving a program written in C.

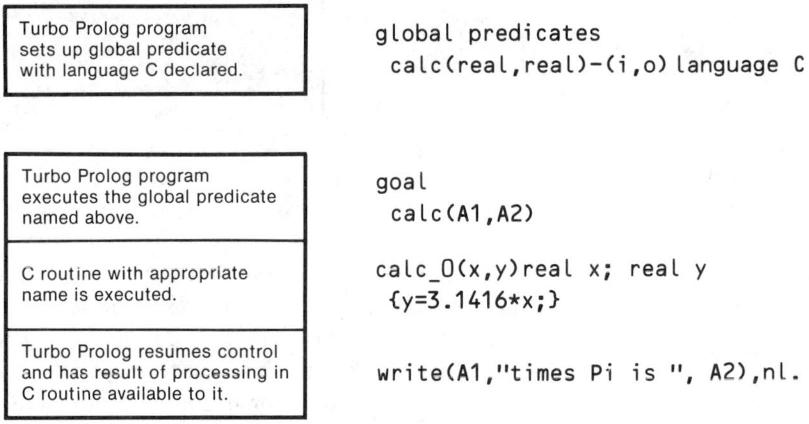

```
Turbo Prolog program            global predicates
sets up global predicate          calc(real,real)-(i,o) language C
with language C declared.


Turbo Prolog program            goal
executes the global predicate     calc(A1,A2)
named above.

C routine with appropriate      calc_0(x,y)real x; real y
name is executed.               {y=3.1416*x;}

Turbo Prolog resumes control
and has result of processing in write(A1,"times Pi is ", A2),nl.
C routine available to it.
```

Figure 7-3
Direct call interaction

The processing of the direct call method of program interaction is straightforward and easy to understand. It does, however, require careful coding in the Turbo Prolog program making the call. You will delve into this in greater detail in a few moments. Right now, let's look at the basic processing requirements.

Flow of Direct Call Interactions

When Turbo Prolog interacts with an external program written in another language through the direct call technique, there are a number of rules to follow:

1. A global predicate must be declared. The Turbo Prolog program must include a global predicates section that declares one or more predicates to be external to the program and explicitly identifies the language in which these predicates are written.

2. Flow control pattern(s) must be included. In the global predicates section, the flow pattern(s) of the predicate must be explicitly provided.

3. The predicate must be used in a goal or statement. The predicate declared as external is then used exactly as if it were a Turbo Prolog goal or statement. It is simply stated, with the

appropriate number of parameters, in the appropriate place in the program.

4. The external program name must follow a convention. Because of the possibility of alternate or compound flow patterns in global predicates, Turbo Prolog automatically assigns an appendage to the predicate name. This appendage must be explicitly included in the name of the external language routine being called.

Let's take a closer look at each of these rules and use some examples to clarify what they mean. (Don't be concerned if you don't understand everything about the examples and what they are doing at this point. These are "dummy" routines created solely for these examples.)

Global Domain and Predicate Declarations

As you saw in chapter 2, Turbo Prolog assumes that all predicates and domains in an individual program are local to that program. This is true even though the program may be only one module in a Turbo Prolog project. To enable more than one program in a single project to use the same predicate and its associated domain values, predicates and domains must be explicitly declared as global.

Declaring domains as global is identical to declaring any domain, except key words identify the declarations as global domains instead of simple local domains.

```
global domains
   value = string
   vallist = integer*
```

After a domain is declared global in this way, its value is available to any other program in the multiprogram project. This includes programs written in languages other than Turbo Prolog.

Declaring global predicates is more complex than declaring global domains. In most respects, a global predicate's declaration is identical to that of an ordinary local predicate. The differences are in the inclusion of flow pattern information about the predicate and the necessity of defining the language in which the external procedure is written if it is not another Turbo Prolog program.

Flow Pattern Declarations

Return your attention to the program code in figure 7-3. The global predicates declaration at the top of this figure is:

```
global predicates
   calc(real,real) - (i,o) language C
```

The first part of this declaration is quite familiar. It is an ordinary predicate declaration that describes a predicate named calc that is associated with two parameters, both real numbers. But that is where the similarity ends.

Following this otherwise ordinary predicate declaration is a hyphen followed by the expression (i,o). This is the flow pattern for this predicate.

> **Note:** Flow patterns and their explicit declaration are unique
> to Turbo Prolog. If you are planning to develop applications
> in other dialects of Prolog, be sure to check that version's
> method of handling external calls written in other languages.

Any flow pattern description in Turbo Prolog consists of two or more letters enclosed in parentheses and separated by commas. The two allowable letters are i and o. The i stands for input and the o for output. These terms are a bit misleading but their use will become clear in a moment.

Each argument in the global predicate's declaration must have an i or an o associated with it in every flow pattern description. (As you will see, there may be multiple flow patterns in a single predicate declaration.)

You can think of arguments whose position corresponds to an i in a flow pattern description as being known at the time the predicate is called. In contrast, those positions that have an o in the flow pattern description are unknown at the time the predicate is invoked. In figure 7-3, there is only one flow pattern. It indicates that the first real number following the calc predicate is known at the time the call is made and that the second is unknown. In other words, if both values are variables, the first is instantiated before the predicate is called and the second is not.

If you look at the goal statement in figure 7-3, you'll see that the predicate is invoked with two variable names, A1 and A2, as arguments. Because of the flow pattern description, A1 must be instantiated before this point and A2 must not be instantiated. The external procedure simply multiplies the known argument, A1, by Pi and returns the answer in the unknown variable, A2. If you invoked the calc predicate with A1 uninstantiated, an error condition would result.

Expected Uses of i and o

In most external calls to procedures written in languages other than Turbo Prolog, at least one argument has a flow pattern of o, indicating it is unknown when the procedure is called. If this were not the case, the Turbo Prolog code and the external program would not have a common variable to store and retrieve the result of a procedure. In other words, there would be no vehicle by which the two programs could interact.

Multiple Flow Patterns

One of the most powerful features of Prolog is its ability to be reversible. The same predicate used to process specific argument values can be used to generate them. A simple example is the sum predicate, which adds two numbers:

```
sum(X,Y,Z) :- Z = X + Y.
```

If you supply two known values for the first two arguments, the sum predicate instantiates the variable Z to their sum:

```
Goal: sum(3,9,S).
S = 12
1 Solution
Goal:
```

But if you instead supply the first value and the sum, the predicate calculates with equal facility the difference of those two values:

```
Goal: sum(3,D,12).
D = 9
1 Solution
Goal:
```

This reversible feature can be used quite powerfully in sophisticated programs of the type you will work with when you finish this book. Other languages require two separate routines to perform such seemingly different processes as addition and subtraction.

In the previous situation, if you wanted to use both versions of the sum predicate in a project, you would declare the predicate as follows:

```
global predicates
  sum(integer,integer,integer) - (i,i,o) (i,o,i)
      language C
```

If you try to invoke the sum predicate with the second argument known but the first unknown, you cause an error because the first integer argument can only be known when the predicate is called, regardless of which of the two valid forms you are using.

Declaring the Language

As mentioned, in Turbo Prolog you explicitly declare the language in which the external reference used by the predicate is written. There are a host of technical reasons—some hinted at in the Turbo Prolog reference manual and all beyond the scope of this book—to declare explicitly the language in which the external procedure is written. Suffice it to say that it makes for more efficient compilation and execution of your Turbo Prolog programs.

By the way, all external calls in a single Turbo Prolog project do not need to be written in the same language. Each predicate must have its own language declaration in any event, so mixing languages is valid.

External Procedure Naming Convention

There is one final general rule to be observed in creating Turbo Prolog external program calls. As you have seen, there is the possibility of multiple flow patterns in a predicate's definition and usage. In addition, any given predicate can have a number of variant forms, where the number of arguments (in technical Prolog talk, its *arity*) varies from one use to another.

The language in which the external calls are written, unless it is Prolog, cannot simply mix and match these variants and multiple flow pattern definitions at will as Turbo Prolog does. Each specific use of the predicate must have, in all likelihood, a separate definition in the external program. To differentiate among all possible variations in use in the external program, Turbo Prolog adds an underscore and an integer to the end of the predicate name before it calls the external procedure.

Returning to the sum predicate declaration in which we provided two flow patterns—one for addition and one for subtraction—Turbo Prolog expects to find procedures named sum_0 and sum_1. If the flow pattern in the sum predicate at the time it is called is (i,i,o), then sum_0 is called. If the flow pattern is (i,o,i), then Turbo Prolog invokes the external procedure sum_1.

This means you must write a separate procedure for each type of call the Turbo Prolog program might make to an external predicate. This is true even if you have no variants and no multiple flow patterns: the external procedure in that case will have to be called sum_0.

Summary

This chapter introduced the interaction between Turbo Prolog and external procedures written in C, Pascal, FORTRAN, and assembly language. You saw that there are two basic methods by which this interaction can take place: the use of an intermediate file and the direct call of an external routine declared as a global predicate. You learned the rules for using direct calls and studied flow patterns and their declaration.

Chapter 8 focuses on specific languages in which to write these external calls. It builds on the principles established in this chapter to demonstrate through examples how to construct, compile, and execute externally written programs in other languages. If your program interacts with other high-level languages, the next chapter is quite useful. If you need to interact with DOS, chapter 9 contains additional helpful information.

Chapter **8**

Interfacing with Programs in Other Languages

This chapter discusses some specific issues in writing Turbo Prolog programs that interact with programs in other languages. Turbo Prolog, following the lead of other Prologs and taking the process a step further than most, permits access to programs in Pascal, C, FORTRAN, and assembly language. (It also permits flexible access to MS-DOS and PC-DOS, but that is the subject of chapter 9.)

First, the general principles and techniques in designing Turbo Prolog programs to interact with external routines in these other languages are discussed. Then you look at Pascal, C, and assembly language interactions in turn, with a few examples of interface techniques. Although FORTRAN interfaces are not discussed, the general principles and techniques apply equally well to it.

In this chapter, we assume you are familiar with the high-level language used for the external programming. Therefore, no explanations beyond basic descriptions are provided for terminology and concepts, with the exception of those peculiar to Turbo Prolog.

General Design Techniques

You must be aware of four general design issues when you write external procedures in other languages that are called from a Turbo Prolog program:

- declaration of the external procedure
- appropriate procedure naming in the external program
- proper use of parameters
- selection of the large memory model

The first two issues were addressed in chapter 7. A discussion of the other two follows.

Proper Use of Parameters

Parameters are passed between Turbo Prolog and external routines written in other languages (except assembly language) through the 8086 processor's stack. Table 8-1 shows the various data types in Turbo Prolog and their size implementation. If the parameter is passed from Turbo Prolog to the external routine, it is pushed onto the stack as a 32-bit pointer to the memory location where the return value must be stored before control returns to Turbo Prolog. Input parameters passed to Turbo Prolog are pushed directly onto the stack; the size of the parameter on the stack depends on the data type.

Table 8-1
Turbo Prolog Data Types

Type	Stored As
integer	2 bytes
real	8 bytes (using IEEE format)
char	1 byte (2 bytes when pushed onto the stack)
string	4-byte double-word pointer to null-terminated string
symbol	4-byte double-word pointer to null-terminated string
compound	4-byte double-word pointer to record

Many language compilers, including Microsoft C, Microsoft Pascal, and Turbo C, allow the programmer to choose between 16-bit and 32-bit pointers. Turbo Prolog requires that all pointers be 32-bit values.

Stack management becomes an issue if the external routines are written in any language other than C. All other languages must remove from the stack any parameters except those being returned to Turbo Prolog. C handles this process automatically, so the C programmer can ignore the issue of stack management in interactions with Turbo Prolog.

Using the Proper Memory Model

Many high-level languages and virtually all implementations of C allow the programmer to choose a large or small memory model when compiling and linking programs. Turbo Prolog requires that you always use the large memory model when programming external routines if the option is available.

Interfacing with C

The easiest high-level language supported by Turbo Prolog to interface is C. Turbo C is designed with "hooks" that greatly facilitate such interfaces, but calling external routines written in Microsoft C is also straightforward. This section provides a short example of a useful C routine and shows how it can be implemented and called from Turbo Prolog.

The C Routine   This small routine is written in Microsoft C, Version 4.0. It counts the number of characters in a text file, excluding control characters, carriage returns, and linefeeds, and returns the answer as an integer.

```
int_acrtused;
count_em (name)
  char *name
{
  FILE *fpt;
  INT i=0;
  INT c;
  fpt = fopen(name,"rb");
if (fpt==NULL) {
  printf("Could not open %s\n",name);
  exit(); }
printf("Opened %s\n",name);
c=0;
WHILE(c!=EOF) {
  c=fgetc(fpt);
    if(c>=0X20) i++; }
  fclose(fpt);
return(i)
}
```

Note the strange looking line at the beginning of this program:

```
int_acrtused;
```

This prevents a link error. (The origin of this link error is unclear.) It is only required if you prepare this file for the Microsoft C compiler.

If you are using a Microsoft C compiler, Version 4.0 or later, enter this program and save it as COUNTEM. You'll use this file name in the compilation and linkage instructions later in this chapter.

The Prolog Program   The following Turbo Prolog program uses the C program you have just saved as COUNTEM. In real-life programming, this would be a small part of a much larger project rather than a program. But this small routine serves our purposes.

```
global predicates
  _count_em(string,integer) - (i,o) language C
    predicates
  char_count(integer)
goal
  char_count(X).
clauses
  char_count(Count) :-
```

```
clearwindow,
write("Enter the file name: "),
readln(Filename),
_count_em(Filename,Total),
write("There are ",Total," characters in the
  file.").
```

Notice that in both the Turbo Prolog program and the C listing, an underscore character is placed in front of the name of the C predicate to be called. This is required by Microsoft C's methods of calling external routines. If you are using a different C compiler, this may not be necessary, but including it will not cause a problem.

Type this program into Turbo Prolog and save it as CHRCOUNT.PRO. You'll use this name in further processing steps.

Compiling the C Program

To compile the C program COUNTEM.C so that it can be linked with Turbo Prolog, use this compilation sequence:

```
msc /Gs /AL COUNTEM.C
```

The /Gs option turns off stack checking. The /AL arguments result in the use of the large memory model, as required by Turbo Prolog.

When this compilation process is complete, a file called COUNTEM.OBJ exists on your disk.

Compiling the Prolog Program

Next, you compile CHRCOUNT.PRO as an executable file using the built-in Turbo Prolog compiler. First, use the Options selection from the Compile menu to choose a file of type .EXE. Then choose the Compile option. This creates a new object file, CHRCOUNT.EXE.

Linking the Two Programs

Now let's create a project file with the same name as the main file it contains. (This is a requirement.) The new file, CHRCOUNT.PRJ, contains this line:

```
CHRCOUNT+COUNTEM+
```

After you create the project file, select Compile Project under the Options pull-down menu, give Turbo Prolog the name of the project file, and choose the Compile option.

Using Other C Compilers

We selected the Microsoft C compiler because of its widespread use. The interface with other C compilers is similar to that described for the Microsoft C compiler, but each compiler has its own idiosyncrasies. For example, Lattice C requires the definition of a group of public symbols usually found in the Lattice C initialization code before you can use external routines.

Be sure to read your C compiler's documentation, especially as it relates to interfacing with external procedures, before attempting to build a project that relies on interaction between Turbo Prolog and C.

Interfacing with Pascal

Turbo Prolog can also call external predicates written in Pascal. The examples in this chapter use Microsoft's Pascal compiler. Turbo Prolog will not be compatible with Turbo Pascal until Borland releases Pascal Version 4.0. At that time, documentation will be included in the Turbo Pascal manual regarding the interface. Turbo Prolog is compatible only with Version 3.2 or higher of Microsoft Pascal.

The procedures in this discussion should work equally well with other implementations of Pascal, provided they have the ability to compile source code to an object file (type .OBJ).

The Pascal Module
In Microsoft Pascal, use the module type to define your program. This avoids the need to provide overhead programming, which is only required if the program runs as a standalone subsystem. This module presents the doubling and halving example mentioned previously.

```
program TWOHALF;
var a,b: integer;
procedure two_times_0(VAR a: integer; VARS b:integer);
begin
  b:=2*a;
end;
procedure two_times_1(VARS a: integer; VAR b:integer);
begin
  a:=b/2;
end;
```

Notice that we have defined two procedures, following the Turbo Prolog naming convention, so that `two_times_0` performs doubling and `two_times_1` takes care of halving.

Note, too, that the unbound variable in each of the two procedures is passed as a `vars` parameter. This is mandatory. Without this approach, Microsoft Pascal will use 2-byte pointers for these variables. As you saw earlier, Turbo Prolog requires 32-bit pointers for all such transfers. Type this program and save it as TWOHALF.PAS.

The Prolog Program
As in the C example, we will demonstrate a small and simplistic Turbo Prolog program that calls the Pascal code and displays the response.

```
global predicates
  two_times(integer,integer) - (i,o),(o,i) language
    Pascal
predicates
  run
  chooseop(char)
clauses
  run :-
    clearwindow,
    write("Enter an integer: "),
    readint(In),
    write("Enter D to double it, H to divide it by two:
     "),
    readchar(Op),
    chooseop(Op).
  chooseop(Op):-
    (Op='D' or Op='d'),
    two_times(In,Result),
    write("Your number doubled is ",Result),
    nl.
  chooseop(Op):-
    (Op='H' or 'h'),
    two_times(Result,In),
    write("Your number halved is ",Result),
    nl.
  chooseop(_):-
    write("Sorry, I didn't understand your choice.").
```

Type this program into Turbo Prolog and save it as TWOTIMES.PRO.

Compiling and Linking the Modules

Compile the Pascal TWOHALF program with the following commands:

```
PAS1 TWOHALF
PAS2
```

This creates the file TWOHALF.OBJ on the disk.

Now compile the Turbo Prolog program TWOTIMES.PRO into an object file. Define a new .PRJ file called TWOTIMES.PRJ to include these two newly created object files. The project file should consist of the line:

```
TWOTIMES+TWOHALF+
```

Finally, compile the project using the techniques discussed previously:

1. Select the Compile Module option from the Options menu.

2. Give the name TWOTIMES for the project file.

3. Select the Compile option from the Options menu.

The program is now ready to run. Simply type TWOTIMES from the DOS prompt and follow the directions.

Interfacing with Assembly Language

Because of the very nature of assembly language, there are a few additional rules when writing Turbo Prolog programs that interact with external procedures written in assembly code. In this section, we explain those rules and then turn to an example from the Turbo Prolog reference manual for an explanation of the processes. Finally, we look at some nicely predefined macros to be used with Turbo Prolog for further insight into the process of interfacing assembly language routines and Turbo Prolog.

New Rules for Assembly Language Programmers

The Intel 8086 microprocessor and its related CPUs (including the 80286 and the 80386) allow the programmer to define subroutines as being FAR or NEAR. Subroutines defined as NEAR work somewhat more efficiently than those defined as FAR. There are other subtle and (for our purposes at least) trivial differences.

But Turbo Prolog removes the choice. Any assembly language routine interfaced with Turbo Prolog must define subroutines as FAR.

The second new rule is that all assembly language routines must save the value of BP on entry and restore it prior to exiting. Finally, be sure that your assembly language routines return (RET) with a value that tells the system how many bytes of parameters to pop off the stack. It is your program's responsibility to manage this.

An Example from the User's Manual

Normally, I frown on the inclusion of examples from the user's manual in a programming language book, because the reader has probably read the user's manual and is looking for help beyond what it provides. But I have decided to include some information from the manual for two reasons. First, the example in the original manual is printed incorrectly. This misprinting, which is corrected in an errata sheet sent with Version 1.1, has caused some confusion. Second, it provides a compact and yet usable example that enables you to understand better the macros introduced after this discussion.

The Assembly Language Routine

In the Turbo Prolog manual, on pages 157 through 159, an assembly language routine is described. This routine doubles the value of an integer passed to it and returns the result. Here is the correct code for the example, complete with explanatory comments furnished by Borland International's technical support staff:

```
A_PROG      SEGMENT     BYTE
            ASSUME      CS:A_PROG
PUBLIC      DOUBLE_0
DOUBLE_0    PROC        FAR             ;FAR required, see text
            PUSH        BP              ;save old BP
            MOV         BP,SP           ;set up bp to access
                                        ;parameters
            MOV         AX,[BP]+10      ;move input parm to AX
            ADD         AX,AX           ;double the input parm
                                        ;in AX
            LES         DI,DWORD PTR [BP]+6  ;load ES,DI
                                        ;with pointer to
                                        ;output parameter
            MOV         ES:[DI],AX      ;store AX at ES:[DI]
            POP         BP              ;restore old BP register
            RET         6               ;return, popping
                                        ;parameters off stack

DOUBLE_0    ENDP
A_PROG      ENDS
            END
```

Type this program into your system using your favorite text editor and save it as ASMPROG.ASM, the name you'll use through the rest of this discussion.

The Turbo Prolog Program

Here is a Turbo Prolog program that uses the DOUBLE routine you just coded in assembly language:

```
global predicates
  double(integer,integer) - (i,o) language asm
goal
  write("Enter an integer: "),
  readint(A),
  nl,
  double(A,B),
  write("Double that value is ",B),
  readchar(_).
```

A fairly common problem in coding assembly language routines to be accessed from Turbo Prolog is the misuse of the language parameter to the global predicates declaration. Many people have a tendency to use the full word *assembler* instead of the key word asm. Doing so results in a cryptic:

```
Error 429 - No Error Messages
```

with the cursor on the second *s* in *assembler*.

Type this program into Turbo Prolog and save it as DOUBLE.PRO.

Assembling, Compiling, and Linking the Modules

Assemble ASMPROG.ASM to object code according to the rules of the assembler you are using. Then compile DOUBLER.PRO to an .OBJ file. Create a project file called DOUBLER.PRJ with the following contents:

```
DOUBLER+ASMPROG+
```

Now use the usual routine for linking the two routines:

1. Select the Compile Module option from the Options menu.
2. Give the name DOUBLER for the project file.
3. Select the Compile option from the Options menu.

The program is now ready to run by typing DOUBLER at the DOS prompt.

Macro Set for Predicate Declaration

CompuServe user and Turbo Prolog fan David J. Rodman came up with a set of very useful macros that permit assembly language programmers to define—with the ease that comes with macro assembly language programming techniques—callable predicates for use with Turbo Prolog.

Following is Rodman's file PROLOG.MAC, complete with his notes (I have edited some for clarity and format). In the next section, one of Rodman's suggested uses for these macro definitions is presented.

```
;prolog.mac:
;macros for Prolog-callable assembler routines
;David J. Rodman
;NO RIGHTS RESERVED
;Macros defined here:
;    PRED        NAME
;Defines NAME as a global and initializes the offset
;calculations.
;
;    INARG       NAME,TYPE
;Declares NAME to be an input argument of type TYPE,
;which must be one of CHAR, INTEGER, REAL, STRING,
;SYMBOL, or COMPOUND.
;The given name may be used subsequently to access
;the passed value.
;
;OUTARG       NAME
;Declares NAME to be an output argument, and defines
```

```
;it for easy access.
;
;    ENDPRED
;terminates a predicate properly, clears the stack,
;returns
;
;Enter a predicate.
;PRED defines ENDPRED to terminate this predicate
;properly.
;IMPORTANT NOTE: Arguments must be declared in reverse
;                order or correct stack offsets will
;                not be generated.
PRED      MACRO     NAME
          PUBLIC    NAME
&NAME     PROC      FAR
          PUSH      BP
          MOV       BP,SP
RETVAL    =         0              ;initializes size of
                                   ;activation record
;Define a new ENDPRED macro with the name of this
;predicate.
ENDPRED   MACRO
          POP       BP
          RET       RETVAL
&NAME     ENDP
          PURGE     ENDPRED
ENDM
ENDM
;Declare an input argument by name and type.
;The name is used to create a value that can be used
;easily to access the argument.
;If the argument type is character, for example, the
;easiest way to access it is as BYTE PTR [BP+OFFSET],
;which is just how it will be declared here.
;When this macro is finished with your argument, you
;can access it by name and the PTR type and correct
;offset will be defined for you.
INARG     MACRO     NAME,STYPE
          LOCAL     ARGSIZ
ARGSIZ    =         0
          IFIDN     <&STYPE>,<INTEGER>
          ARGSIZ    = 2
          DECLARE   NAME,WORD
          ENDIF
          IFIDN     <&STYPE>,<CHAR>
          ARGSIZ    = 2
          DECLARE   NAME,BYTE
          ENDIF
```

```
        ;REAL would probably be accessed a byte at a time.
                IFIDN     <&STYPE>,<REAL>
                ARGSIZ    = 8
                DECLARE   NAME,BYTE    ;change to WORD or
                                       ;DWORD if you like
                ENDIF
                IFIDN     <&STYPE>,<STRING>
                ARGSIZ    = 4
                DECLARE   NAME,DWORD
                ENDIF
                IFIDN     <&STYPE>,<SYMBOL>
                ARGSIZ    = 4
                DECLARE   NAME,DWORD
                ENDIF
                IFIDN     <&STYPE>,<COMPOUND>
                ARGSIZ    = 4
                DECLARE   NAME,DWORD
                ENDIF
                IF        ARTSIZ EQ 0
                IF2       .ERR
                          &OUT INARG
                          SYMBOL &NAME
                          DECLARED
                          WITH INVALID
                          &STYPE
                ENDIF
                ENDIF
RETVAL   =               RETVAL+&ARGSIZ
ENDM
;Declare an output argument.
;Much simpler, because this is always a DWORD pointer.
OUTARG   MACRO           NAME
RETVAL   =               RETVAL + 4
ENDM
;Declaration of a pointer
;(Internal macro--you can safely treat this
;as a black box.)
DECLARE  MACRO           NAME,SIZE
                DCL       <&NAME>,<&SIZE>,%RETVAL
ENDM
DCL      MACRO           NAME,SIZE,OFFSET
&NAME    EQU             &SIZE PTR [BP+6+&OFFSET]
ENDM
```

The code is sufficiently well commented, so further discussion is unnecessary.

Like all assembly language macros, this program can be used by simply passing proper arguments to existing macro routines and letting the assembler expand the code.

Next, you'll look at a routine supplied by Rodman as a demonstration of how this collection of code should be used with Turbo Prolog.

An Example Using Macros

This macro is called FILLSTR_0. Its accepts a Turbo Prolog predicate call as follows:

```
fillstr(X,'#',10)
```

and binds X to the string ##########. The global declaration for the call is:

```
fillstr(string,char,integer) - (o,i,i) language asm
```

To design this macro using the previous template, create an assembly language file that looks like this (again, comments are edited and need not be coded into your program):

```
TITLE EXAMPLE -DEMONSTRATE PROLOG.MAC MACROS
INCLUDE \INCLUDE\PROLOG.MAC
;Substitute directory information for yours
;DAVID J. RODMAN
;NO RIGHTS RESERVED
DATA      SEGMENT     PUBLIC BYTE 'DATA'
          ASSUME      DS:DATA
STRNG     LABEL       BYTE
          DB          128 DUP(0)   ;largest string
                                   ;we will create
                                   ;(arbitrary)
DATA      ENDS
CODE      SEGMENT     BYTE
          ASSUME      CS:CODE
          PRED        FILLSTR_0
          INARG       LENGTH,INTEGER   ;length to create
          INARG       FILLCHR,CHAR     ;char to fill with
          OUTARG      STRADDR          ;put address of
                                       ;built string here
          LEA         DI,STRNG         ;prepare to build
                                       ;string in DATA seg
          PUSH        DS
          POP         ES               ;ES:DI is destination
          MOV         AL,FILLCHR
          MOV         CX,LENGTH
          CMP         CX,128           ;must be less
          JC          BLDSTR
          MOV         CX,127           ;truncate buildstring
```

```
            REP       STOSB          ;string filled, needs
                                     ;NULL terminator
            XOR       AL,AL
            STOSB                    ;now string is built
            LES       DI,STRADDR     ;ES:DI is where to put
                                     ;DWORD ptr to string
            LEA       AX,STRNG
            STOSW
            MOV       AX,DS
            STOSW
            ENDPRED
    CODE    ENDS
    END
```

As you can see from the comments, this assembly language routine sets up a macro expansion that uses the AL and CX registers to build a string of up to 128 characters, truncating the string if a value greater than 128 is provided as an argument.

Summary

In this chapter, you examined the use of C, Pascal, and assembly language externally defined predicates within Turbo Prolog programs. You saw that there are several global requirements associated with such calls regardless of the language in which the external procedures are written. You also saw that by using a set of predefined macro expanders you can create quick and easy external assembly language predicates that guarantee proper stack management and parameter passage.

In chapter 9, you turn your attention to DOS interface techniques and use many of the approaches defined in this chapter to examine the use of DOS interrupt handling strategies.

Chapter **9**

Interfacing with the System

This chapter describes how Turbo Prolog interacts with your computer's DOS and other parts of the system. It explains how to call programs outside Turbo Prolog, how to deal directly with DOS-level commands, and how to access your computer's memory directly. We also discuss the use of RS-232 serial ports using one built-in Turbo Prolog routine and several that are included in the Turbo Prolog Toolbox routines.

In much of this chapter, we assume a reasonable amount of experience with the operating system. If experimenting with DOS isn't to your liking, feel free to skip this chapter.

Calling External Programs

In chapter 8, you looked at how to interface Turbo Prolog with programs written in other languages. In this discussion, the focus is on how to call the programs themselves, not to return some value to Turbo Prolog but rather to perform some external function.

The Turbo Prolog built-in predicate `system` can call any program stored external to Turbo Prolog as a batch or command file, that is, any file with an extension of .BAT, .EXE, or .COM. The use of the predicate is straightforward. Suppose you have a file called SAM.BAT on the logged disk drive, and you want to execute it within a Turbo Prolog program. You could simply code a line like this:

```
system(sam).
```

On encountering that line, Turbo Prolog goes to the disk, uses the current DOS path to locate the file, and executes it. When the external program finishes executing, control returns *immediately* to Turbo Prolog. This last point is important. If you are calling an external program that displays information on the screen (such as a specialized directory routine), you may have to modify the external program to pause when it is finished and wait for the user to press a key to return to Turbo Prolog. Otherwise, the displayed information disappears so rapidly that it is useless.

One way to do this is to use the redirection capabilities of DOS and route the output through the DOS MORE filter. For example, you could execute the file D.COM by setting up a batch file called D1.BAT. In this file, you would have just one line:

```
D¦MORE
```

The program will pause at each screenful and before returning control to Turbo Prolog.

> **Note:** You cannot pass command-line parameters to a .BAT file or other file from Turbo Prolog. If, for example, you have a .BAT file that invokes your favorite word processor and normally takes an argument when called, that argument cannot be passed directly from Turbo Prolog. Using an intermediate file approach and modifying the .BAT file to read that file for its parameter(s), rather than expecting them to be passed directly through the command line, is the only effective way to deal with this limitation.

If the external program you are calling returns some value to Turbo Prolog and if you do not want to link the program directly into your code using the techniques described in chapter 8, then you should pass the information by writing it to a file.

DOS Interaction

Any DOS command that exists as an explicit file can be invoked by the system predicate (discussed in the preceding section). However, sometimes you want to deal with DOS at a lower level. For those situations, you can use Turbo Prolog's potent built-in bios predicate.

> **Note:** The bios predicate is not for the beginning programmer. It accesses DOS and memory at very low levels, where the potential to "clobber" memory and interfere with the proper operation of programs is quite high. Don't use the bios predicate without a modicum of understanding of what the DOS BIOS calls do.

bios Predicate Basics

To begin, we should note that Borland has misnamed the bios predicate. The predicate is used to access not only ROM BIOS routines but also DOS service routines. In fact, it is probably more often used for the latter than for the former.

A major part of the functionality of MS-DOS and PC-DOS is

found in a special ROM chip in your system called the ROM BIOS chip. The term *BIOS* stands for *Basic Input/Output System.* In at least some sense, this chip's contents give your computer its personality. IBM PC workalikes (also called "clones") essentially replace IBM's BIOS chip with a compatible one of their own design.

The Turbo Prolog built-in bios predicate permits access to the routines stored in that ROM chip. It also permits direct access to interrupts handled directly by DOS without resorting to the ROM BIOS chip. Many of the most useful interrupt routines are serviced by DOS rather than by BIOS. Turbo Prolog handles these interfaces by the conventional approach of setting up the contents of one or more registers and calling an appropriate DOS or BIOS interrupt routine. An interrupt routine essentially tells the BIOS that you want to do something unusual. The BIOS stops its normal mode—which is waiting for you to press a key to give it a command—and pays attention to the information in its registers. ROM BIOS calls accessible through the bios predicate have a format similar to that shown in figure 9-1.

```
bios($21,reg(AX,BX,CX,DX,SI,DI,DS,ES),reg(AXO,BXO,CXO,DXO,SIO,DIO,DSO,ESO)).
```

| INTERRUPT NUMBER | REGISTERS AT ENTRY TO INTERRUPT | VARIABLES FOR REGISTERS AT CONCLUSION OF INTERRUPT |

Figure 9-1
Format of the bios predicate

Most of the DOS commands you will want to carry out within Turbo Prolog require the use of the AX register and interrupt 33 (hexadecimal 21, shown as $21 in the examples). There are other important interrupts in the BIOS, but we will concentrate on this one because it enables all the routines that are collectively referred to as *extended DOS commands.* Thus, most of the bios predicate calls look something like this:

```
bios($21,reg(AX,0,0,0,0,0,0,0),reg(Q,_,_,_,_,_,_,_)).
```

In some programs, you use additional registers, but the format and content are similar to this listing. Incidentally, the content of the AX register is usually given as a calculation of 256 times some value. This latter value tells the interrupt what you want to do. Consult your DOS manual for the meanings of the interrupts, and the contents of the AX register required to accomplish your objectives.

(The value 256 derives from the fact that the AX register is two bytes wide. The first (high-order) byte and the second (low-order) byte both contain a binary value. To put any value into the high-order byte of the AX register, you multiply the value by 256. For example, if you want to place 12 in the register, first you multiply 256 by 12, which is 3072. Expressed in hexadecimal notation, 12 is C and 3072 is C00. The two zeros fill the low-order byte of the two-byte AX register, leaving C in the high-order byte.)

A Small Example The following small program finds out what version of DOS you are running and displays it.

```
predicates
  dosversion(real)
clauses
  dosversion(Ver) :-
    AX=48*256,
    bios(33,reg(AX,0,0,0,0,0,0,0),
reg(VN,_,_,_,_,_,_,_)),
    Minor=VN div 256,
    Major = VN - 256 * Minor
    Ver = Major+Minor/100.0.
```

If you type this program into Turbo Prolog, save it, and run it, the interaction is similar to the following (the DOS version may vary depending on which version you are using):

```
Goal: dosver(Version).
Version=3.1
True
Goal:
```

Notice that the value **48*256** is placed into the 8086's AX register with a two-step process. First you assign the value to a variable, then you put that variable in the position assigned to the register in the **reg** compound structure. Typically, such **bios** calls use the register names as they appear in the CPU register set: AX, BX, CX, DX, ST, DT, DS, and ES. But if you want to return the value in the register after the call is complete, you have to use different variable names in the two **reg** structures in the **bios** call.

In the previous example, we chose **VN** (an acronym for version number) as the name of the AX register on return from the execution of the interrupt. You can also name the register differently as you call it. Either approach is acceptable. These are simply variable names, and associating them with the corresponding 8086 register names is only convenient, not required.

Other `INT21` **Calls** The interrupt you will work with most often is called `INT21` because its hexadecimal value is 21. Every such call requires a value to be placed in the AX register. This value determines what the interrupt will cause DOS to do. Some of the calls require values to be placed in other registers as well. For example, if you want to find out how much disk space there is on a disk, you must place a number in register DX that tells DOS which disk you are interested in knowing about.

On most MS-DOS and PC-DOS machines running DOS Version 2.1 or later, these interrupts are explained in detail in the book that is the equivalent of the IBM *DOS Technical Reference*. Other books on MS-DOS, however, might prove to be better resources for this data.

Assembly Language Access

You do not need to use the Turbo Prolog bios predicate if you know assembly language programming. You can simply code the interrupt and register-handling instructions directly in assembly language. It is, however, much easier to code a bios predicate call than to handle the same assignment with an assembly language routine.

Following is an assembly language routine that accomplishes the same thing as the previous Turbo Prolog program: it returns the DOS version number in use. (The original program was written by Dave Baldwin and distributed in a message on CompuServe.)

```
PUBLIC      getdosvers_0
dosvers     SEGMENT    PUBLIC         "CODE"
getdosvers_0      PROC  FAR
            PUSH       BP
            MOV        BP,SP
            MOV        AH,30H         ;set up for DOS version
                                      ;call (see text)
            INT        21H
            MOV        BH,AH          ;save AH
            LDS        SI,DWORD PTR [BP+10]   ;address of
                                      ;Major version
            XOR        AH,AH
            MOV        [SI],AX
            MOV        AL,BH          ;get minor version
                                      ;number
            LDS        SI,DWORD PTR [BP+6]  ;address for
                                      ;Minor version
            MOV        [SI],AX
            POP        BP
            RET        8
GETDOSVERS_0      ENDP
DOSVERS     ENDS
END
```

Notice the line that places the hexadecimal value 30 into the AH register. This translates to a decimal value of 48, which is the value used in the previous Turbo Prolog program using the bios call. You do not need to multiply the value $30 by 256 because in assembly language you have direct access to both halves of the AX register—AH (high-order byte) and AL (low-order byte). By depositing the value directly into the high register, AH, you accomplish the same thing as multiplying by 256 in the Turbo Prolog program.

Here, for the record, is the Turbo Prolog program that uses the assembly language routine you have just examined.

```
PROJECT "GETDOS"
global predicates
  getdosvers(integer,integer) - (o,o) language asm
predicates
  run
clauses
  run :-
    getdosvers(Major,Minor),
    write(Major, " ", Minor).
goal
run.
```

Memory Manipulation

There may be times when you want to store items at specific places in your computer's memory or retrieve information from specific addresses. For example, when moving information between programs, it is often convenient for the two programs to "agree" on where in memory to store information for the other program to retrieve (as discussed in chapter 7).

Turbo Prolog supplies three predicates that permit you to examine and change directly the contents of your computer's RAM: membyte, memword, and ptr_dword.

You might also want to see how Turbo Prolog has allocated the stack, heap, and trail regions. For this purpose, Turbo Prolog supplies the storage predicate. We will start with the storage predicate and then examine the other three more direct manipulation routines.

Examining Turbo Prolog's Memory Use

Using Turbo Prolog's built-in storage predicate, you can examine, but may not alter, the amount of space allocated in the three run-time memory areas used by the Turbo Prolog system: stack, heap, and trail. These sizes can be reset using other techniques. The storage predicate returns three real values. The first is the size of the stack presently allocated, the second is the heap size, and the third is the size of the trail portion of memory.

The storage predicate looks like this:

```
storage(Stack,Heap,Trail).
```

The size of the stack can be set to a range of 600 to 4000 16-byte paragraphs by the Miscellaneous option in the Setup menu. The trail is normally not allocated in Turbo Prolog because it is generally not needed. However, if you have a program that requires the trail, you can set it with the trail compiler directive. By default, the memory left over after the stack, the trail, and two other areas used by Turbo Prolog have been set aside is assigned to the heap. Therefore, the size of the heap is not directly subject to manipulation.

You can use the `storage` predicate to determine if your program is about to run out of space. You can then take appropriate action to prevent a hard system crash caused by an out-of-memory condition.

Direct Memory Manipulation

Information may be stored in and retrieved from memory locations in byte-sized or word-sized increments using the Turbo Prolog built-in predicates `membyte` and `memword`. The two instructions are identical, except `membyte` deals with data a byte at a time, and `memword` handles two-byte words at one time.

In calling either predicate, the first two arguments are the segment and offset portions of the memory location being addressed. The third parameter is either the value to store at that location or a variable to which the contents of that location are bound. In other words, if the third parameter is a byte or word, it is stored at the address provided. If it's a variable, the contents of that location are read into memory and assigned to that variable.

For example, suppose you want to retrieve a byte of information stored at memory location 00B0:4C00. The Turbo Prolog predicate call looks like this:

```
membyte($00B0,$4C00,Whatsit).
```

To store the numeric value 14.023 at that same location, you have to allocate a word of storage (floating-point numbers occupy two bytes):

```
memword($00B0:$4C00,14.023).
```

String Storage and Retrieval

The operation of the third built-in Turbo Prolog predicate for memory manipulation, `ptr_dword`, is similar to `membyte` and `memword`. Experienced DOS programmers recognize this as a shorthand way of describing double-word pointers. To store or retrieve a string stored in memory using this predicate, you supply either the string value or a variable to which the contents are assigned, followed by the segment and offset address portions of the memory location.

Thus, if you want to retrieve a string now stored at 00D0:123B, you would code a Turbo Prolog call like this:

```
ptr_dword(Stringval,$00D0,$123B).
```

This predicate assumes a null-terminated string, such as that automatically generated by C programs. If you are retrieving a Pascal string or other string terminated by some character other than a null, you have to use `membyte` or `memword` calls in a loop until the end of the string is reached.

Serial Ports and the Toolbox

Turbo Prolog, as it comes from Borland International, has one built-in routine to deal with I/O ports on your system. The low-level `portbyte` predicate sends or receives information from a port address on the PC. Borland's Turbo Prolog Toolbox, however, has a range of serial port manipulation predicates. In this section, we briefly discuss `portbyte`, then examine some (though not all) of the Toolbox's add-on predicates for serial port management.

The `portbyte` Predicate

Direct access to your computer system's I/O ports is available through the Turbo Prolog built-in predicate `portbyte`. Its format is shown in figure 9-2.

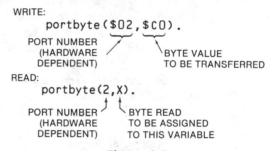

Figure 9-2
Format of the `portbyte` predicate

When you call `portbyte` with the second argument as a variable, Turbo Prolog reads the next byte at that I/O port and stores its decimal equivalent in the variable. If you pass a byte as the second argument, that byte is output to the designated port. The port numbers identified with the various ports on your system depend on the type of system you are using and the numbers and kinds of ports installed. Consult your DOS manual and user guides for more information.

The biggest drawback to the `portbyte` routine is that it does not buffer input through a port. Data simply continues to arrive at the port. While your program is servicing one byte of data—storing or manipulating it—many other bytes may arrive at the port and be lost before the next `portbyte` call is executed.

Similarly, timeout problems can arise in communicating with other devices when `portbyte` is in write mode. To use this predicate as a true communications tool, you have to set up your own routine (probably in assembly language) to service hardware interrupts so that no data is lost during transmission.

RS-232 Interfaces through Toolbox Routines

The Turbo Prolog Toolbox contains a number of routines in object code format to access and control the RS-232 ports on your system. Included are routines that permit you to open, monitor, and close an RS-232 communications port. These routines provide full buffering and can be interrupt-driven. You can also control the size of buffers used for input and output, and the baud rate, parity, word length, stop bits, and transmission protocol used by your communications programs.

Because these Toolbox routines are not written in Prolog, the source code is not available with the Toolbox programs. But accessing them is easy. If you are writing a program that requires special control over RS-232 port I/O operations, you should consider using these routines.

Other System Routines

There are two other minor system routines to discuss. You can use Turbo Prolog's `date` and `time` built-in predicates to set and retrieve the current date and time. The `date` predicate takes three integer arguments. If they are bound when the predicate is called, the year is set to the value of the first integer, the month to the value of the second, and the day to the value of the third. If they are uninstantiated when the call is made, they are bound to the current settings for those values. Thus, you could have this kind of exchange with Turbo Prolog:

```
Goal:date(1987,4,3).
True
Goal:date(Y,M,D).
Y=1987, M=4, D=3
1 Solution
Goal:
```

The `time` predicate works the same way except it requires four arguments, all integers. The first represents hours, the second represents minutes, the third represents seconds, and the last represents hundredths of a second.

Summary

Several levels at which you can interact with parts of your computer system reside outside Turbo Prolog but might be of interest to it. You can use `system` to call other programs that exist as batch or executable files. To execute low-level DOS routines directly with interrupts, you can use the Turbo Prolog `bios` built-in predicate with appropriate arguments to registers. Direct access to memory locations for both reading and writing is available with the `membyte`, `memword`, and `ptr_dword` predicates.

You can gain some measure of interaction with your system's RS-232 serial ports by the `portbyte` predicate. But buying the Turbo Prolog Toolbox and using its RS-232 routines is vastly preferable if your work in this area is serious and on-going. Finally, you can control the system clock with the `date` and `time` predicates, which also permit you to examine the present contents of these areas of memory.

In chapter 10, your focus shifts from external programs to external databases.

Chapter 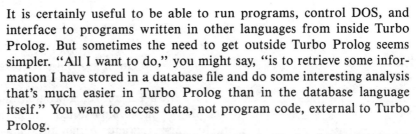 **10**

Using External Data Files

It is certainly useful to be able to run programs, control DOS, and interface to programs written in other languages from inside Turbo Prolog. But sometimes the need to get outside Turbo Prolog seems simpler. "All I want to do," you might say, "is to retrieve some information I have stored in a database file and do some interesting analysis that's much easier in Turbo Prolog than in the database language itself." You want to access data, not program code, external to Turbo Prolog.

Doing so is certainly feasible with Turbo Prolog, though it is not as easy as you might think. In this brief chapter, you look at the process of reading and writing information prepared by other programs: databases, spreadsheets, and word processors. The general information in this chapter can be used with any program. In chapter 11, you look at some of the predicates available in the Turbo Prolog Toolbox to access Borland Reflex, Lotus 1-2-3, Symphony, and dBASE II, III, and III Plus files more directly. So if you need to access files generated by one of those tools, you can skip this chapter and read chapter 11.

The most complex application involving external data files we can describe involves the following steps.

1. Preparing the data inside the external program for use by the Turbo Prolog routine.

2. Exporting the data from that external program to an intermediate file in a form Turbo Prolog can use.

3. Defining the Turbo Prolog data structures to accommodate the incoming data.

4. Running the Turbo Prolog program to access and modify the contents of individual records in the data file.

5. Importing the revised file back into the original program.

There are simpler intermediate designs. For example, if your program does not modify any data in the file, you can omit steps 4 and 5. But by looking at the most complex set of processing steps, you'll appreciate the techniques and complexities in external data file management through Turbo Prolog. Let's look at each of these steps.

Preparing the Data

For this discussion, we assume you are running an external database program with a file record structure like that shown in figure 10-1. As you can see, each record has four fields: a name, an age, a salary, and a personnel rating.

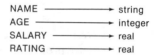

```
NAME   ──────────▶ string
AGE    ──────────▶ integer
SALARY ──────────▶ real
RATING ──────────▶ real
```

Figure 10-1
Database file structure

You will write a Turbo Prolog program that requires from this file only the employee's name, salary, and rating; the ages of employees are irrelevant for this program. Within the database program you must select only those fields needed by the Turbo Prolog program, and you must sort the records by name (or some other criterion if it makes more sense). You may also want to perform some sort of selection process on the data. For example, you may want to select only employees who earn more than $19,000, but less than $30,000, per year.

After you determine what data should be placed into the external file and the order in which it should be stored, you are ready for the next step.

Exporting the Data

Almost all database management systems can export information to an external file. Generally, the process is simple. You tell the program the file, fields, and sort order to use and the name of the file in which to store the results. The program does the rest.

Sometimes, though, there are complications. As a rule, these wrinkles are positive: they give you more control over the format of the data as it is stored on the disk. For example, you may have a choice of delimiters (field separators): tabs, quotation marks, commas, or combinations of the three. Sometimes you have the option of storing information in the file with some widely used format (for example, using SYLK and DIF).

Because of the way Turbo Prolog handles such files, it is safest to use a simple comma-delimited file format. Output the data so that each field is on a separate line, if your database manager allows it. This makes manipulation of the data by your Turbo Prolog program almost painless. Most database managers, however, do not have that feature, so you'll have to be concerned about how your Turbo Prolog program will know where each field starts and ends. We'll cover that subject in more depth shortly.

Sometimes the export data function disguises itself as a report function that prints the report to a disk file (without headers, footers, and page numbers). Whatever the details, the objective is to create a file containing ASCII text, comma delimited if possible. If you can get one field per line, so much the better.

Defining the Turbo Prolog Structures

There is very little to the next step, defining the Turbo Prolog structures. After you know what fields are being exported from the database to the intermediate file (from which you read the information), you only need to decide which form of the `read` statement to use in retrieving that data from a text file.

For example, suppose the database program does not permit one field per line as an export option. You will want your Turbo Prolog program to read the information a record at a time, probably with the `readln` predicate, and then separate the fields internally. We'll have more to say about that in a moment.

If you can get one field per line in the output from the database, then a collection of `read` statements is used. For example, if you are using the sample file and storing only the employee's name, salary, and rating, the read loop would look something like this:

```
/* initialization and loop control code would precede
    this program segment */
readln(EmployeeName),
readint(Salary),
readreal(Rating),
/* manipulation routines follow */
```

You may find yourself in a kind of hybrid situation: you can get one field per line but they are all ASCII strings delimited by quotation marks, even the numbers. With Turbo Prolog's string-handling capabilities, this poses no particular problem. Here's how the same fragment of code would look if you converted each piece of information to its proper form as it was read in from the text file:

```
/* initialization, etc. */
readln(EmployeeName),
/* no conversion necessary; you want a string */
readln(Temp),
str_int(Temp,Salary),
readln(Temp),
str_real(Temp,Rating),
/* manipulation, etc. */
```

Turbo Prolog has routines to convert from strings to real numbers, integers, and characters. Because strings are equivalent to symbols, the only data structure you can't convert directly is a compound structure. But databases don't create ASCII files with compound data structures, so that's not a problem in this application.

But what if your database doesn't permit you to save information on the file one field at a time? Your Turbo Prolog program will then have to read in one entire record at a time and separate the elements into their specific values for each field. The task is not easy, but it is fairly straight-forward. Here is one way to do it. (Again, all initialization and processing code is eliminated in the code fragment.)

```
readln(Rec).
extract(Fld,Rec) :-
  fronttoken(Rec,Fld,Rest),
  /* do something with Fld: write it, assign it, etc. */
  extract(_,Rest).
  /* use anonymous variable to avoid failure */
```

You search through the input string one character at a time with the frontchar predicate until a comma is found. Then you convert each character before the comma to a string with the str_char predicate, and assemble these separate strings into one string. (Turbo Prolog is not well suited to index through a string. Prolog handles lists better than it does strings. As a result, it might be wise to write the predicate that looks for the comma and handles the indexing as an external Pascal or C routine. Writing such a procedure in either of those languages would be quite simple.)

Accessing and Modifying the Records

As you read each record from the ASCII file exported from the database, you cannot simply write it back out to the same place after modification. Instead, you use a second file to store the modified records in the same order in which they were retrieved. The process is simple.

Open a second file for writing after opening the ASCII input file for reading. Then read a record from the input file, modify its contents (if necessary), and write the new record to the output file. Be sure to close both of the files when processing is complete.

Importing Revised Data

Importing the modified data file back into the database is as simple as exporting it, perhaps even simpler. You already know the format, so just set up your database to import records, tell it the format, and proceed.

Why Go through This?

Manipulating data stored in an external database file is not straightforward in any language, as you can tell. Unless the programming language has built-in "hooks" to give you direct access to the records as the database program stores them, you'll have to export the data, manipulate it, rewrite it, and import it.

In the next few years, one of the primary uses for Turbo Prolog and other nonprocedural languages will be in the design and construction of "intelligent front ends." Programs that help naive or untrained users enter information into databases and spreadsheets with more accuracy and confidence, and help them figure out what has happened when they fail to do so, will be a major product thrust of the next few years. This is particularly true of a spreadsheet application. With most spreadsheets, it is impossible to catch input errors until they produce a calculation mistake. A Turbo Prolog program that edits information being entered, checks its integrity, and then provides it to the spreadsheet could save many more hours of effort than the extra time required to export and import the data.

Summary

It is possible, though not easy, to access information in database files created by external database programs. If you are not working with dBASE II, III, or III Plus or with either of the major spreadsheet packages from Lotus, you can still get at the data by exporting it to a file that Turbo Prolog can read and, if necessary, modify. It is easier to do this if the program that generates and stores the data can create files that are comma delimited and formatted as one field per line. Most databases can do that. Even if yours cannot, you can still get at the information, but it takes more programming effort.

Speaking of effort, in chapter 11 you'll see how the Turbo Prolog Toolbox's built-in routines to directly access major database and spreadsheet data files can greatly streamline the process described in this chapter.

Toolbox Access to Database and Spreadsheet Files

This chapter describes the routines available in Borland's Turbo Prolog Toolbox to access information in dBASE III files. The Toolbox also includes routines to access files in Borland's own Reflex product as well as Lotus 1-2-3 and Symphony, but those are not discussed in this chapter. The principles are identical in any case.

  After you briefly review these predicates and their use, the discussion turns to how you can create custom predicates to directly access data stored by any other database or spreadsheet program. The only requirement is that you have access to certain information about that program's data file structure.

dBASE File Access

The Turbo Prolog Toolbox includes a number of predicates to write programs that access information stored in dBASE III files. The routines only work with dBASE III Version 1.1 or later. The example programs furnished by Borland in the Turbo Prolog Toolbox manual only read information from dBASE III files; they do not write new records to the database. There is no theoretical reason why you couldn't develop an equivalent set of routines that write data as well.

  Our purpose is not to restate material in the Toolbox documentation. However, to gain a clear understanding of the discussion that follows, we must provide a brief sketch of how to use these dBASE III access predicates in Turbo Prolog programs. You'll analyze the routines in the Toolbox source code listing to see what you can learn about dBASE file structures. With that background, you can make some observations about how to use this program as a model to create Turbo Prolog interfaces to other databases.

Using the Predicates

The dBASE files comprise a project called XDBASE3.PRJ. Open that file and examine it. Check that the second line, which calls for the inclusion of `real_ints`, is associated with the proper subdirectory path information, depending on how you've set up your directories. If you are using a special configuration file for the tools predicates as suggested in the Borland manual, you will want to remove the path entirely because you are already in the subdirectory that contains the file.

Now you are ready to compile the file. Choose the Project item from the Options menu and then select Compile from the same menu. After the compilation, as usual, you'll be asked if you wish to run the program. Type *y* and in a few moments your screen appears similar to figure 11-1. The program displays all four records retrieved as a group and then singly, before displaying the Turbo Prolog master screen.

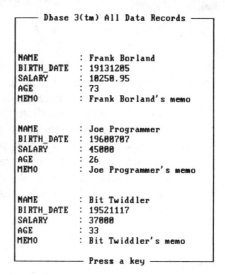

```
┌──── Dbase 3(tm) All Data Records ────┐
│                                      │
│                                      │
│  NAME        : Frank Borland         │
│  BIRTH_DATE  : 19131205              │
│  SALARY      : 10250.95              │
│  AGE         : 73                    │
│  MEMO        : Frank Borland's memo  │
│                                      │
│                                      │
│  NAME        : Joe Programmer        │
│  BIRTH_DATE  : 19600707              │
│  SALARY      : 45000                 │
│  AGE         : 26                    │
│  MEMO        : Joe Programmer's memo │
│                                      │
│                                      │
│  NAME        : Bit Twiddler          │
│  BIRTH_DATE  : 19521117              │
│  SALARY      : 37000                 │
│  AGE         : 33                    │
│  MEMO        : Bit Twiddler's memo   │
│                                      │
└──────────── Press a key ─────────────┘
```

Figure 11-1
Screen when dBASE III access begins modifying the project

You could use these routines immediately in your programs by simply changing the file name in the program and setting up your own new database file with dBASE III. Then you would modify the portions of the program that define the record structure so that they match the structure of your database.

That's about all there is to it. The proper positioning of the file's read operations and the translation of data from a binary format to a human-readable one are transparent to your program.

Examining the Structure

In the program called DBASE.PRO, you can see a large number of file-reading instructions that produce somewhat unintelligible data. You'll look at those lines in some detail to learn how a dBASE III file is structured. This, in turn, tells you how to analyze other database files to enable Turbo Prolog access to their contents.

During the execution of the `Init_Dbase3` predicate, the Turbo Prolog program reads the header of the dBASE file (in a predicate called `rd_dbase3_dBaseHeader`) and then it reads the field names for each field in the file (in the predicate `rd_dbase3_fieldDescL`). This is the key procedure in terms of file structure.

Reproduced here, for convenience in the discussion, is the `rd_dbase3_dBaseHeader` predicate:

```
rd_dbase3_DbaseHeader(TotRecs):-
  ignore(4),
  read_long(TotRecs),
  ignore(24).
```

The first and third lines rely on yet another Turbo Prolog Toolbox program called READEXT.PRO. This program contains a number of convenient data translation predicates for accessing information stored in a format other than ASCII format. The `ignore` predicate simply skips over the reading of the number of bytes passed to it as an argument. So the header-reading predicate in the dBASE III access program skips the first four bytes, which contain information irrelevant to our use of the file, and reads a 32-byte value that stores the total number of records in the file.

Take a look at figure 11-2, which is a hexadecimal dump of the contents of the sample file in the Toolbox documentation. Notice that the first four bytes contain the values 83, 56, 0A, and 0B. The next bytes contain the values 04 and 00.

```
← ↑ ↓ → LineUpDn  0..9)speed  G)oto  H)ex  S)et  PgUp  PgDn  Home  End  Return
000000   83 56 0a 0b  04 00 00 00  c2 00 32 00  00 00 00 00   .V.......2.....
000010   00 00 00 00  00 00 00 00  00 00 00 00  00 00 00 00   ...............
000020   4e 41 4d 45  00 00 00 00  00 00 00 43  0f 00 32 7f   NAME.......C..2.
000030   14 00 00 00  00 00 00 00  00 00 00 00  00 00 00 00   ...............
000040   42 49 52 54  48 5f 44 41  54 45 00 44  23 00 32 7f   BIRTH_DATE.D#.2.
000050   08 00 00 00  00 00 00 00  00 00 00 00  00 00 00 00   ...............
000060   53 41 4c 41  52 59 00 00  00 00 00 4e  2b 00 32 7f   SALARY.....N+.2.
000070   08 02 00 00  00 00 00 00  00 00 00 00  00 00 00 00   ...............
000080   41 47 45 00  00 00 00 00  00 00 00 4e  33 00 32 7f   AGE........N3.2.
000090   03 00 00 00  00 00 00 00  00 00 00 00  00 00 00 00   ...............
0000a0   4d 45 4d 4f  00 00 00 00  00 00 00 4d  36 00 32 7f   MEMO.......M6.2.
0000b0   0a 00 00 00  00 00 00 00  00 00 00 00  00 00 00 00   ...............
0000c0   0d 00 20 46  72 61 6e 6b  20 42 6f 72  6c 61 6e 64   .. Frank Borland
0000d0   20 20 20 20  20 20 20 31  39 31 33 31  32 30 35 31          191312051
0000e0   30 32 35 30  2e 39 35 20  37 33 20 20  20 20 20 20   0250.95 73
0000f0   20 20 20 35  20 4a 6f 65  20 50 72 6f  67 72 61 6d      5 Joe Program
000100   6d 65 72 20  20 20 20 20  20 31 39 36  30 30 37 30   mer     1960070
000110   37 34 35 30  30 30 2e 30  30 20 32 36  20 20 20 20   745000.00 26
000120   20 20 20 20  20 32 20 42  69 74 20 54  77 69 64 64        2 Bit Twidd
000130   6c 65 72 20  20 20 20 20  20 20 20 31  39 35 32 31   ler        19521
000140   31 31 37 33  37 30 30 30  2e 30 30 20  33 33 20 20   11737000.00 33
000150   20 20 20 20  20 20 20 33  20 4d 61 72  79 20 4d 61        3 Mary Ma
000160   72 74 69 6e  20 20 20 20  20 20 20 20  20 31 39 35   rtin          195
000170   30 30 32 32  37 33 37 30  30 30 2e 30  30 20 33 36   0022737000.00 36
```

Figure 11-2
Hex dump of sample dBASE III file

The number of records in the file is stored in a dBASE III structure, with the least significant byte first. Thus, the number of records stored in the database is 0004. As you might recall from running the program and from figure 11-1, that is a correct record count. (Incidentally, the predicate read_long is also contained in the file READEXT.PRO. It reads a 2-byte value where the low-order byte comes first.)

Now let's see how the XDBASE3.PRO program reads the list of field names and related information into memory in the rd_dbase3_fieldDescL predicate.

```
rd_dbase3_fieldDescL([[FldName¦FldNameL],[fldDesc
    (Type,Len)¦FldDescL]):-
  readchar(Ch),
  Ch<>'\013',
  !,
  read_strArr(10,Name),
  frontchar(FldName,Ch,Name),
  readchar(T),
  conv_FldType(T,Type),
  ignore(4),
  readchar(L),
  ignore(15),
  rd_dbase3_FieldDescL(FldNameL,FldDescL).
rd_dbase3_FieldDescL([],[]):-readchar(_).
```

Beginning at the first position after the 24 bytes the previous predicate ignored, this predicate reads the first character and ensures that it is not a carriage return (hexadecimal 13). The carriage return character is used in dBASE III files to indicate the end of the field description area. For the first read in figure 11-2, this means reading the value at location $20, which is 4E. It is not a carriage return, so the program reads the next 10 characters and appends the first character read to these 10 to give an 11-character field name.

The next byte is the description of the data type. The next 4 bytes contain address information, which is not significant in this process, so these bytes are skipped. The next byte contains the length of the field. The next 15 bytes are unneeded data. Reading of the next field description begins 32 bytes after the last description began.

Following along with this description and figure 11-2, you'll find that the first field in the record is called NAME, is type C (character data in dBASE parlance), and is 20 characters ($14) long. The next field is called BIRTH_DATE, is type D (date), and is 8 characters long. You should be able to decipher the rest of the file structure.

Look at address C0, and you'll find $0D, which is ASCII 13 (carriage return). This marks the end of the field description area and the start of the actual file data. As you can see in the ASCII representation of the hexadecimal dump, the data does indeed begin at this point.

You know from the header that there are four records in the file. All but the last part of the fourth record are seen in one screen dump, as shown in figure 11-2.

Customizing Your Own Direct Access

If you are adventuresome and if the use of an intermediate ASCII file is not a good solution, use what you learned from the XDBASE3.PRO program to create customized Turbo Prolog programs that directly access information stored in other databases. Before you can do so, however, you need to answer these questions:

- What is the structure and content of the file's header record?
- Where and how is information about the fields stored?
- Where and how is data stored?
- What special characters, if any, are used as field or record delimiters?

The best way to discover the structure of the database's files is to "take one apart" with a hexadecimal dump, as you did previously. You must first know the structure of the file from the programmer's standpoint, so that you will recognize where field descriptions begin and end, where field lengths are described, and the like. For example, the file structure of the dBASE III workalike from Paperback Software International, VP-Info, closely parallels that of dBASE III. Some database programs provide full documentation, either in user manuals or on request (sometimes with a special license fee), describing their file structures. Others require you to do some detective work, and some may not yield even to the best investigative techniques.

But if you can find the answers to the previous questions, you are well on your way to designing a Turbo Prolog program that uses the techniques in the Toolbox's dBASE III samples to access your database program's data files.

> **Note:** Be sure to include the two files that handle proper reading and data type conversion—REALINTS.OBJ (or its C equivalent, REALINTS.C, which is also supplied on the Toolbox disks) and READEXT.PRO. You may also want to use a copy of XDBASE3.PRO or DBASE3.PRO as a starting point, editing those files rather than typing one from scratch.

The Toolbox can be a very useful addition to your Turbo Prolog library if you are interested in directly accessing data files created by other database managers. If you need access to dBASE III, Lotus 1-2-3, or Symphony files, the Toolbox supplies routines that handle such interaction with great facility. If you are working with some other external database or spreadsheet program, you can design your own Turbo Prolog program to access those files using the techniques in the Toolbox programs and the expanded discussion in this chapter.

Summary

In this chapter you saw in detail how to use the Turbo Prolog Toolbox's built-in routines to access a dBASE III file. By extension, you can use the Toolbox to access files written using other databases and spreadsheets.

This chapter concludes the discussion of interactions between Turbo Prolog and the world outside its boundaries. In chapter 12, you begin to focus on an application to which Prolog has long been known to be well suited—natural language processing.

Part 3

Natural Language Processing in Turbo Prolog

Overview of Natural Language Processing

With this chapter you begin part 3, which describes an interesting and powerful application for Prolog called *natural language processing,* or NLP. When you have finished reading and working through the programs, you will have gained:

- a deeper appreciation for the power of Turbo Prolog
- a basic understanding of NLP concepts and issues

This chapter presents an overview of NLP and provides a framework for the rest of the discussion. Chapter 13 examines simple parsing techniques in a *context-free grammar.* In chapter 14, the level of grammatic complexity is taken one step further with an *augmented transition network* approach to grammar and parsing.

This chapter begins with some background in NLP and why it is important. Then some basic terms and concepts needed throughout the rest of part 3 are explained. Finally, you take a brief look at where NLP has come from and where it is today. Along the way, you'll learn about programs with interesting names like ELIZA, LUNAR, SHRDLU, LIFER, MARGIE, SAM, and PAM.

Why Natural Language Processing?

Next to expert systems, no other AI topic has caught the current imagination like natural language processing. It has been commercialized to a limited degree and it is certain that in the next year or two, it will be exploited to a much greater extent. You can't yet "talk" to your computer, but you can type in nearly plain English into some computer programs and they respond as expected (most of the time).

This aspect of NLP—making machines easier for humans to use—is in the forefront. It has found particular application in database programs (through CLOUT, a natural-language front end for Microrim's

R:Base V, Symantec's Q&A and its Intelligent Assistant, and GURU's CHAT mode) and more recently to spreadsheets (with HAL from Lotus). Even with these programs, though, true NLP has not arrived. True user-friendliness—in the sense that we can portray a program as being as friendly as a . . . well, a friend—is still on the horizon. But it is getting closer all the time.

Making systems easier to use is not the only value in NLP. At least two other objectives are frequently cited by NLP researchers and investigators as reasons for viewing NLP as an important aspect of current computer software development.

First, by exploring and studying NLP, you gain a better understanding of how humans store, think about, and communicate knowledge. This aspect of AI research is often overlooked in the press as it sensationalizes all the things that AI can—and cannot—do. But among AI researchers, this insight into human thinking, decision-making, and communication processes is far more important than supplying products that emulate those processes.

Second, a long-time dream of computer scientists has been to put the computer to work in helping to avoid and resolve international conflict. One vehicle for doing this is machine translation of human languages. (It is amazing how many international conflicts, even today, are directly caused by miscommunication. The topic is beyond the scope of our discussion, but interesting nonetheless.) Some limited success has been achieved in moving written text from one human language to another in a way that speakers of the target language found acceptable. But research has a long way to go before developing a system that can be relied on to clarify, rather than further confuse, the human communication process.

NLP will be a major theme of any serious computer user's reading and thinking in the next few years. Gaining an appreciation of it now can be quite helpful.

There was another, more practical reason for choosing to explore NLP rather than, for example, expert systems in this book. The application of Prolog to the world of expert systems has been well covered. (See, for example, Carl Townsend's *Mastering Expert Systems with Turbo Prolog,* also published by Howard W. Sams & Co.) But NLP has been ignored as far as treatments accessible to the interested observer who lacks degrees in linguistics and computer science. Many books about NLP exist, but for the most part they use LISP or discuss the subject in a more theoretical way. (An important exception is the readable but sometimes dense *Prolog and Natural Language Analysis* by Dr. Fernando C. N. Pereira and Stuart M. Schieber, published by Stanford and the University of Chicago presses.)

Basic Terms and Concepts

In this section, you are provided with a vocabulary within which a discussion of NLP can be held. Even though some of these terms may seem familiar, be sure you understand them thoroughly before reading the rest of part 3. In computer science and linguistics, as with most other arenas of human knowledge, special terminology often seems like everyday words. The result can be grave misunderstandings.

This is not a complete or comprehensive discussion of the vocabulary of NLP research. It is, rather, a presentation of the terms important to this discussion of NLP.

A Definition of NLP

First, we'll define natural language processing. Let's start with a simple and circular definition and then work our way out of it.

> **Definition:** Natural language processing is a branch of artificial intelligence. Its goal is to design computer systems that can understand natural language.

Notice at the outset that NLP is not confined to a specific human language. Responding to English-like commands may be perfectly fine for a computer in Schenectady, but the user in Paris is not going to be amused, or particularly helped, by such a device. But this definition begs the question of what natural language is. Let's see if we can come up with a definition that is sufficiently formal to satisfy linguistics experts and yet understandable to the rest of us.

> **Definition:** Natural language is the use of words and symbols to communicate between humans. It consists minimally of vocabulary and sentence structure, and rules about how those two objects work together.

It is worth noting that some languages fitting this terse definition are not really natural, but artificial. Natural languages, in the most precise use of the term, grow spontaneously in human culture. Artificial languages are consciously invented. Often, artificial languages are devised for computer programming. But at least one artificial language is in relatively widespread human use. Esperanto, designed by Polish researcher L. L. Zamenhof in the late 19th century, is spoken by an estimated eight million people from virtually every country.

Now you may begin to get an appreciation for what is involved in NLP. Natural language is a form of agreement among members of a culture or subculture as to what words and symbols mean and how they are to be put together. The word *bird* means *a living object with wings and feathers that flies through the air* only because there is a general agreement among this culture that when we say *bird,* that is what we mean. If you and I agreed that when we use the word *bird* we mean *a young girl, probably attractive,* we may find ourselves better understood in Liverpool than in Chicago. If, instead, we decide that *bird* means *a long, leisurely walk in the woods,* we will know precisely what we mean by *Let's go for a bird* but others will find us a bit strange.

Similarly, we have agreement about how we put words together to form sentences. A declarative sentence (one that states a fact) generally has the pattern of a subject followed by a verb optionally followed by an object. *I program computers* is such a sentence, with *I* the subject, *program* the verb, and *computers* the object. If I said instead *Program I computers* or *Computers program I,* the degree to which I communicate is lessened. In the last example, you might even think I am a robot and don't understand grammar very well. (We'll have more to say about the word *grammar* shortly.)

So far, so good. A natural language is an agreed-upon set of symbols, most of which are words, that we put together in well-defined ways to communicate with other humans. How does an NLP program fit into this? Let's take a leap and define an NLP program. The words in italic in the next definition are defined in the remainder of this section.

> **Definition:** A natural language processing program is a set of software instructions designed to accept input from a human, and *parse* that input into manageable components called *terminals* and *nonterminals*. Such a program uses a *grammar* to determine if the input constitutes a valid sentence or other structure in the *syntax* of the grammar. Ultimately, the program applies rules to determine the meaning of the sentence in its *context*.

Parsing a Computer Program

When you were in school, if you were fortunate (or unfortunate) enough to have an English teacher who taught you how to diagram sentences, you've done a lot of parsing in your life. Parsing is the process of taking apart a stream of text and breaking it into logical components according to some rules.

Most computer programming languages, including Prolog, are parsed as part of the process of interpreting programs that you write in those languages. In a programming language, the parser consists of a three-step processor, as depicted in figure 12-1.

The first step is the scanning process, sometimes called *lexical analysis*. This step breaks the input text into logical components, or tokens. For example, in a C compiler, the lexical analyzer would break this line of input:

```
Num = addit(Val1,Val2);
```

into the following logical components:

```
Num
=
addit
(
Val1
,
Val2
)
;
```

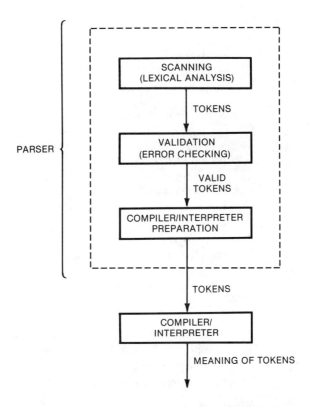

Figure 12-1
Parsing process in a computer language

Sometimes the token corresponds to a single letter or symbol, as in the case of the parentheses, comma, equal sign, and semicolon. Sometimes, it more closely resembles a word, as with `Num`, `addit`, `Val1`, and `Val2`. Depending on the rules of the language—and therefore the design of the scanner—a single token might consist of two or more symbols joined, as in the Pascal assignment operator `:=` for example. Prolog's `if (:-)` is another example.

After the scanner breaks the input stream into its component parts, it performs error checking. In most cases, this means ensuring that there are no symbols in the input stream that are illegal because of their form. In formal terms, the process *validates* the input as consisting of valid symbols in the context of the rules of the language.

Then the parser prepares the tokens for the next step in language processing. Sometimes this step is a non-step because the data as it is tokenized is already usable by the next step in the process. In some cases, though, a great deal of modification or transformation must take place before the text can be passed to the next stage of processing.

Parsing in English

Let's apply the same three-step process to a parser designed to process English rather than a programming language. The scanner part of the process is inherently easier, at least at the levels of English that we deal with in this book. The scanner simply breaks the input stream into single units of words and punctuation. Given the sentence:

```
A boy ran fast.
```

a parser divides the text into five tokens: *A, boy, ran, fast,* and the period at the end of the sentence. A word in this sense is any collection of letters and numbers terminated by a space or a punctuation symbol. If the word ends with a punctuation symbol, then it is really two words: the group of characters up to the punctuation mark and the punctuation mark itself.

At the next phase of parsing natural language text, the parser applies the rules of the *grammar* to the tokens passed to it by the scanner. We'll have more to say about grammars, but for now you should understand that the major task of this phase is ensuring that the tokens combine to form a valid sentence according to the rules of the grammar.

The final step in parsing natural language text is applying the meanings of symbols to the symbols themselves so that they are properly interpreted. This is the part of natural language processing that remains to be conquered by AI programmers, though much progress has been made in recent years.

Grammars and Their Purpose

Clearly, the grammar of a language is a major determinant of meaning. The word *can,* for example, may be used as a verb (as in *She likes to can vegetables*), a noun (*Put that in the can*), or an auxiliary verb (*You can do it*). A grammar can clarify this issue by determining the position of the word in the sentence in relation to other words.

Although there have been some attempts to define grammarless natural language processors, most successful efforts employ a grammar. A grammar is a precise, concise, and easily automated way of describing a language and its rules.

Grammar Components: Terminals and Nonterminals

A grammar is a formal description of a language. It describes symbolically what constitutes comprehensible input in terms of the language's rules. Seen another way, it *is* the language's rules. All grammars consist of two basic types of objects: nonterminals and terminals. A sentence (or other basic unit of language) is defined as consisting entirely of terminal symbols.

Let's look at an example. Figure 12-2 describes a brief and incomplete grammar for an English declarative sentence.

Each symbol contained in angle brackets, like < SENTENCE >, is a nonterminal. All other symbols are treated as terminals. Sentences are written using terminals. Nonterminals are not used in sentences directly. Rather, the nonterminal symbolizes the type of terminal that can occupy a position.

```
<SENTENCE> ──────▶ <ARTICLE> <NOUN> <VERB>.
<ARTICLE> ──────▶ A
<ARTICLE> ──────▶ An
<ARTICLE> ──────▶ The
<NOUN> ──────▶ boy
<NOUN> ──────▶ girl
<NOUN> ──────▶ dog
<VERB> ──────▶ runs
<VERB> ──────▶ plays
<VERB> ──────▶ cries
```

Figure 12-2
A partial grammar: English declarative sentence

Interpreting figure 12-2, then, we can say that this grammar defines (in linguistic terms, *generates*) a language consisting of sentences beginning with an <ARTICLE> followed by a <NOUN> followed by a <VERB>, and ending with the terminal symbol we call the period. (This structure is nearly identical to the structure used in the discussion of modular programming in part 1.) An <ARTICLE>, in turn, is defined as any of the terminal symbols *A, An,* or *The.* A <NOUN> is the terminal symbol *boy, girl,* or *dog.* Finally, a <VERB> is the terminal symbol *runs, plays,* or *cries.*

In terms of this grammar, then, the following are valid sentences:

A girl runs.

A boy cries.

The dog plays.

A dog cries.

A boy plays.

But the following sentences would not be validated by this gram- for the reasons indicated:

he girl runs.   First letter is not capitalized.

dog cries   No period at the end.

1 apple plays.   The word *apple* is not a known noun.

the grammars we discuss in the rest of part 3 are more complex
but they are constructed in the same way. They start with the
t (<SENTENCE> in most cases, but possibly <PRO-
or <STATEMENT> in examples of programming lan-
d divide it into constituent nonterminals and terminals until
als remain.

functional, all nonterminals must lead, directly or indirectly,
l. No nonterminal can be left unexpanded. In the previous
example, if you leave out all the terminals associated with
al <NOUN>, you could never construct a valid sentence
ar.

nt to see what a complete grammar looks like, read the
hapter 12 in your Turbo Prolog reference manual, where

a full grammar of Turbo Prolog is presented. As you will see, a grammar can be quite complex.

Historical Perspective

Work in NLP for computers dates back to the 1940s, when computers first appeared. The field known as *computational linguistics* focuses on the use of computers to deal with linguistic symbols and structures. Very early in its history, this branch of computer science was used to develop word indexes, contextual concordances, and program cross-referencers.

Past this surface-level activity, the next major focus was on machine translation between human languages. This seemingly easy goal proved elusive and led to a great deal of frustration with computers and their limitations. These frustrations are reminisicent of those that haunt the AI world today.

Early Work   In the 1960s, serious work in NLP began. The timing was a result of the confluence of a number of developments, including:

- vast increases in hardware power
- development of high-level languages, including LISP, capable of real symbolic manipulation
- linguistic breakthroughs by Noam Chomsky

Of the dozens of programs that emerged from this first-blush attempt to deal with natural language using the computer, three stand out as both interesting and valuable: SAD-SAM, BASEBALL, and ELIZA.

SAD-SAM

The acronym SAD-SAM stands for *Syntactic Appraiser and Diagrammer-Semantic Analyzing Machine.* It was developed in 1963 at the Carnegie Institute of Technology by Robert Lindsay. This program, like most early systems, focuses on a narrow domain of knowledge. Specifically, SAD-SAM deals with family relationships and genealogies. It has limitations, notably in the fact that it assigns only one connection or relationship to a given description. For example, it cannot determine whether a boy eating his aunt's spaghetti is enjoying the cooking of his father's sister or sister-in-law.

But within the framework with which it was designed to communicate, SAD-SAM does a more than adequate job for a pioneer piece of software.

BASEBALL

In 1963, Bert Green and his Lincoln Laboratories colleagues wrote a program called BASEBALL that permits the user to use reasonably

English-like speech to retrieve facts about a single American League baseball season.

The program has a rich dictionary and uses heuristics to resolve ambiguities in the phrasing of questions. Overall, it is an impressive program capable of answering a broad range of questions about the subject it "knows" about.

ELIZA

ELIZA, the most famous natural language program, was written by Joseph Weizenbaum in the mid-1960s at MIT. Scaled-down versions of the program—often sold under the rubric of artificial intelligence—are available on most modern microcomputers.

The program uses a technique called *pattern matching* to simulate a dialog between the user and itself. The program poses as a therapist, taking cues from the user's inputs to phrase questions and prompt for more data as needed. As the user enters responses, the computer matches them to known patterns and offers a response that a human therapist might conjure up in real life. The following sample interaction with ELIZA lets you determine how realistic its responses seem to be. (ELIZA's responses are in uppercase letters.)

```
I am angry.
WHY ARE YOU ANGRY?
Because my girlfriend made me come here.
YOUR GIRLFRIEND MADE YOU COME HERE?
She says I am angry too much.
WHAT DO YOU THINK MAKES YOU ANGRY?
I am not angry.  She just thinks I am.  Women are all
    alike.
IN WHAT WAYS?
They're always nagging at us.
CAN YOU GIVE ME A SPECIFIC EXAMPLE?
I am too nervous to think right now.
DO YOU THINK THAT COMING HERE WILL HELP YOU NOT TO BE
    NERVOUS?
I hope so.
TELL ME MORE ABOUT YOUR GIRLFRIEND
```

ELIZA is a tricky program. It is so realistic that many people who used the program thought they were interacting with a real therapist. When they found out it was a psychological experiment, some of them were angry. (Weizenbaum set out to create a parody of natural language processing when he wrote ELIZA. He was undoubtedly surprised by the degree to which people took the program seriously.)

Growing out of his work with ELIZA and other studies and experiences, Weizenbaum has become an advocate of the position that AI can never really succeed in completely emulating human thought and communication.

LUNAR   LUNAR is an NLP program designed to aid scientists in classifying and retrieving information about the moon rocks brought back to earth from the Apollo 11 mission. The program accepts English sentences as inputs and translates them into formal Structured Query Language (SQL) requests. The computer then processes these requests.

This program has been in frequent use as geologists basically untrained in the use of computers have learned how to retrieve information from the system. Here is an example of a query posed by a geologist, the program's interpretation of the query in SQL, and the program's response. (This example first appeared in *The Artificial Intelligence Handbook,* edited by Avron Barr and Edward Feigenbaum.)

```
Request:
  (DO ANY SAMPLES HAVE GREATER THAN 13 PERCENT ALUMINUM)
Query Language Translation (after parsing):
  (TEST (FOR SOME X1 / (SEQ SAMPLES) : T ; (CONTAIN X1
    (NPR* X2 / \'AL2O3) (GREATERTHAN 13 PCT))))
Response:
  YES
```

LUNAR uses an augmented transition network parsing approach, which you will learn more about in chapter 14.

SHRDLU   One of the most famous and often emulated NLP programs is Terry Winograd's SHRDLU. This program deals with a small, artificially created universe, called the *blocks world,* that contains several blocks of different sizes, shapes, and colors. It interacts with the user, who commands an imaginary robot inside this blocks world, telling it to move certain blocks in certain ways.

Here is a sample interactive session with SHRDLU (adapted from Margaret Boden's excellent AI introduction, *Artificial Intelligence and Natural Man*). The scenario begins with several blocks and pyramids of different sizes and colors that are stacked on each other, inside each another, and on a table top:

```
pick up the big red block.
OK.
grasp the pyramid.
I DON'T UNDERSTAND WHICH PYRAMID YOU MEAN.
find a block which is taller than the one you are
    holding and put it into the box.
BY "IT," I ASSUME YOU MEAN THE BLOCK WHICH IS TALLER
    THAN THE ONE I AM HOLDING.  OK
```

```
what does the box contain?
THE BLUE PYRAMID AND THE RED BLOCK.
```

This has the appearance of a very sophisticated NLP program. In fact, within the limited domain about which it has been given knowledge, SHRDLU is capable of quite astonishing feats. The explanation the program furnishes for the ambiguous *it* in this example demonstrates its sophistication.

Winograd, now at Stanford University, is a pioneer in the NLP field. SHRDLU was his first attempt at such a program; he has since taken the art well beyond this level.

MARGIE, SAM, and PAM

At Yale University's Artificial Intelligence Lab, Dr. Roger C. Schank and his colleagues have for years worked on a theory of natural language called the Conceptual Dependency (CD) theory. The root principle in CD theory is that if two sentences have identical meanings, you should be able to represent them identically. This is true even across human language lines. For example, if two sentences, one in French and one in English, have the same meaning, their representation should be the same.

CD represents ideas as collections of *semantic primitives* that include primitive acts and primitive states. Relations among these components are called *dependencies*. CD theorists strive to keep the number of primitives small. A primitive act can include such things as PROPEL, which is defined in CD theory as applying physical force to an object, PTRANS, the transfer of the physical location of an object, and ATRANS, the transfer of an abstract relationship such as ownership.

State primitives in CD include HEALTH, MENTAL STATE, and PHYS-ICAL STATE. Any of these is subject to alteration by a CD primitive act. Such states are associated with positive and negative integer values, so that HEALTH(-10) means dead and MENTAL STATE(+10) means joyous or ecstatic.

Using CD theory, we can express the sentence *Dan gives Carolyn a book* as Dan ATRANS (book) to Carolyn. ATRANS is the CD act that describes transferring possession or ownership. The more complex *Don told Mary that Carolyn was happy* can be represented as Don MTRANS (Carolyn BE MENTAL+STATE(5)) to Mary. MTRANS represents the transfer of mental information between people (or even within a person).

One final significant idea in CD theory is that anything in a sentence that is implicit must be made explicit when the sentence is represented. Let's look at the sentence *John eats the spaghetti with a fork*. The CD representation of this sentence conveys the idea that John's mouth is involved in the act, and the concept that the fork is used to contain the spaghetti. Even the idea that John has to move the fork for this to happen is encoded so that the result is:

```
John INGEST spaghetti (fork (John
       MOVE(mouth))(spaghetti(CONTAIN))).
```

The first major project at Yale to use CD theory and portray its value was MARGIE (an acronym for Meaning Analysis, Response Generation, and Inference on English). It has three major components:

- a conceptual analyzer, which converts English sentences to CD representations
- an inference generator, which deduces facts from the propositions stated in the CDs (see text)
- a text generator, which converts the CDs into English sentences

In the mid-1970s Schank, his colleague Robert Abelson, and some of their graduate students began to develop NLP systems that could deal with text in larger than one-sentence blocks. SAM (Script Applier Mechanism) and PAM (Plan Applier Mechanism) resulted. These programs use CDs as the middle language, or interlingua, into which input text is translated. From that point on, PAM and SAM deal with only the CD structures, not the top structures of the sentences themselves.

A *script* is a standardized sequence of events that describes some typical human behavior. A script can be devised, for example, for a trip to the grocery store, a visit to the doctor, or a picnic. Schank and Abelson believe that humans have such scripts in their minds and that these scripts permit them to put communication into an appropriate context.

Each script provides information about the players in the scenario, the props (inanimate objects), the events (in proper sequence), and the relations to other events. Each script is also associated with a goal. Figure 12-3 shows how a script for a trip to the grocery store might be designed (though it could be more complex).

The goal of the script is to buy groceries. Notice the 13-step process involves all the props and both players. Some scripts have many more players and props and require dozens of steps.

What is important about scripts is that they provide a framework or a context for natural language processing. Getting a bill in the grocery store is somewhat different from getting one in the mail or in a restaurant, and much different from getting one if you happen to be the governor. Scripts enable NLP systems to place such ambiguous communication into a context from which meaning can be derived.

Using scripts, SAM can answer questions about a story without explicitly being told everything. For example, if the computer is given a story in which the customer left the store before paying for the groceries, it would conclude that the customer did not take the groceries with him (unless it had an alternate script for theft!) from the fact that payment isn't mentioned.

PAM takes a slightly different approach. A script is a fairly explicit description of a scenario; a plan is a list of goals, and methods for accomplishing them. Plans are thus sketchier and capable of greater

PLAYERS: customer, cashier
PROPS: groceries, cart, aisles, shelves, food items,
             cash register, bag, price, bill, money
GOAL: obtain groceries
SCRIPT:

1. Customer goes (travels) to store (earlier script)
2. Customer gets cart
3. Customer pushes cart down aisle
4. Customer transfers food items from shelves to cart
5. Customer reaches last aisle
6. Customer goes to cash register with cart
7. Cashier enters each item's price into cash register
8. Cashier transfers groceries to one or more bags
9. Cashier tells customer amount of bill
10. Customer transfers money to cashier to pay bill
11. Cashier transfers money to cash register
12. Customer pushes cart out of store
13. Customer transfers bags to vehicle

Figure 12-3
CD script for a grocery store trip

generalization than scripts, but the computer program using a plan must be able to infer more from its environment. From the two-sentence story fragment *Dan was thirsty. He looked for a glass.* A plan-oriented system can understand that the ultimate goal is to PTRANS some liquid from where it now resides into Dan by the INGEST process. Finding a glass to contain it is an intermediate goal.

CDs and spin-offs like scripts and plans are the state of the art in NLP today. Programs that handle such processes are very large and generally written in a symbol-processing language like LISP, though Prolog is used extensively for this work as well.

Natural-Language Front Ends

This journey into the world of NLP theory and research has demonstrated the immense complexities when you attempt to write computer programs that "understand" even the simplest English sentences and the concepts they embody. The field is wide open for new developments and techniques.

But bringing NLP into a more realistic position for today, natural-language front ends for databases and spreadsheets are the current marketing rage and promise to stay that way for some time. Much of this work traces its roots to the studies of Gary Hendrix while he was employed at SRI International, a research group. Hendrix created a program called LIFER, an off-the-shelf natural-language front-end processor that developers can use to implement NLP front ends in their products. Hendrix later left SRI International and founded Symantec, which makes a database program and word processor combination called Q&A that uses LIFER-like technology.

With a natural-language front end, the user can extract data from a database or spreadsheet without needing to know much if anything about programming or template design. For example, the user should be able to find out the salaries of all marketing employees by typing the sentence *Tell me all the salaries of my marketing department personnel.* The program parses the user's entry and either fulfills the request or, if it stumbles on a word or idea, asks the user for clarification.

In addition to the parser, LIFER has a second component. Because LIFER was designed for developers, it permits the designer to specify a grammar and an interpretation. This means LIFER is a general-purpose front-end product from which other front ends can be developed.

Several other database and spreadsheet applications—using LIFER directly or only its ideas—now have natural-language front ends. GURU, a combined expert system shell, database, spreadsheet, telecommunications, graphics, and word-processing package from Micro Data Base Systems, has an embedded NLP system called CHAT. R:Base V has an option called CLOUT that permits the user to access data in a database with English sentences. I have already mentioned Q&A from Symantec. And of course there is HAL, a natural-language front end for Lotus 1-2-3 spreadsheet design and use.

Each of these programs deals with a very small subset of the English language within a more or less well-defined environment. Within those limits, each can do fairly sophisticated English language interface management. More and more of these programs showing greater and greater "understanding" and sophistication will appear in the next few years. And some of them will be written in Prolog.

Summary

By now, you may be wondering where Prolog fits into all of this. As you will see in the next two chapters, Prolog is ideally suited to dealing with NLP problems. Using Prolog, you can efficiently express vocabularies as unary Prolog facts and process grammars as rules. Prolog incorporates definite clause grammars (DCGs) as a nearly inherent part of its structure. It is no accident that a great deal of serious NLP work in this country is being done in Prolog.

Simple Parsing and Context-Free Grammars

This chapter explores the concept of a *context-free grammar*. Such a grammar lends itself particularly well to computer implementations because it does not require the program to keep track of adjacent symbols and deal with multiword groups. Context would add an enormous level of complexity that is well beyond the scope of this discussion.

Context-Free Grammar: A Formal Definition

Examined formally, a context-free grammar is one in which the left side of each rule has only one symbol. This is in contrast to a context-sensitive grammar, in which each side of the production rule may have multiple symbols. In fact, a context-sensitive grammar by definition adds a symbol or symbols for context to the left side of the rule.

Figure 13-1 is an example of a context-free grammar that could be used to generate and analyze a small range of sentences in an NLP application.

As you can see, each production, or rule, in figure 13-1 contains only one nonterminal symbol on its left. The terminals are the English words associated with <DETERMINER>, <VERB>, and <NOUN>.

Context-Free Grammars Lead to Tree Structures

Context-free grammars do not deal with the semantic issues of what the words and sentences mean. With this limitation, why are they used in NLP applications? There are a number of reasons, all related to programming issues. The most significant of these is that a context-free grammar lends itself to a tree representation. Trees are important ways of conceptualizing data structures in Prolog and many other languages.

Figure 13-1
A context-free grammar

For example, figure 13-2 shows the tree that results from mapping the derivation of the sentence *A dog plays ball*. Such a tree is called a *derivation tree* because it reveals the derivation of the sentence in the framework of the grammar.

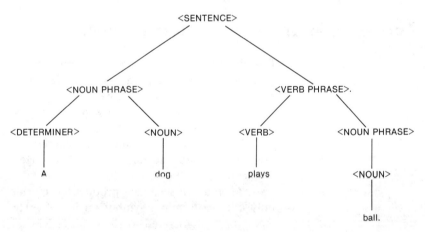

Figure 13-2
Derivation tree for *A dog plays ball*

Notice the symbol <SENTENCE> at the top of the tree. In the context-free grammar defined in figure 13-1, this is the start symbol. All definitions take place in the framework of a sentence as defined by the grammar. From the first production, we determine that a <SENTENCE> consists of a <NOUN PHRASE> and a <VERB PHRASE>. This is the second level of the tree diagram in figure 13-2.

A <NOUN PHRASE> in turn consists of a <DETERMINER> and a <NOUN>, and a <VERB PHRASE> includes a <VERB>

and a <NOUN PHRASE>. These substitutions make up the third level of the mapping tree in figure 13-2. At this point, all but one of the nonterminal symbols can be associated with a terminal in the vocabulary of the grammar. The only exception is the word *ball,* which is not a <NOUN PHRASE> in the same sense as *a dog* is because it lacks a <DETERMINER>. There is, however, another production that defines a <NOUN PHRASE> as consisting only of a <NOUN>. Because *ball* is defined as a <NOUN> in the vocabulary of the context-free grammar, the sentence passes.

Figure 13-3 is a derivation tree of a sentence that the grammar will not accept.

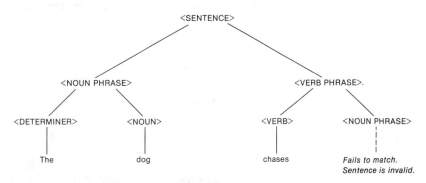

Figure 13-3
Derivation tree for *The dog chases barks*

The sentence, *The dog chases barks* is rejected by the grammar because *barks* does not meet the criteria of the production, which defines a <VERB PHRASE> as consisting of a <VERB> and a <NOUN PHRASE>. *Barks* is not defined as a noun in the vocabulary of the grammar. The sentence, therefore, fails to pass the test of this context-free grammar.

Notice, however, that by adding a new production defining the word *barks* as a <NOUN>, we can force the grammar to accept this sentence.

The importance of this observation about context-free grammars and corresponding derivation tree structures is that Prolog deals with data structures in a tree-like manner. Lists and compound objects can both be represented by trees. These are the most common types of data structures in a Prolog program. If you can reduce any grammar—or, more generally, any kind of algorithm or data structure—to a tree representation, you can be certain that Prolog will deal with it effectively and efficiently.

One major reason Prolog works so well for NLP applications is that is automatically backtracks through collections of alternative rules until it finds a set of rules that solve the problem. This exhaustive search aspect of a parser—inherent in Prolog—is often quite difficult to implement in other programming languages.

Context-Free Grammars and Prolog

With this background, you are ready to examine how to implement a context-free grammar in Turbo Prolog. You will start with a very simplistic program that demonstrates the principles in such a design. From there, you will be prepared to move to a more complex grammar capable of dealing with a broader range of inputs.

The following listing is a Turbo Prolog program that recognizes a single sentence pattern: <ARTICLE> <NOUN> <VERB>. Its input must be in the form of a list. This is a somewhat inconvenient form of data entry, but for the moment the focus is on parsing a sentence rather than the construction of the internal representation of the sentence itself.

```
domains
  symlist=symbol*
predicates
  article(symbol)
  sentence(symlist)
  noun(symbol)
  verb(symbol)
clauses
sentence([Word1,Word2,Word3]):-
  article(Word1),
  noun(Word2),
  verb(Word3).
article(a).
  article(an).
  article(the).
  noun(tree).
  noun(ball).
  noun(programmer).
  verb(falls).
  verb(bounces).
  verb(codes).
```

Type, save, and then run this Turbo Prolog program. Your input to the program is in the form:

```
sentence([word1,word2,word3]).
```

with individual words separated by commas. The period at the end is optional but the square brackets denoting list notation are not. Figure 13-4 shows four different goal statements posed to the program and the program's response to each.

Notice that the first, second, and fourth goal statements present sentences that the program accepts (sentences fitting the pattern and using words that the program has been told about). The third sentence,

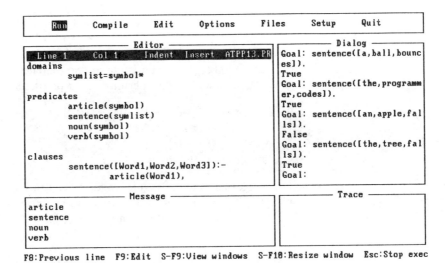

Figure 13-4

Four interactions with the limited parsing program

an apple falls, is within the proper sentence format, <ARTICLE> <NOUN> <VERB>, but the word *apple* is not in the program's limited vocabulary. The sentence fails and the Turbo Prolog response to the goal statement is False.

It is easy to see from this example why implementing context-free grammars is so straightforward in Turbo Prolog. The elements of the grammar—notably terminals like *a, programmer,* and *bounces*—can be represented as unary Prolog facts.

Sentence Definition

The only rule in the context-free grammar program just listed is the description of a sentence as consisting of three words in a list separated by commas (because that is how Turbo Prolog and most other implementations of the language handle lists). The first word must match the Prolog fact pattern:

```
article(Word1)
```

Three such words are present in the knowledge base as it stands. The occurrence of any of these words in the first position of the list satisfies the first of the rule premises. Similarly, the second word must match the Prolog fact pattern:

```
noun(Word2)
```

and the third must match the pattern:

```
verb(Word3)
```

Any new sentence structure you want to implement in the program can use this rule's format as a template from which to design new rules. To demonstrate this, let's make it possible for this small program to recognize a compound sentence consisting of two sentences joined by the word *but*.

The new rule that permits this type of sentence looks like this:

```
sentence([W1,W2,W3,W4,W5,W6,W7]):-
   sentence([W1,W2,W3]),
   W4=but,
   sentence([W5,W6,W7]).
```

Notice that this rule requires a sentence to consist of seven "words": two three-word sentences that comply with our previously defined production rule for a sentence, joined at the fourth position by the word *but*. Formally, this is stated as follows:

```
<ARTICLE> <NOUN> <VERB> but <ARTICLE> <NOUN> <VERB>
```

Remember that the word *but* is a terminal and should not be enclosed in angle brackets in the formal notation.

Now you can present `goal` statements like those in figure 13-5 and expect the program to respond correctly. If either side of the symmetrical sentence structure defined with the new rule does not match the previous rule for a sentence or if the fourth word is anything other than *but,* the program rejects the sentence.

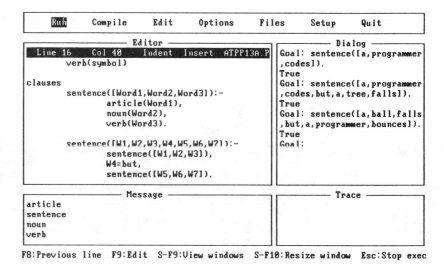

Figure 13-5
Interacting with the more complex parser

Expanding the Program's Vocabulary

Adding to the vocabulary of the program is quite easy. You simply add facts to the knowledge base with the proper functors so that the new words are recognized by the program during the parsing of a sentence.

Note: Don't forget that Turbo Prolog, unlike most conventional versions of the language, requires that all like predicates be grouped together in the program.

Here is a sample listing of how the program looks after adding a number of words to its vocabulary. Feel free to add your own nouns and verbs to the list, following the same format shown here.

```
domains
  symlist=symbol*

predicates
  article(symbol)
  sentence(symlist)
  noun(symbol)
  verb(symbol)

clauses
sentence([Word1,Word2,Word3]):-
  article(Word1),
  noun(Word2),
  verb(Word3).
sentence([W1,W2,W3,W4,W5,W6,W7]):-
  sentence([W1,W2,W3]),
  W4=but,
  sentence([W5,W6,W7]).
article(a).
article(an).
article(the).
noun(tree).
noun(ball).
noun(programmer).
noun(table).
noun(house).
noun(car).
noun(butterfly).
noun(radio).
noun(chess_set).
noun(person).
verb(falls).
verb(bounces).
verb(codes).
verb(lives).
verb(flies).
verb(stands).
verb(waters).
verb(travels).
verb(drives).
verb(communicates).
```

```
verb(plays).
verb(is_cluttered).
verb(walks).
```

Extending the Grammar

This grammar program is fairly primitive. For example, it does not allow phrases and clauses consisting of more than one word to be parsed as a group. In that sense, it is not as complete as the context-free grammar in figure 13-1, even though it has a wider vocabulary.

Let's expand our context-free grammar experiment to handle phrases. The following program listing accomplishes what we want. Note that we have reverted to our smaller initial vocabulary for simplicity of demonstration and testing. Feel free to add whatever words you like to this vocabulary.

```
domains
  symlist=symbol*
predicates
  sentence(symlist)
  append(symlist,symlist,symlist)
  noun_phrase(symlist)
  verb_phrase(symlist)
  article(symlist)
  noun(symlist)
  verb(symlist)
clauses
  append([],L,L).
  append([H1|L1],L2,[H1|L3]) if
    append(L1,L2,L3).
  sentence(Input) if
    append(L1,L2,Input) and
    noun_phrase(L1) and
    verb_phrase(L2).
  noun_phrase(Sublist) if
    append(L1,L2,Sublist) and
    article(L1) and
    noun(L2).
  verb_phrase(Sublist) if
    append(L1,L2,Sublist) and
    verb(L1) and
    noun_phrase(L2).
  verb_phrase(Sublist) if
    verb(Sublist).
article([a]).
article([an]).
article([the]).
noun([tree]).
noun([ball]).
```

```
noun([programmer]).
verb([falls]).
verb([bounces]).
verb([codes]).
```

This program takes advantage of the fact that the `append` list manipulation predicate, like all other Prolog predicates, has a compound flow pattern. If used in what you might think of as its "usual" way, it joins two lists, producing a third. For example:

```
append([a,b,c],[d,e,f],L3).
L3=[a,b,c,d,e,f]
```

However, if you call the `append` predicate with the first two arguments uninstantiated and supply the third argument, Prolog produces a list of all possible decompositions of the furnished list into sublists. Here is an example:

```
append(L1,L2,[a,b,c]).
L1=[], L2=[a,b,c]
L1=[a], L2=[b,c]
L1=[a,b], L2=[c]
L1=[a,b,c], L2=[]
```

In this program, the `append` predicate is used in this second way. Each time the `sentence` and `noun_phrase` predicates try to determine the validity of a list passed to them by the user or the program, they use the `append` predicate to decompose the list into its component parts to determine if any of these lists qualifies as a recognizable segment of a valid sentence.

Notice also that the terminals—article, noun, and verb—are defined as lists rather than symbols. This is in keeping with the way the `append` predicate works. It breaks lists into sublists but always produces a list. If you define these terminals as symbols, the program never identifies a sentence as valid.

As you can see from figure 13-6, you can now pose goals that include phrases and obtain expected results. The first sentence is recognized by the first program as well as the last, but the second sentence is understood only by the most recent version of the program. The third sentence is invalid in both programs and is included to demonstrate that this last program behaves exactly as expected.

Sentence Analyzer

On the *Library and Sample Programs* disk included with Turbo Prolog, there is a program called SANAL.PRO. (It is furnished with Borland's free upgrade from Version 1.0 to Version 1.1.) This program is an elaborate demonstration of a context-free grammar.

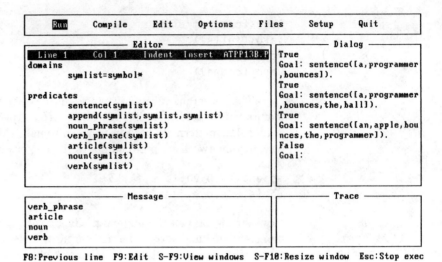

Figure 13-6
Interacting with the complex phrase grammar

Not only does the SANAL program analyze a sentence, it draws a derivation tree of the sentence on the screen and permits you to examine and update the vocabulary stored in a database file on the disk. See figure 13-7. The vocabulary in the program's database file is shown in figure 13-8.

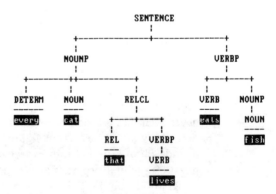

SENTENCE=every cat that lives eats fish

PROLOG OBJECT=sent(nounp(determ("every"),"cat",relcl("that",verb("lives"))),verbp("eats",nounp(none,"fish",none)))

write a sentence:

Figure 13-7
Screen output from SANAL

The SANAL program permits the entry of strings rather than lists. Load the program and note the s_sentence predicate, the key predicate you should examine to understand the program in greater detail. Note, too, that in the domains section of the program, several domains are defined as compound objects.

NOUNS	RELATIONALS
leo	that
vibeke	who
katrine	whoom *[sic]*
jon	which
finn	
max	VERBS
cat	love
food	like
fish	hate
prolog	live
man	eat
woman	ate
	sleep
DETERMINERS	
a	
an	
the	
some	
all	
every	
this	
that	

Figure 13-8
Vocabulary recognized by SANAL

If you experiment with different sentence structures in SANAL and in the three programs created in this chapter, you will gain an appreciation for the strengths and weaknesses of this approach to parsing in Prolog. Expand the range of sentence structures recognized by the programs in this chapter so that you understand what can and cannot be done and how grammatical rules are expressed in Turbo Prolog.

Summary

In this chapter, you learned about context-free grammars and their implementation in Turbo Prolog. You saw that a context-free grammar is flexible. As you developed three increasingly complex and powerful programs in Turbo Prolog, you moved from analyzing simple sentences to examining and understanding complex sentences, finally including phrases in the parse strategy as well.

Finally, you looked briefly at the SANAL.PRO program provided by Borland International with Turbo Prolog Version 1.1. You saw how it works and gained some clues into its inner operations as an NLP program.

As you move to chapter 14, you'll turn your attention to a different type of grammar known as an augmented transition network, or ATN. This grammatical definition—more flexible and useful than a context-free grammar—builds on many of the key concepts of parsing introduced in this chapter.

Augmented Transition Network Grammars

This chapter describes a very powerful grammar representation called an *augmented transition network* (ATN). ATNs are seen by many as the current state of the art, at least in terms of systems actually in use. An understanding of how ATN parsers work will add greatly to your appreciation of NLP.

We begin with a bit of historical and theoretical background as a framework for the discussion. Then we present the ATN diagrams for the grammar we will implement. Finally, we present an ATN program written by Vermont high school student and Turbo Prolog hacker Tom Emerson just for this book.

Background

ATNs made their debut in the early 1970s as a result of research by William A. Woods, a well-known natural language specialist with one of the pioneering AI firms. In developing the ATN concept, Woods built on the idea of a *finite-state transition diagram* (FSTD), a method of portraying machine-based systems of all types that had been in use for a number of years. An FSTD looks something like figure 14-1, where the nodes are specific states of the machine and the arcs represent actions that change the state.

Figure 14-1 is an over-simplified machine-state diagram. Real-life diagrams often contain hundreds, even thousands, of nodes with overlapping arcs connecting all nodes in a complex network.

Woods saw the power in these diagrams and applied their logic to language analysis. In the process, he created a grammatic design that can be applied to any recursively definable language, which covers a great deal of linguistic territory.

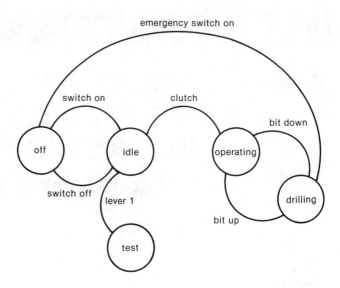

Figure 14-1
A finite-state transition diagram (FSTD)

Theoretical Framework

In an FSTD, each node represents, at least potentially, a *final state* of the machine. The machine can be left in that state indefinitely and nothing untoward will happen as a rule. Also, there is no decision-making in an FSTD: it is simply a description of how to move from one legal final state to another legal final state.

Woods extended the idea of an FSTD with tests and side effects, and thus made them theoretically powerful enough to recognize any language that might be recognized by a computer. To appreciate fully the impact of these advances, you must look at two intermediate stopping points on the road to the ATN: FSTDs (revisited) and recursive transition networks (RTNs), from which ATNs grew.

FSTD Operation

An FSTD can deal only with the simplest of grammars. To see this, look at figure 14-2. The start state for this FSTD is the leftmost node and the final state is shown as concentric circles. The center state is an intermediate state, INT1. This is a classic FSTD segment. What happens if you pass the phrase *the wonderful program* to this FSTD?

You begin at the START state. Noting that the leftmost word in the parse string is *the,* follow along the arc labeled *the.* This leaves you in the center state, INT1, with the words *wonderful* and *program* still to parse. If your vocabulary indicates that *wonderful* is an adjective, you loop through the <ADJECTIVE> arc and return to the INT1 node with only the word *program* left to parse. Again, assuming the vocabulary has defined *program* as a noun, you move along the next arc marked <NOUN> and reach the final state. Because you have reached

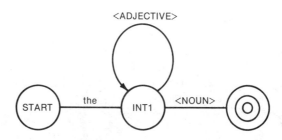

Figure 14-2
FSTD for grammar segment

the final state, you can declare that *the wonderful program* is an acceptable input to this parser.

Recursive Transition Networks

Such a parser is very linear and does not work for most kinds of input you
want to parse in an NLP system. One missing element is that of recursion,
i.e., the ability to have an arc that is labeled with a nonterminal invoke a
subnetwork. Recursion permits you to reuse nonterminals as often as
needed in parsing input.

To overcome these problems and to add recursion, you'll move to
the next level of complexity of transitional parsers, a recursive transition
network (RTN). Figure 14-3 presents a fragment of such a network.

If you presented the string *The shy programmer in the pinstriped
suit wrote this code* to the grammar in figure 14-3, it would parse it into
these components:

```
<NOUN PHRASE>: The shy programmer in the pinstriped suit
<PREPOSITIONAL PHRASE>: in the pinstriped suit
<NOUN PHRASE>: the pinstriped suit
<VERB>: wrote
<NOUN PHRASE>: this code
```

Note the interaction among the subnetworks. Any subnetwork can
call any other, including itself. The <PREPOSITIONAL PHRASE>
subnetwork, for example, contains a <NOUN PHRASE> subnetwork.
It should also be evident from this discussion that some of the arcs are
nondeterministic. In other words, there are multiple possible arcs to be
investigated at some points in the parse.

An RTN can handle a context-free grammar quite nicely, but this is
hardly sufficient power for the major NLP tasks that need to be addressed.

Power of ATNs   With the addition of tests before an arc is taken and actions after an arc
is followed, an ATN becomes a powerful way of representing language.
At points where more than one arc is possible, the system can be de-

signed to test conditions (for example, the word pattern that has already been parsed or the framework within which the text is being analyzed) to determine which arc is most likely to yield a positive result. Similarly, an action after an arc is followed could include a requirement to rearrange the remainder of the input so parsing is more direct and efficient or correct.

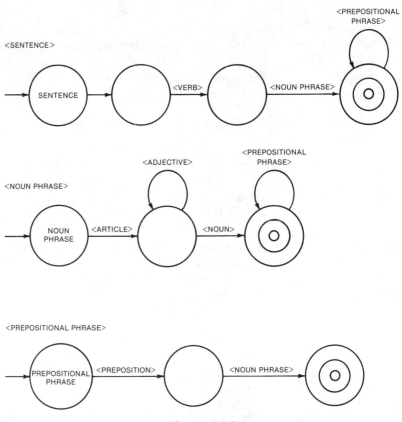

Figure 14-3
A recursive transition network (RTN) fragment

In every other respect, an ATN operates and looks like an RTN. But with this added power, true NLP becomes feasible with even very complex grammars.

Before you move to the discussion of the specific ATN grammar and Turbo Prolog program, pause to note one known weakness of ATN grammars. They rely heavily on syntax. This restricts their ability to deal with ungrammatical utterances that may nonetheless be meaningful. But the other kinds of grammars you have seen (and those yet to be discussed) have the same weakness, in addition to others.

An ATN Grammar

We will develop a parsing program for the ATN grammar depicted in figure 14-4. The node labels are identical to those used in the program itself.

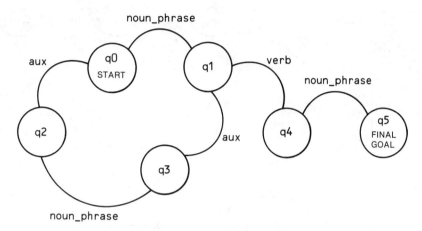

**Figure 14-4
An ATN grammar**

The start state is q0. Notice that you immediately have a choice between two branches, one requires a noun phrase and the other requires an auxiliary verb as the first element in the string being parsed. The transition q0-q1-q3-q4 is identical to q0-q1-q3 except the former also contains an auxiliary verb.

Notice that the nonterminal noun_phrase recurs in the ATN grammar of figure 14-4. In fact, there are three arcs labeled noun_phrase. But you have not defined a noun_phrase anywhere in the diagram. That's because a noun_phrase subnetwork is created as shown in figure 14-5. Again, the same node labels are used for easy cross-referencing.

Implementing an ATN

The ATN.PRO program, listing 14-1, is at the end of this chapter. The program implements the grammar described in figures 14-4 and 14-5. Its vocabulary is as follows:

```
Proper Nouns:  john, mary
Nouns: boy, girl, baby
Verbs: run, smile, likes, like
Auxiliary:  can
Adjectives: very, pretty, little
Determiner (article): the
```

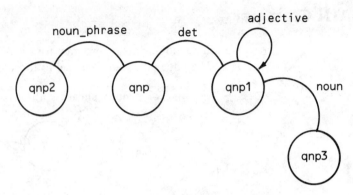

Figure 14-5

The noun_phrase subnetwork of an ATN grammar

If you enter and run the program, you will encounter two error messages indicating that a variable is not bound in a particular clause. Ignore these warnings and press the F10 key.

Let's take a look at some sample runs of the program to get a better idea of what it can and can't handle. Figure 14-6 shows a very small sentence entered into the ATN parser and successfully parsed. Notice that the text is entered as a string, with no capital letters and no punctuation (including no period at the end).

```
────────────────────────ATN PARSER────────────────────────
ATN Parser Version 3.2
By Tom Emerson

Enter sentence to be analyzed-->mary likes john


Transition from node: q0 to node: q1 [noun_proper("mary")]
Transition from node: q1 to node: q4 verb("likes")
Transition from node: q4 to node: q5 [noun_proper("john")]

Completed at node: q5

Parse:
[noun_phrase([noun_proper("mary")]),verb("likes"),noun_phrase([noun_proper("jo
hn")])]
Press the SPACE bar
```

Figure 14-6

Simple successful parse in ATN program

The information displayed shows the nodes from which and to which the transition is made. The first transition—made when the ATN program detects a noun_phrase because of the presence of a proper noun—is q0-q1. Inside the noun_phrase subnetwork, the pro-

gram makes a qnp-qnp2 transition. The parser's next transition is from
q1 to q4. The arc that connects those nodes is labeled verb
and you can see that *likes* is listed as a verb in the vocabulary of the
program.

The move from q4 to q5, the final node of the ATN grammar,
requires a noun_phrase, which appears as *john*. This proper noun
makes the same qnp-qnp2 transition that *mary* triggered. The sentence
is passed because the parser reached a final node with no more text to
parse.

A more complex sentence, *the very pretty little girl can smile,* is
shown in figure 14-7. But notice that the program still only requires
three main grammar transitions to pass the sentence. That is because *the
very pretty little girl* is a noun_phrase handled in the noun_phrase
subnetwork. In that subnetwork, the transition list would appear as
follows:

qnp-qnp1-qnp1-qnp1-qnp3

Note that the list appearing at the end of the program's run has only
three components: the noun phrase, an auxiliary verb, and a verb.

```
----------ATN PARSER----------
ATN Parser Version 3.2
By Tom Emerson

Enter sentence to be analyzed-->the very pretty little girl can smile


Transition from node: q0 to node: q1 [det("the"),adj("very"),adj("pretty"),adj
("little"),noun("girl")]
Transition from node: q1 to node: q3 aux("can")
Transition from node: q3 to node: q4 verb("smile")

Completed at node: q4

Parse:
[noun_phrase([det("the"),adj("very"),adj("pretty"),adj("little"),noun("girl")]
),aux("can"),verb("smile")]
Press the SPACE bar
```

Figure 14-7
More complex successful parse

Finally, look at figure 14-8. Here we try a sentence, *the very little
boy runs,* for which no verb is defined in the vocabulary. The parser
finds the noun_phrase using a transition list of:

npq-npq1-npq1-npq3

But when it returns to the main grammar network, the noun_phrase cannot find a verb or an auxiliary to connect to, so the parse fails. The parser tells you at which node the parse failed and displays the amount of the sentence that could be parsed and what remained to be examined.

```
                              ─ATN PARSER─
ATN Parser Version 3.2
By Tom Emerson

Enter sentence to be analyzed──>the very little boy runs


Transition from node: q0 to node: q1 [det("the"),adj("very"),adj("little"),nou
n("boy")]

Sentence failed at node: q1
Parsed: [noun_phrase([det("the"),adj("very"),adj("little"),noun("boy")])]
Left: ["runs"]
Press the SPACE bar
```

Figure 14-8
Unsuccessful parse attempt

Summary

This chapter introduced the idea of an augmented transition network (ATN). You saw how an ATN is derived from a finite-state transition diagram (FSTD). You also saw how an ATN, building on the concept of the FSTD, can parse a very wide range of languages indeed. You examined a small ATN grammar and a Turbo Prolog program implementing that grammar. This concludes our necessarily brief look at NLP.

Listing 14-1

```
/*          Augmented Transition Network Parser
                      Version 3.2
                    by Tom Emerson
*/
/*   NOTE:  During compilation, the compiler will report
            a VARIABLE NOT BOUND IN CLAUSE... error
            twice: in the _append_ predicate and in the
            _trans_ predicate.  This is normal.  Press
            F10 to continue with the compilation.
*/
```

```
domains
  list = string*
  form_list = class*
  class = noun(symbol) ; verb(symbol;
    adj(symbol) ; det(symbol);
    aux(symbol) ; noun_proper(symbol);
    noun_phrase(form_list) ; prep_phrase(form_list).
predicates
  append(form_list,form_list,form_list).
  separate(string,list).
  dictionary(class,list,list).
  arc(symbol,symbol,class).
  terminal(symbol,list).
  trans(symbol,symbol,form_list,list,list).
  ptrans(symbol,symbol,symbol,list,class,form_list).
goal
  clearwindow,
  makewindow(1,7,7,"ATN PARSER",0,0,25,80),
  write("ATN PARSER Version 3.2").
  write("\nBy Tom Emerson"),
  nl,nl,
  write("Enter sentence to be analyzed-->"),
  readln(Sentence),
  separate(Sentence,S),
  nl,
  trans(q0,Nq,Parse,S,S1).

/*  The sentence to be analyzed is sent to the parser
    in the fourth argument of the previous _trans_
    predicate.
*/

clauses
  append([],X,X):- !.
  append([H|L],L1,[H|L2]) :-
    append(L,L1,L2).

  separate(S,[H|T]):-
    fronttoken(S,H,S1),!,
    separate(S1,T).
  separate(_,[]).

dictionary(noun_proper(john),[john|X],X).
dictionary(noun_proper(mary),[mary|X],X).
dictionary(noun(boy),[boy|X],X).
dictionary(noun(girl),[girl|X],X).
dictionary(noun(baby),[baby|X],X).
dictionary(verb(run),[run|X],X).
```

Listing 14-1 (cont.)

```
dictionary(verb(smile),[smile|X],X).
dictionary(verb(likes),[likes|X],X).
dictionary(verb(like),[like|X],X).
dictionary(aux(can),[can|X],X).
dictionary(adj(very),[very|X],X).
dictionary(adj(pretty),[pretty|X],X).
dictionary(adj(little),[little|X],X).
dictionary(det(the),[the|X],X).

arc(q0,q1,noun_phrase(_)).
arc(q0,q2,aux(_)).
arc(q1,q4,verb(_)).
arc(q1,q3,aux(_)).
arc(q2,q3,noun_phrase(_)).
arc(q3,q4,verb(_)).
arc(q4,q5,noun_phrase(_)).
arc(qnp,qnp1,det(_)).
arc(qnp,qnp2,noun_proper(_)).
arc(qnp1,qnp1,adj(_)).
arc(qnp1,qnp3,noun(_)).

terminal(q4,[]).
terminal(q5,[]).

trans(Lq,Nq,Parse,S1,SO):-          /* Transition */
  dictionary(Class,S1,SO),
  arc(Lq,Nq,Class),
  write("\nTransition from node: ",Lq," to node: ",Nq,"
    ",Class),
  append(Parse[Class],P1),
  !,
  trans(Nq,_,P1,SO_).

trans(Lq,_,Parse,S1,_):-            /* End of ATN */
  terminal(Lq,S1),
  bound(Parse),
  nl,nl,
  write("Completed at node: ",Lq),
  nl,nl,write("Parse:"),nl,
  write(Parse).

trans(Lq,_,Parse,SO,_):-           /* Noun Phrase */
  arc(Lq,Nq,noun_phrase(_)),
  ptrans(qnp,Nq,Lq,SO,noun_phrase(_),Parse).

trans(Lq,_,Parse,SO,_):-           /* Failure */
  bound(parse),
```

```
      nl,nl,
      write("Sentence failed at node: ",Lq),
      nl,write("Parsed: ",Parse),
      nl,write("Left: ",SO).

ptrans(Bq,Nq,Lq,SO,noun_phrase(X),Parse):-
      dictionary(Class,SO,S1),
      arc(Bq,Zq,Class),
      append(X,[Class],P1),
      !,
      ptrans(Zq,Nq,Lq,S1,noun_phrase(P1),Parse).

ptrans(_,Nq,Lq,SO,noun_phrase(Pr),Parse):-
      bound(Pr),
      write("\nTransition from node: ",Lq," to node: ",Nq,"
         ",Pr),
      append(Parse[noun_phrase(Pr)],P1),
      !,
      trans(Nq,_,P1,SO,_).
```

Turbo Prolog Power:
Math and Logic

Chapter 15

Problem Solving

This chapter begins part 4, which is devoted to a collection of programs that have one thing in common: they solve some sort of problem. Not all computer programs solve problems. At least, not directly. A word-processing program, for example, does not solve a problem. Rather, it accepts text and commands from a user, saves text on a disk, and formats and prints the result. It may, in the process, be said to solve a problem for the user, but it is not primarily a problem-solving program.

In chapter 16, you'll see a program that uses Turbo Prolog's built-in logic to deal with the famous Master Mind puzzle. The computer creates a random pattern of colors. You try by deduction to guess the colors and the order in which they appear. This process is a classic problem-solving assignment for a logic program.

Chapter 17 presents a problem solver of a different sort—a mortgage calculator that proves that Turbo Prolog's much maligned number-crunching capability is greater than expected.

The next two chapters examine programs that revert to the more classic AI problem-solving world. In chapter 18, it's the well-known problem of the farmer with a goat, a wolf, a cabbage, and a small rowboat. He must get them all safely to the other side, but leaving some of them together will destroy his objective. Chapter 19 demonstrates how to use Turbo Prolog to design solutions to those annoying word problems in puzzle books. You're given only a few clues, but they turn out to be just enough to figure out the solution. You may be surprised at how quickly Turbo Prolog does this task!

Finally, in chapter 20, there's a more mathematical problem. In list processing, it's often important to know the minimum and maximum values in a list. The program in this chapter shows you an elegant and efficient way to do this.

Before you delve into the programs themselves, though, let's take a look at the question of problem solving and how Prolog (and, more specifically, Turbo Prolog) is suited to this common AI task.

What Is Problem Solving?

It may seem unnecessary to dwell on the definition of problem solving, but its theoretical aspects are important. Basically, a logic programming language like Prolog solves a problem by finding its way through a *state space*. Any problem that lends itself to a state space diagram can be dealt with powerfully and elegantly by a Prolog program.

State Space Diagrams   A state space diagram is a graph depicting all possible states in which a problem can find itself and the connecting arcs from one state to another. (You encountered a form of state space diagrams in chapter 12 when you learned about finite-state transition diagrams, or FSTDs.)

Figure 15-1 is the state space diagram for a puzzle in which three coins, starting with two heads and one tail, must be converted to all heads or all tails by flipping them one at a time. The catch: it must be done in exactly three moves. All combinations of coin positions—all possible states in the puzzle—are shown as circular nodes. The connecting arcs are numbered to show which coin is flipped to move from one state to another. These paths are bidirectional, but not all arcs are bidirectional.

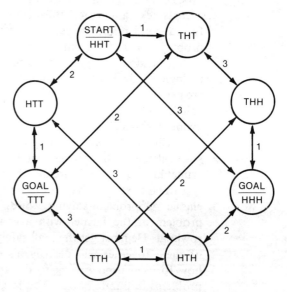

Figure 15-1
State space diagram of three coins puzzle

The state space diagram, then, shows all possible states and moves. In the three coins puzzle, there are eight possible states, and only three moves: flip over coin 1 (move 1), coin 2 (move 2), or coin 3 (move 3).

A Prolog program to solve this problem must begin with a representation of this state space diagram, identify the start and goal states, and "know" the possible moves. From there, solving the puzzle is a simple matter of searching. The design of this program is left to you as an exercise.

Search Strategies

This brings you to the other important idea in problem solving: searching. At least four identifiable search strategies are available when searching any space state for a solution:

- "brute force" method, which involves no intelligence but simply looks at all possible alternatives until it finds the right one
- depth-first search, in which the program follows a given path to its ultimate conclusion and, if unsuccessful, backtracks to the next previous level and checks the next path until it finally finds a solution
- breadth-first search, in which all possible paths are followed to a specific level in the search space and then each is pursued one additional level, and so on, until one of them results in a solution
- "best-first" method, in which some AI concepts are used to determine which of the available paths is most likely to result in a solution

Most computer programs use a brute force method and follow a depth-first strategy. That is what you will encounter for the most part in this book as well. Best-first searches are just being implemented in high-powered computer systems. In a few years, they will become very important in many problem-solving programs, but today they are not sufficiently understood.

There is no way of determining, in general, whether a depth-first or breadth-first search will result in a more efficient solution to a given problem. The nature of the problem, the structure of the state space, and the constraints placed on the solution are all factors.

Importance of Problem Solving

In artificial intelligence research, searching is a major issue. In an expert system design, for example, the user generally poses a goal statement to the system, and the program tries to gather enough information with enough certainty to present the user with a solution, a way of achieving the stated goal.

Similarly, as you saw in part 3, NLP programs quite often become dedicated to the task of proving that a given set of inputs does indeed comprise a valid sentence in the defined grammar. This is a kind of problem solving as well.

It is no accident that we often talk of Prolog programs in terms of goals and queries rather than functions and procedures. The user who interacts with Turbo Prolog does so in response to a goal, which is what drives the program to operate the way it does. The user prompt is the word `goal` in Turbo Prolog rather than the more traditional, but far more cryptic, `?-` in "standard" Prolog. Prolog is often referred to as a backward-chaining, goal directed language. That description is accurate and goes a long way toward explaining why Turbo Prolog programs that solve relatively sophisticated problems are still small enough to fit in this book.

The ideas, concepts, techniques, and strategies in searching form a major part of current AI programming methodologies and tasks. By the time you finish reading part 4, you will have a good grasp of the subject and an appreciation for how it is implemented in Turbo Prolog.

Now let's turn to chapter 16 and dive into our first problem-solving program.

Chapter **16**

Master Mind

In this chapter you look at a program, written by Israel del Rio, that plays a game of Master Mind against the user. The computer "thinks" of a combination of colors. The user tries to deduce what colors appear in the pattern and in what order they appear. The game itself is quite old and is available in many versions. Some use colors, others use numbers and letters.

This version is notable for its user interface, which is intuitive and nicely done, and for its use of database structures to manage the user's guesses. It is also one of the better organized Turbo Prolog programs you're likely to encounter, so you can learn something about programming style from it as well.

The Problem

Guessing games are fun. But they can be frustrating, too. Even a simple child's game like "Button, button, who's got the button?" is impossible to solve if there aren't clues like *you're getting warmer* and *cold, very cold.*

Master Mind without clues could only be solved by guessing. The problem is that four slots filled with a choice of six colors that can be repeated results in 1,296 permutations and combinations of possible colors. At 30 seconds per guess (allowing for entry time, computer response time, and consternation time), it takes 648 minutes, or about 11 hours, to guess all of them. And you know everything is always in the last place you look for it.

The people who invented this diabolical game in the first place were faced with the problem of how to devise clues that guided the player toward a right solution without giving the solution away. Their plan was ingenious. After each guess, the computer (or the other human player) tells the player how many colors were guessed right in the wrong position and how many were guessed right in the right position. For example, if the computer sets up the pattern blue-red-orange-blue and you guessed blue-orange-blue-magenta, the computer would indicate you had guessed two colors in the wrong position and one color in the right position, for a total of three correct colors.

Obviously, you can use logic to shorten considerably the 11 hours it would take to randomly guess the color combinations. For example, assume that the computer has set up another pattern. Suppose you guess that the combination is blue-orange-blue-magenta and the computer responds by indicating two colors are right and one is in the wrong position.

You can determine which color is in the right position by changing one of them. Suppose you next guess magenta-orange-blue-blue. The computer now tells you that three colors are correct but none is in the right place.

So you put the blue back into the first position and guess blue-orange-blue-blue (the other logical option is to assume magenta was in the right place), and the computer tells you that you again have two colors right and one in the wrong position. So the first blue is in the right position and you can stop looking for any other first-position colors. The process of guessing the combinations ends when all four colors are guessed in the right positions.

The Program

Let's see how del Rio solved this problem with the clever use of database declarations and some other techniques. The program, listing 16-1, is at the end of this chapter. First, let's run the program.

Running the Program

This program works best on a color display. It can still be played with a monochrome display, but it is not nearly as interesting or easy to understand. The screen examples aren't printed in color, so we'll show you as much as possible in black and white and describe the rest in words.

To run the program, simply load it and choose the Run option from the Turbo Prolog menu. After the program compiles, you'll see an instruction screen, which explains how the game is played. See figure 16-1. The message at the bottom of the screen tells you to press any key to start the game. When you do so, you'll see a display that looks like figure 16-2. The game is under way.

There are now three windows on the screen: the Instructions window, the Master Mind window, and the Hints window. Following the directions in the Instructions window, type a *b*, press the right arrow, then pick blue, orange, and magenta for the remaining boxes. The screen appears similar to figure 16-3, depending on what color combination your program chose.

Notice that the computer indicates you have chosen one color in the right position and two colors in the wrong position. Not a bad start! Guess again. This time guess that the first blue is in the right position,

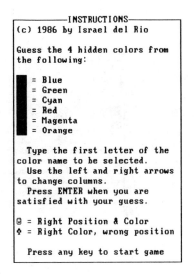

Figure 16-1
Master Mind instruction screen

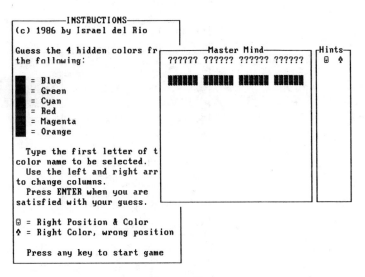

Figure 16-2
Master Mind opening screen

and change the order of the other three letters so that the guess is blue-magenta-blue-orange. The computer response is shown in figure 16-4.

Now you have two colors in the right position and one color incorrectly positioned. But you don't know whether the first blue is one of the correctly positioned colors (though you may suspect it is). Let's try one more guess. This time, swap orange and magenta and replace the second blue with green. So the guess is blue-orange-green-magenta. The

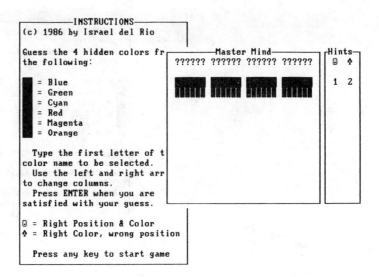

Figure 16-3
First guess and computer response

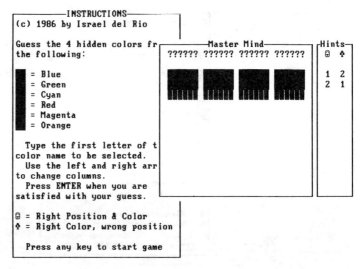

Figure 16-4
Game in progress

result is one color in the right position and three colors in the wrong position. This is real progress! You now know all four colors and it's a simple matter of arranging the last three in the right sequence.

By deduction, suppose you conclude that orange must be in the fourth position and that magenta must be in the second or third. So you try blue-green-magenta-orange and voila! Figure 16-5 shows the results of a correct guess.

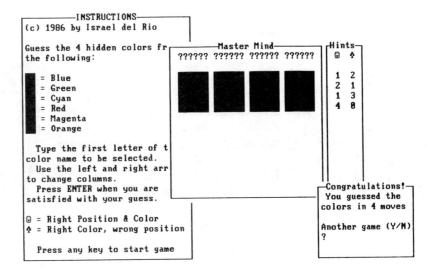

Figure 16-5
Winning screen

Analyzing the Program

In this analysis, the focus is on the way the program handles user input of colors and arrows, the intelligent use of database declarations to avoid a major design pitfall, and the process of checking the user's input against the computer's predetermined color choices.

User Input Handling

When the program is ready for the user to enter color guesses, the predicate getEntry is called. Inside getEntry, the program calls the putcolor predicate.

There are two versions of the getEntry predicate. The first uses the program's readKey predicate to get the user's input and convert it to the form the program expects. It remains true as long as the user does not press the RETURN key. The RETURN key generates an ASCII code of 13, which is what the line:

```
K<>13,
```

means. When the user does press the RETURN key, the first getEntry predicate fails and the second takes over. It is a simple cut that returns control to the calling routine.

As the user enters values through the getEntry predicate, the putcolor predicate changes the color of the space in which the entry is being made. To do so, it uses the attrib predicate defined in the Master Mind program itself. There are three versions of the putcolor predicate. The first is always used, except when the attribute being passed is 0. When the attribute is 0, the second putcolor predicate comes into play. If the user enters a key that does not correspond to one of the color choices available, the system uses the sound predicate to signal the mistake and leaves the color unchanged through the third putcolor predicate.

Notice that two of the attrib predicates are not color attribute selectors but arrow selectors. This is an elegant way of handling the need to move the cursor when the user presses one of the arrow keys. The left arrow generates an ASCII 75 character and the right arrow generates an ASCII 77. Note that the fourth argument to the attrib predicate is an integer defined as domain type displa. The program uses this integer value to determine how to affect the cursor position after reading a key. Only the right and left attribute values affect the fourth argument; colors all have a fourth argument of 0.

Database Declaration Use

If del Rio had designed Master Mind in a conventional, procedural programming language, he almost certainly would have had some difficulty dealing with one issue. If the program updates the list containing the guesses as the user enters them, what happens if the user wants to change a guess? You'd have to backtrack to the square the user wants to change, store the unchanged guesses somewhere, get the new guess, add it to the other guesses in the appropriate spot, and go on. A lot of processing is required to accomplish this task.

Partly because of Turbo Prolog's nonprocedural nature and partly because of its powerful list-handling capabilities, this program doesn't have to concern itself with that problem. Rather, it implements a predicate called read_line. After the user presses the RETURN key inside the getEntry predicate, the main play_game predicate calls play_line. This predicate has four versions. The first looks like this:

```
play_line(Row,4,Res):-Res=Row-2,!.
```

The second argument is the number of exact matches—position and color—found during the evaluation of the user's guesses. (We'll explain in the next section how this evaluation is handled.) When this number is 4, the user has found the solution. This routine subtracts 2 from the row number to determine the number of guesses the user made to reach the conclusion. (There is the first row filled by the system with question marks at the start; because the row has been incremented already by the play_line predicate, you must subtract an additional 1 to get the right answer.)

The second instance of the play_line predicate comes into play when the user reaches line 14 of the display area. This means the user has made 12 guesses, which is the maximum allowed by the game's rules. This version of the play_line predicate simply sets the variable Res to 0 and cuts program execution.

The fourth version of the play_line predicate was already described. It notifies the user that four colors were not entered before pressing RETURN. Turn your attention to the third version of the play_line predicate. It handles all other situations—normal entry of four colors with no complete match detected yet.

This version of the play_line predicate is:

```
play_line(Row,_,Res):-
   init_line(Row,1,'\178'),
   cursor(Row,1),
   getEntry(Row,1),
   read_line(Row,1,[],Selection),
   check_guess(M,C,Selection),
   shiftwindow(2),
   cursor(Row,1),
   write(M," ",C),
   shiftwindow(1),
   NewRow=Row+1,
   play_line(NewRow,M,Res),!.
```

First, this predicate initializes the line about to be used by the user to enter guesses by writing a series of characters that are displayed as a patterned block. This acts as a mask in which the user enters a color. The program uses character 179 for this purpose, though any nongraphic character would do.

After placing the cursor at the first column of the row, play_line gets the user's input, uses read_line to determine what colors were guessed, then uses check_guess to fill in the M and C values: M for a match in which the color and position are right, and C (for close) for a match in which the color is right but the position is wrong. (Actually, C could stand for color, but close sounds more interesting.)

Look at the check_guess predicates in the program. They use the database built-in predicates retract and asserta to modify the memory resident database of guesses being checked. The first version simply ensures that you are starting with clean database files. The second instance of the check_guess predicate sets up Glist so that it contains the list of colors generated by the computer. It then places empty lists in database memory for to_guess and my_guess. Then it calls the predicate check_pos, where the real work of going through the user's guesses one at a time and determining how many exact matches can be found takes place.

The check_pos predicate looks like this:

```
check_pos(X,Y,[H¦Tail],[Z¦Gtail]) :-
   to_guess(GC),
   retract(to_guess(_)),
   asserta(to_guess([W¦GC])),
   my_guess(GG),
   retract(my_guess(_)),
   asserta(my_guess([H¦GG])),
   check_pos(X,Y,Tail,Gtail).
```

When this predicate is called, the first argument, Good_pos, is unbound, the second argument is set to 0, the third argument contains the user's guesses as a list, and the fourth argument contains the computer's color pattern as a list. Because this predicate uses recursion, it divides the two lists into head and tail portions as it begins execution. It then sets up two temporary database storage lists by appending the first element of each of these lists to the previously empty lists initialized for this purpose.

The first time through this predicate, then, the third check_pos version executes and, when it concludes, recurses. But this time, the second instance of the predicate checks to see if the heads of the two new lists are equal. If they are, it adds 1 to the value of Y—which is set to 0 when the predicate is called—and recurses again. This process continues until all four positions have been checked for exact matches. At the conclusion of this sequence, the second argument to check_pos is instantiated to this number.

Next, the program checks the entire list for the number of colors that are found in the original computer list. This work is handled by check_color. It is a much simpler predicate than check_pos, so we won't describe it.

You can see that del Rio used database declarations and predicates quite efficiently to make two separate but related comparisons to the contents of two lists. This is a technique to remember when you are dealing with list manipulation problems in programs of your own design.

Summary

Master Mind is an interesting and entertaining program. But beyond its value as an entertainment program, it contains several interesting techniques you can use to solve problems in your own Turbo Prolog programming. The use of database structures as temporary storage points that still permit the comparison of list contents is a particularly noteworthy idea. User input techniques and validation checking are also nicely handled.

Listing 16-1

```
domains
  colors_list = color*
  color = symbol
  code = integer
  row, column, keycode, attribute, displa = integer

database
  guess_colors(colors_list)
  to_guess(colors_list)
  my_guess(colors_list)
```

```
predicates
  member(color, colors_list)
  append(colors_list, colors_list, colors_list)
  extract_element(color, colors_list, colors_list,
     integer)
  check_color(integer, integer,colors_list)
  colors(code, color)
  select_colors(colors_list)
  is_random(color)
  check_pos(integer,integer,colors_list, colors_list)
  check_guess(integer, integer, colors_list)
  showGuess(colors_list,column)
  get_element(color,integer,colors_list)
  final(integer)
  run
  inform
  putcolor(keycode, row, column,column)
  attrib(color,keycode,attribute, displa)
  readKey(keycode, row, column)
  new_cur(column, displa, column)
  getEntry(row,column)
  ireadchar(char, row, column)
  fakekey(char, row, column)
  init_line(row, column,char)
  read_line(row,column,colors_list,colors_list)
  blink(row,column)
  delay(integer)
  play_game(integer)
  play_line(row,integer,integer)
  allcolors

goal
  makewindow(8,40,0,"",0,0,25,80),
  inform,
  not(run),
  makewindow(8,7,0,"",0,0,25,80).

clauses
/* Some "facts" (tables, just tables) */
  colors(1,"Blue").
  colors(2,"Green").
  colors(3,"Cyan").
  colors(4,"Magenta").
  colors(5,"Red").
  colors(6,"Orange").

  attrib("Blue",98,113,0).
```

Listing 16-1 (cont.)

```
attrib("Green",103,114,0).
attrib("Cyan",99,115,0).       attrib("Red",114,116,0).
attrib("Magenta",109,117,0).
   attrib("Orange",111,118,0).
attrib(left,75,0,-7).
attrib(right,77,0,7).


/* Main module (goal) */

run :-  !,
  play_game(Result),
  final(Result),
  nl,nl,
  write("Another game (Y/N)?"),
  readchar(Another),
  Another = 'y',
  removewindow,
  removewindow,
  removewindow,
  removewindow,
  run, !.

inform :-
  makewindow(6,113,31,"INSTRUCTIONS",0,1,25,34),
  write("(c) 1986 by Israel del Rio"),
  nl,nl,
  write("Guess the 4 hidden colors from\nthe
    following: "),
  nl,
  allcolors.

inform  :-
  nl,nl,
  write("  Type the first letter of the \ncolor name
    to be selected."),
  nl,
  write("  Use the left and right arrows\nto change
    columns."),
  nl,
  write("  Press ENTER when you are\nsatisfied with
    your guess."),
  nl,nl,
  write("\01 = Right Position & Color"),
  nl,
  write("\05 = Right Color, wrong position"),
  nl,nl,
```

```
    write(" Press any key to start game"),
    readchar(_).

  allcolors :-
    attrib(Name,_,Attr,_),
    Attr <> 0,
    nl,
    cursor(Row, Col),
    write("\219\219 = ",Name),
    field_attr(Row,Col,16,Attr),
    fail.

  play_game(Result) :-
    makewindow(12,0,0,"",7,36,16,39),
    makewindow(2,31,116,"Hints",3,61,16,8),
    cursor(0,1),
    write("\01","  ","\05"),
    makewindow(1,112,116,"Master Mind",3,30,16,31),
    select_colors(Y),
    clearwindow,
    init_line(0,1,'?'),
    play_line(2,0,Result),
    retract(guess_colors(_)),
    showGuess(Y, 1), !.

  final(0) :-
    sound(10,5000),
    makewindow(3,87,87,"Sorry!",16,0,8,20),
    clearwindow,
    write(" Maximum number of guesses is 12"), !.

  final(Result) :-
    sound(10,5000),
    makewindow(3,106,6,"Congratulations!",17,59,8,20),
    clearwindow,
    write(" You guessed the colors in ",Result,"
     moves"), !.

/* Randomly selects 4 colors out of 6 */

  select_colors([A,B,C,D]) :- retract(guess_colors(_)),
     !,
  select_colors([A,B,C,D]).

  select_colors([A,B,C,D]) :- is_random(A),
     is_random(B),
is_random(C),
is_random(D),
```

Listing 16-1 (cont.)

```
asserta(guess_colors([A,B,C,D])).

  is_random(X) :- random(Y), Z = (Y * 6) + 0.5,
    colors(Z,X).

/* Evaluates how good the List guess was */

  check_guess(Good_pos, Good_col, List) :-
    retract(to_guess(_)),
    retract(my_guess(_)),
    check_guess(Good_pos, Good_col, List), !.

  check_guess(Good_pos, Good_col, List) :-
    guess_colors(Glist),
    asserta(to_guess([])),
    asserta(my_guess([])),
    check_pos(Good_pos,0,List, Glist),
    my_guess(Mlist),
    check_color(Good_col,0,Mlist), !.

/* Checks how many exact matches occurred */

  check_pos(X,Y,[],_) if X = Y, !.

  check_pos(X,Y,[H¦Tail],[G¦Gtail]) if H = G, Z = Y + 1,
    check_pos(X,Z,Tail, Gtail), !.

  check_pos(X,Y,[H¦Tail],[Z¦Gtail]) :-
    to_guess(GC),
    retract(to_guess(_)),
    asserta(to_guess([W[¦]GC])),
    my_guess(GG),
    retract(my_guess(_)),
    asserta(my_guess([N[¦]GG])),
    check_pos(X,Y,Tail,Gtail).

/* Checks if color okay, but not right position  */

  check_color(X,Count,[]) :- X = Count, !.

  check_color(X,Count,[H¦Tail]) :-
    to_guess(Newlist),
    extract_element(H,Newlist,[], Success),
    Success = 1,
    Count2 = Count + 1,
    check_color(X,Count2, Tail), !.
```

```
    check_color(X,Count,[_|Tail]) :-
      check_color(X, Count, Tail).

/* Extracts an element from a list        */

  extract_element(_,[],NewNew,X) :-
    X = 0,
    retract(to_guess(_)),
    asserta(to_guess(NewNew)), !.

  extract_element(X,[Y|List],Newlist,F) :-
    X<>Y, append(Newlist,[Y],NewNew),
    extract_element(X,List,NewNew,F), !.

  extract_element(_,[_|List],Newlist,X) :-
    X = 1,
    append(Newlist,List,NewNew),
    retract(to_guess(_)),
    asserta(to_guess(NewNew)), !.

/* Performs and verifies one move    */

  play_line(Row,4,Res) :- Res = Row - 2, !.

  play_line(14,_,Res) :- Res = 0, !.

  play_line(Row,_,Res) :-
    init_line(Row,1,'\178'),
    cursor(Row,1),
    getEntry(Row,1),
    read_line(Row,1,[],Selection),
    check_guess(M,C,Selection),
    shiftwindow(2),
    cursor(Row,1),
    write(M," ",C),
    shiftwindow(1),
    NewRow = Row + 1,
    play_line(NewRow,M,Res), !.

  play_line(Row,_,Res) :-
    sound(10,100),
    makewindow(3,64,64,"ERROR",9,26,4,48),
    clearwindow,
    write("You must select 4 colors before pressing
      ENTER"),
    nl,write("      Press any key to continue"),
    readchar(_),
```

Listing 16-1 (cont.)

```
      removewindow,
      play_line(Row,0,Res), !.

  init_line(_,29,_) :-!.

  init_line(Row, Col,V) :-
    cursor(Row, Col),
    write(V,V,V,V,V,V),
    NewCol = Col + 7,
    init_line(Row, NewCol,V), !.

    read_line(_,29, PrevList, List) :- List = PrevList, !.

    read_line(Row, Col, PrevList, List) :-
      scr_attr(Row, Col, Attr),
      attrib(X, _, Attr, _),
      append(PrevList,[X],NewList),
      NewCol = Col + 7,
      read_line(Row, NewCol, NewList, List), !.

/* Reads player entry                          */

    getEntry(Row, Column) :-
      readKey(K, Row, Column),
      K <> 13,
      putcolor(K, Row, Column, NewCol),
      getEntry(Row,NewCol), !.

    getEntry(_, _) :- !.

    showGuess([],_) :- !.

    showGuess([C¦List],Column) :-
      cursor(0,Column),
      attrib(C,Code,_,_),
      putcolor(Code, 0, Column, _),
      Newcol = Column + 7,
      showGuess(List,Newcol), !.

/* Reads typed keys                            */

    readKey(K, Row, Col) :-
      fakekey(X, Row, Col),
      X <> '\0',
      frontchar(Y,X,""),
      upper_lower(Y,Z),
```

```
    frontchar(Z,C,_),
    char_int(C,K), !.

  readKey(K, Row, Col) :-
    fakekey(C, Row, Col),
    char_int(C,K), !.

  fakekey(K,Row,Col) :- ireadchar(K,Row,Col), !.
  fakekey(K,Row,Col) :- fakekey(K,Row,Col).

  ireadchar(K,_,_) :- inkey(L), !, K = L.

  ireadchar(_, Row, Col) :-
    blink(Row, Col), fail.

  blink(Row, Col) :- !,
    scr_attr(Row, Col,Attr),
    delay(600),
    field_attr(Row, Col, 6, 0),
    delay(100),
    field_attr(Row, Col, 6, Attr).

  putcolor(K, Row, Col,NewCol) :-
    attrib(_, K, Attr, _),
    Attr <> 0,
    NewCol = Col,
    write('\219','\219','\219','\219','\219','\219'),
    field_attr(Row,NewCol,6,Attr),
    cursor(Row, NewCol), !.

  putcolor(K, Row, Col, Newcol) :-
    attrib(_, K, _, Disp),
    new_cur(Col, Disp, NewCol),
    cursor(Row, Newcol), !.

  putcolor(_, _, OldCol, NewCol) :-
    sound(2,50), NewCol = OldCol.

  new_cur(Old_col, Disp, New_col) :-
    New_col = Old_col + Disp,
    New_col < 23,
    New_col > 0, !.

  new_cur(_, Disp, New_col) :-
    Disp < 0,
    New_col = 22, !.

  new_cur(_, _, New_col) :-
    New_col = 1.
```

Listing 16-1 (cont.)

```
/** GENERAL-PURPOSE ROUTINES **/

/* Appends two lists to a third list        */

   append([],List,List).
   append([X¦L1], List2, [X¦L3]) if
     append(L1,List2,L3).

/* Gets element #n from a list              */

   get_element(X,1,[Z¦_]) if ! and X=Z.
   get_element(X,Y,[_¦Tail]) :- Counter = Y -1, !,
   get_element(X,Counter,Tail).

/* Verifies if an entry is member of list */

   member(Name,[Name¦_]) :- !.
   member(Name,[_¦Tail]) if member(Name,Tail).

   delay(0) :- !.
   delay(N) :- NN = N - 1, delay(NN).
```

Chapter **17**

A Mortgage Calculator

This chapter presents a Turbo Prolog program written by Eddy C. Vasile. The program is modularly designed, presents a readily adaptable way of implementing menus, and shows that Turbo Prolog can handle number-crunching tasks efficiently.

The Problem

Mortgage amortization was one of the very first useful programs written for microcomputers as they began to become popular in the early 1970s. Traditionally, the writing of such programs has been an exercise assigned to programming students in first-year computer science courses.

The formula for loan payment calculations is well known:

$$M = P * I * C / (C-1)$$

where:

  M is the monthly payment to be calculated
  P is the principal amount of the mortgage or loan
  I is the monthly interest rate (annual rate divided by 12)
  C is I + 1 raised to the power of the term of the loan in months

In its more complete algebraic form, then, the equation looks like this:

$$M = \frac{PI(I + 1)^n}{(I + 1)^n - 1}$$

The other equation you will use calculates the total principal amount that may be borrowed for a given period at a known interest rate when the amount of the desired monthly payment is specified.

The Program

The program in listing 17-1 (at the end of this chapter) handles both of these calculations set forth in the previous equations. Depending on the user's response to the first menu query, the program either calculates the monthly payment or the total amount that may be borrowed under specific circumstances.

Running the Program

When you load and run the program, the goal statement:

```
menu(Choice)
```

results in the program presenting the main menu shown in figure 17-1 and waiting for the user's response. If you enter *1*, the first getnumbers clause is executed. If you enter *2*, the second getnumbers clause is run. If you enter anything else, the menu(Choice) goal fails and the program ends.

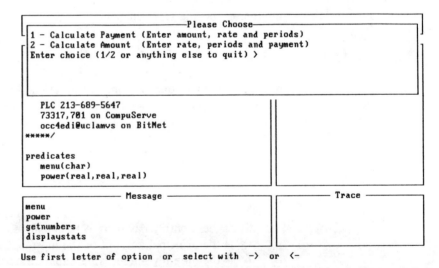

```
                        ─Please Choose─
1 - Calculate Payment (Enter amount, rate and periods)
2 - Calculate Amount  (Enter rate, periods and payment)
Enter choice (1/2 or anything else to quit) >



  PLC 213-689-5647
  73317,701 on CompuServe
  occ4edi@uclamvs on BitNet
*****/

predicates
   menu(char)
   power(real,real,real)

─────── Message ───────              ──── Trace ────
menu
power
getnumbers
displaystats

Use first letter of option  or  select with  ->  or  <-
```

Figure 17-1
Main menu of AMORT program

If you choose 1, Calculate Payment, the program asks for the base mortgage amount, base interest rate, and term of mortgage in years. If you choose 2, Calculate Amount, the program asks for the desired monthly payment, the base interest rate, and the term of the mortgage in years. This prompting (for either choice) is handled in a new Window 1 (replacing the original menu's window), which is defined with a makewindow statement in each of the two getnumbers clauses. See figure 17-2.

```
┌─────────────────Enter Loan Data for Payment Calc────────────────┐
│ Please enter the base mortgage amount > 220000                   │
│ Please enter the base interest rate % > 12.5                     │
│ Enter the number of years in mortgage > 20                       │
│                                                                  │
│                                                                  │
│                                                                  │
├────────────────────────────────────────────┐                   │
│   PLC 213-689-5647                           │                   │
│   73317,701 on CompuServe                    │                   │
│   occ4edi@uclamvs on BitNet                  │                   │
│ *****/                                       │                   │
│                                              │                   │
│ predicates                                   │                   │
│   menu(char)                                 │                   │
│   power(real,real,real)                      │                   │
├─────────────── Message ──────────────┐  ┌──── Trace ────────────┤
│ menu                                  │  │                       │
│ power                                 │  │                       │
│ getnumbers                            │  │                       │
│ displaystats                          │  │                       │
└───────────────────────────────────────┘  └───────────────────────┘
Use first letter of option  or  select with  ->  or  <-
```

Figure 17-2
Information request windows in AMORT

After the answers are entered, the program calculates the requested value and displays the result using the `displaystats` clause. The screen looks like figure 17-3 at the end of the run.

```
┌─────────────────────────Please Choose─────────────────────────┐
│ 1 - Calculate Payment (Enter amount, rate and periods)         │
│ 2 - Calculate Amount  (Enter rate, periods and payment)        │
│ Enter choice (1/2 or anything else to quit) >                  │
│                                                                 │
│                                                                 │
├───────────────────────────────────────────┐  ││               │
│   PLC 213-689-5647                          │  ││               │
├───────────────────20 Year Loan Statistics──────────────────────┤
│ Loan Amount        =    220000.00                               │
│ Interest Rate      =        12.500                              │
│ Monthly Payment    =      2499.51                               │
│ Number of Payments =       240                                  │
│ Total Payments     =    599882.21 (With Rounding Adjustments)   │
│ Total Interest     =    379882.21                               │
│ Hit any key to continue.                                        │
├─────────────────────────────────────────────────────────────────┤
│ power                                       │  ││               │
│ getnumbers                                  │  ││               │
│ displaystats                                │  ││               │
└─────────────────────────────────────────────┘  └────────────────┘
Use first letter of option  or  select with  ->  or  <-
```

Figure 17-3
Sample run of AMORT

After you have typed in or downloaded the AMORT.PRO program, run it twice with sample data and check the results. This will ensure that the program has been properly entered.

Analyzing the Program

You will examine AMORT.PRO by looking at its streamlined form of menu handling, its calculations, and its display of results using the often-overlooked `writef` predicate.

Menus

The one menu in the program appears in the `menu` clause. Notice that the program creates a window and then uses `write` predicates to display the two available alternatives. It then uses `readchar` to accept the user's answer.

In the next lines, the program checks to make sure that the character read is a 1 or a 2. It does this by using the ASCII sort sequence for characters rather than the numeric comparison approach because of the use of `readchar` to accept the user's answer. If the user's answer, stored in the `Choice` variable, is not both less than or equal to 2 and greater than or equal to 1, the `menu` predicate fails and the program ends without its goal being satisfied.

Calculations

Loan and mortgage amortization programs involve addition, subtraction, multiplication, and division, as well as the calculation of exponents.

The monthly interest rate is calculated in the `getnumbers` predicates by the line:

```
Rate=IntRate/1200
```

Suppose you entered 15% as the interest rate, which is stored in the real number variable named `IntRate`. The program calculates the monthly interest rate as 15/1200, or .0125% per month.

Similarly, the program accepts the term of the mortgage in years and converts it to months by multiplying the user's input (stored in the variable `Years`) by 12:

```
NumPeriods = Years * 12
```

Calculating the interest rate factor, `C`, involves two steps:

1. Adding 1 to the interest rate per month (`Rate`) and storing the result in the variable `Temp`.
2. Using the `power` clauses to raise the value of `Temp` to the power indicated by the period in months of the mortgage.

This line in the `getnumbers` clause carries out the last calculation:

```
power(Temp,NumPeriods,PowerNum)
```

The `power` clauses, annotated by Vasile in his original program, check to see which of the three arguments is already bound and then carry out the right exponentiation or root extraction.

Turbo Prolog, like many microcomputer languages, does not contain explicit exponentiation and root extraction functions that directly operate on real numbers. The calculations in the `power` clauses rely on well-established relationship rules in mathematics using the numerical constant *e*. These values are natural logarithms (ln), as contrasted with base algorithms such as base 10 logarithms (usually abbreviated log).

Multiplying `B` by the natural log (`ln`) of `A` in the first `power` clause and then calculating its natural power with the `exp` function results in `A` being raised to the `B` power. The natural log calculations in the other `power` clauses follow similar patterns and rules.

Formatted Output with `writef`

Notice that the `displaystats` clause includes six lines that all begin with the built-in Turbo Prolog `writef` predicate. As Vasile's comment indicates, this is quite similar to the formatted `write` statement, which is familiar to C programmers. In Turbo Prolog, the programmer must supply formatting information for the display of numeric values. (The `writef` predicate can be used with non-numeric data, but is not often used that way.)

With the judicious use of spaces following the text labels *Loan Amount, Interest Rate, Monthly Payment, Number of Payments, Total Payments,* and *Total Interest,* the program positions the equal signs that precede each displayed numeric value so that they are aligned. The alignment of the numeric display is then managed by the use of the format specifiers, which begin with a percent sign and end with the letter `f`. (The format specifier could also end with e, f, or g, depending on how you want to display the numeric values.) Figure 17-4 explains the `writef` print specifier format.

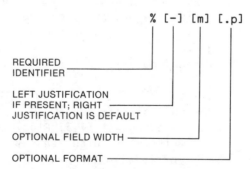

```
% [-] [m] [.p]
```

REQUIRED IDENTIFIER

LEFT JUSTIFICATION IF PRESENT; RIGHT JUSTIFICATION IS DEFAULT

OPTIONAL FIELD WIDTH

OPTIONAL FORMAT

number = floating point precision or maximum string length
e = display real numbers in exponential notation
f = display real numbers in fixed-decimal notation
g = use shortest format

Figure 17-4
Print specifier format for `writef` predicate

As it turns out, Vasile could have omitted the f at the end of each print specifier because that is the default value. But it makes the program more understandable.

Summary

This neat little program demonstrates that Turbo Prolog fans need not apologize for the language's lack of computational capability. Turbo Prolog can carry out highly useful and powerful calculations, even if it does lack some of the niceties of more math-oriented languages.

You could extend the AMORT program so that it displays a table of all payments, showing how much of each payment is applied to principal and how much to interest, along with a declining loan balance. This addition is not difficult and might be fun to make as you delve more deeply into the power of Turbo Prolog.

Listing 17-1

```
/*****
This program illustrates Turbo Prolog's
number-crunching ability by calculating
mortgage amortizations.
Eddy C. Vasile
73317,701 on CompuServe
*****/

predicates
  menu(char)
  power(real,real,real)
  getnumbers(real,real,real,real,char)
  displaystats(real,real,real,real)

goal
  menu(Choice).

clauses
  menu(Choice):-
    makewindow(1,31,3,"Please Choose",1,1,8,78),
    write("1 - Calculate Payment (Enter amount, rate and
      periods)\n"),
    write("2 - Calculate Amount  (Enter rate, periods
      and payment)\n"),
    write("Enter choice (1/2 or anything else to quit) >
      "),
    readchar(Choice),
    Choice<='2',
```

```
    Choice>='1',
    getnumbers(PresValue,Rate,NumPeriods,
      Payment,Choice),
    displaystats(PresValue,Rate,NumPeriods,Payment),
    removewindow.

  getnumbers(PresValue,Rate,NumPeriods,Payment,Choice):-
    Choice='1',
    free(Payment),
    makewindow(1,31,3,"Enter Loan Data for Payment
      Calc",1,1,8,78),
    write("Please enter the base mortgage amount > "),
    readreal(PresValue),
    write("Please enter the base interest rate % > "),
    readreal(IntRate),
    Rate=IntRate/1200,
    write("Enter the number of years in mortgage > "),
    readreal(Years),
    NumPeriods=Years*12,
    removewindow,
    Temp=1+Rate,
    power(Temp,NumPeriods,PowerNum),
    Payment=PresValue*(Rate/(1-1/PowerNum)).

  getnumbers(PresValue,Rate,NumPeriods,Payment,Choice):-
    Choice='2',
    free(PresValue),
    makewindow(1,31,3,"Enter Loan Data for Amount
      Calc",1,1,8,78),
    write("Please enter the desired monthly payment >
      "),
    readreal(Payment),
    write("Please enter the base interest rate % > "),
    readreal(IntRate),
    Rate=IntRate/1200,
    write("Enter the number of years in mortgage > "),
    readreal(Years),
    NumPeriods=Years*12,
    removewindow,
    Temp=1+Rate,
    power(Temp,NumPeriods,PowerNum),
    PresValue=Payment/(Rate/(1-1/PowerNum)).


/*****
Prolog tries hard to give you what you ask for.
If the variables Base and Exponent are bound
(i.e., values assigned) then Result is calculated.
If Base and Result are bound and Exponent is free
```

Listing 17-1 (cont.)

```
then a solution is returned for Exponent.
*****/

  power(A,B,C):-
    bound(A),
    bound(B),
    C=exp(B*ln(A)).
  power(A,B,C):-
    bound(A),
    bound(C),
    B=ln(C)/ln(A).
  power(A,B,C):-
    bound(B),
    bound(C),
    A=exp(ln(C)/B).


  displaystats(PresValue,Rate,NumPeriods,Payment):-
    NumYears=NumPeriods/12,
    str_real(YearString,NumYears),
    concat(YearString," Year Loan
     Statistics",WindowText),
    YearRate=Rate*1200,
    TotalPayment=Payment*NumPeriods,
    TotalInterest=TotalPayment-PresValue,

/*****
Open window number 2 (red letters on light blue
background in original--changed to high-white
on black, and white edges), from col 1 to 78, from row
10, 10 rows deep.
*****/

    makewindow(2,15,7,WindowText,10,1,10,78),
    shiftwindow(2),

/*****
Formatted write like C or TURBO BCD
*****/

    writef("Loan Amount        =%15.2f",PresValue),nl,
    writef("Interest Rate      =%16.3f",YearRate),nl,
    writef("Monthly Payment    =%15.2f",Payment),nl,
    writef("Number of Payments =%12.0f",NumPeriods),nl,
    writef("Total Payments     =%15.2f (With Rounding
     Adjustments)", TotalPayment),
    nl,
```

```
writef("Total Interest    =%15.2f",TotalInterest),
nl,
write("Hit any key to continue."),
readchar(_),
removewindow.
```

Classic Logic Problem

There is a class of logic problems that involves a similar scenario: a group of objects, some of which are animate, a vehicle, and a distance to travel. The vehicle contains a limited amount of space and certain combinations of objects are inherently dangerous. The object of the logic puzzle is to find a way to transport all the objects safely to the other side of the river, road, mountain, or other path.

One classic variation on this theme is the Missionaries and Cannibals problem, which involves three missionaries, three cannibals, and a river. The river is crossed with a small boat that can only hold two people. It is unsafe for the missionaries to be left on either bank of the river if they are outnumbered by cannibals. (I dealt with this problem in some depth in my book, *Artificial Intelligence Programming for the Macintosh,* published by Howard W. Sams & Co.)

In this chapter, you look at another variation of this theme. In this problem, a farmer must cross a river with a goat, a wolf, and a cabbage. It is often referred to as the FWGC problem (farmer, wolf, goat, and cabbage). FWGC is a classic that has been dealt with by many Prolog programmers in college classrooms and boring research laboratories. The particular program you will examine is available on CompuServe and many other electronic bulletin board systems. (The author's name has been lost to obscurity.)

The Problem

Dealing with logic problems of this type raises some interesting programming issues. The state of the "universe" as known to the program at any point must be both easy to express and subject to testing. In other words, you must be able to see where all of the "players" are at any point. Furthermore, you don't want the program to repeat the same pattern of movement over and over, so typically you make it illegal for the same situation to recur. For example, if the farmer picks up the wolf with the goat on the left bank, and picks up the cabbage with the wolf on the right bank, you don't want to repeat that scenario.

Finally, some game states are illegal. In essence, you spend a lot of time in a Turbo Prolog program of this sort examining, altering, and testing the state of the objects in the program to ensure that they are legal and not repetitive.

The problem in this puzzle is shown in figure 18-1. The illegal combinations, as you can see, are goat-cabbage and wolf-goat. Wolves don't like cabbages, so that combination is safe.

```
W = WOLF
G = GOAT
C = CABBAGE

W ⎫                      W ⎫  WRONG!
G ⎬ START                G ⎭  WOLF EATS GOAT.
C ⎭

G ⎫  WRONG!              W ⎫
C ⎭  GOAT EATS CABBAGE.  C ⎭  OKAY
```

Figure 18-1
FWGC puzzle diagram

The Program

The program, listing 18-1, is at the end of this chapter. I have edited the original author's opening comments to avoid repetition and to clarify some points. The program itself, however, appears as originally written.

Running the Program

Because the program includes an internal goal statement (discussed in detail later), running the program requires no intervention on the user's part. Simply choose the Run option from the Turbo Prolog menu and the program executes. The display looks like figure 18-2.

Because of the way the goal statement is structured and the way the moves are ordered, the same solution is presented each time you run the program. Are there other possible solutions? We'll talk about modifications to the goal statement and the sequence of move predicates that result in other solutions.

The bottom window's display changes after each move. A delay is built into the program. Without this delay, the moves would be displayed too fast.

Analyzing the Program

In this section, you examine the driving predicates in the FWGC program: the goal statement, the go predicate, and the path predicates. You'll also examine how the move statements are ordered and try to determine what would happen if you altered their sequence.

```
┌─────────────────────Solutions─────────────────────────────────────┐
│                                                                    │
│A solution is:                                                      │
│The farmer takes the goat from west of the river to east           │
│The farmer crosses the river from east to west                     │
│The farmer takes the cabbage from west of the river to east        │
│The farmer takes the goat from east of the river to west           │
│The farmer takes the wolf from west of the river to east           │
│The farmer crosses the river from east to west                     │
│The farmer takes the goat from west of the river to east           │
│                                                                    │
│Press the SPACE bar                                                 │
│                                                                    │
└────────────────────────────────────────────────────────────────────┘
```

```
┌─────────────────────the river─────────────────────────────────────┐
│      WEST              river                        EAST           │
│──────────────────────────────────────────────────────────────────│
│                  Farmer   =>  =>  =>            Farmer             │
│                  river                          Wolf              │
│                  Goat     =>  =>  =>            Goat              │
│                  Cabbage  =>  =>  =>            Cabbage           │
└────────────────────────────────────────────────────────────────────┘
```

Figure 18-2
FWGC puzzle program

The goal Statement

The program includes a goal statement that dictates what the program does when it is run. After making two windows on the screen, the program calls the driving predicate, go, supplying as arguments two structures that describe the starting state (first) and the goal state of the problem. The puzzle begins with the four participants on one bank, and the objective is to get them to the opposite bank. The goal, logically enough, looks like this:

```
go(state(east,east,east,east),state(west,west,west,west,
    )).
```

The go Predicate

The heart of this program is the go predicate called by the last statement in the goal. Let's take a look at how it works.

The predicate is declared as:

```
go(STATE,STATE)
```

STATE is defined as a four-element structure consisting of the key word state followed by four values of type LOC. LOC, in turn, is defined as having a value of either east or west.

The first predicate used by go is path. This predicate appears in the program listing as follows:

```
path(S,G,L,L1):-move(S,S1),
  not(unsafe(S1)),
```

```
not(member(S1,L)),
path(S1,G,[S1|L],L1),!,
path(G,G,T,T):- !.
```

The second clause is carried out when the final state of the problem —the solution—is reached. When the start state equals the goal state, the problem has been solved. The start state is modified to reflect the constantly changing state of the system.

The first instance of the path predicate carries out the moves and checks their validity. Notice that when this path predicate is first called by the go predicate, the arguments it receives are the start state, the goal state, a list replicating the start state in list form, and an unbound variable, L. Because PATH is defined as a list of objects of type STATE in the domains section of the program, and because path is defined as having a PATH as its fourth argument, it follows that this argument is ultimately a list that is a path.

Move Sequences

The move predicate executes a move. The move is chosen from a collection of all possible combinations of two objects (one of which must be the farmer), and the farmer by himself. Each time through the move cycle, the program first tries to move the farmer and the wolf. To do so, they have to be on the same bank of the river, as shown by the fact that the variables X (for the farmer) and Y (for the wolf) are in the same positions in the first two arguments to the state predicate. The path predicate looks at the consequences of this move to ensure that it does not create a condition that is unsafe or has already been tried. Two unsafe conditions are described by two instances of the unsafe predicate. If either of these situations arises from the move, the move fails because the not(unsafe (S1)) condition has not been met.

Similarly, if the move doesn't lead to an unsafe situation, the path predicate next checks to see if this scenario has already been tried in this run. If it has, the condition not(member(S1,L)) fails and the move is not made.

If all of the conditions are met and the move is accepted, the final statement in the first path clause is executed:

```
path(S1,G,[S1|L],L1),!.
```

This statement does two things at once. First, it appends the new situation, S1, to the front of the growing list of situations already seen by the program. Then it uses this situation as the new start state for another recursive run through the path predicate. This processing continues until there is no S different from G, in which case the second path clause executes, indicating that a solution has been found.

When the solution has been found, control returns to the go predicate, which prints the various steps used to solve the puzzle. The rest of the program deals primarily with displaying the results of the run to the user.

Altering the Program

You can try two things to see how the program works internally. First, modify the goal statement so that the starting position does not have all of the items on the east bank when the program begins. Try various combinations. What happens when you put in an unsafe condition at the start of the program? Does the program catch the problem? If not, how could you modify the program to correct this?

You could decide to remove the goal statement completely and enter goals interactively. If you do, however, be sure that your typed goal statement includes the creation of the two windows or an error condition results. If you want to use this approach repeatedly, put the window-generating clauses inside the go predicate and then you can type your goal as follows:

```
go(state(east,west,west,east),state(west,west,west,
    west)).
```

The second thing you can do to experiment with the program is to alter the sequence of move statements. Use the Turbo Prolog built-in editor's cut-and-paste capability to reorder them. Then run the program with the original goal statements and some of your own design. What do you learn about the importance of the order of move statements? Are there some combinations that result in the program "hanging?"

Summary

FWGC uses a brute force method of problem solving. It simply cycles through all available alternatives without "thinking" about what step might be most reasonable. It simply looks at the situation, tries an alternative, determines if the new situation is acceptable or not, and reacts accordingly.

As you saw in chapter 15, many computer programs designed to solve problems and puzzles work this way. Although the brute force method might not seem particularly intelligent, it is one of the things at which a computer really excels. It can try thousands of alternatives in the time it takes us to analyze a handful of options.

Listing 18-1

```
/*
The state of the system is indicated by stating
where the farmer, the goat, the wolf, and the cabbage
are located:
state( Farmer, Wolf, Goat, Cabbage )

The problem is that a state must only be visited once,
and some states are illegal.  This is checked by unsafe
    and member.
```

Listing 18-1 (cont.)

The go predicate can be called with a start state and a
    final state:
go(state(east,east,east,east), state(west,west,west,
    west)).*/

```
domains
  LOC  = east ; west
  STATE = state(LOC,LOC,LOC,LOC)
  PATH = STATE*

predicates
  go(STATE,STATE)/* Start of the algorithm */
  path(STATE,STATE,PATH,PATH)/* Finds a path from one
    state to another */
  move(STATE,STATE)/* Transfer a system from one side to
    another*/
  opposite(LOC,LOC)/* Gives a location on the opposite
    side*/
  unsafe(STATE)/* Gives the unsafe states */
  member(STATE,PATH)/* Checks if the state is already
    visited */
  write_path(PATH)
  write_move(STATE,STATE)
  show_move(STATE,STATE)
  delay(integer)
  showside(LOC,LOC,string)

Goal
  makewindow(3,7,7,"the river",15,0,10,80),
  makewindow(1,7,7,"Solutions",0,0,15,80),
  go(state(east,east,east,east),state(west,west,west,
    west)).

clauses
  go(S,G):-
    path(S,G,[S],L),
    nl,write("A solution is:"),nl,
    write_path(L),
    fail.

  path(S,G,L,L1):- move(S,S1),
    not( unsafe(S1) ),
    not( member(S1,L) ),
    path( S1,G,[S1¦L],L1),!.
```

```
path(G,G,T,T):-        !.    /* The final state is
    reached */

move(state(X,X,G,C),state(Y,Y,G,C)):-opposite(X,Y). /*
    FARMER and WOLF */
move(state(X,W,X,C),state(Y,W,Y,C)):-opposite(X,Y). /*
    FARMER and GOAT */
move(state(X,W,G,X),state(Y,W,G,Y)):-opposite(X,Y). /*
    FARMER and CABBAGE */
move(state(X,W,G,C),state(Y,W,G,C)):-opposite(X,Y). /*
    ONLY FARMER */

opposite(east,west).
opposite(west,east):-!.

unsafe( state(F,X,X,_) ):- opposite(F,X).  /* The wolf
    eats the goat */
unsafe( state(F,_,X,X) ):- opposite(F,X).  /* The goat
    eats the cabbage */

member(X,[X¦_]).
member(X,[_¦L]):-member(X,L).

write_path( [H1,H2¦T] ) :- write_move(H1,H2),
   delay(32000),
   delay(32000),
   delay(32000),!, show_move(H1,H2),
   write_path([H2¦T]).
write_path( [] ).

write_move( state(X,W,G,C), state(Y,W,G,C) ) :-!,
   write("The farmer crosses the river from ",X," to
   ",Y),nl.
write_move( state(X,X,G,C), state(Y,Y,G,C) ) :-!,
   write("The farmer takes the wolf from ",X," of the
   river to ",Y),nl.
write_move( state(X,W,X,C), state(Y,W,Y,C) ) :-!,
   write("The farmer takes the goat from ",X," of the
   river to ",Y),nl.
write_move( state(X,W,G,X), state(Y,W,G,Y) ) :-!,
   write("The farmer takes the cabbage from ",X," of
   the river to ",Y),nl.

/* Show the move across the river */

show_move( state(X,W,G,C), state(Y,W,G,C) ) :-!,
   shiftwindow(3),clearwindow,
```

Listing 18-1 (cont.)

```
    write("          WEST                    river
      EAST"),nl,
    write(" ----------------------------------------------
      ------------------------ "),nl,
    showside(X,Y,"Farmer "),
    showside(W,W," Wolf  "),
    showside(G,G," Goat  "),
    showside(C,C,"Cabbage"),
    shiftwindow(1).

show_move( state(X,X,G,C), state(Y,Y,G,C) ) :-!,
    shiftwindow(3),clearwindow,
    write("          WEST                    river
      EAST"),nl,
    write(" ----------------------------------------------
      ------------------------ "),nl,
    showside(X,Y,"Farmer "),
    showside(X,Y," Wolf  "),
    showside(G,G," Goat  "),
    showside(X,Y,"Cabbage"),
    shiftwindow(1).

show_move( state(X,W,X,C), state(Y,W,Y,C) ) :-!,
    shiftwindow(3),clearwindow,
    write("          WEST                    river
      EAST"),nl,
    write(" ----------------------------------------------
      ------------------------ "),nl,
    showside(X,Y,"Farmer "),
    showside(W,W," Wolf  "),
    showside(X,Y," Goat  "),
    showside(X,Y,"Cabbage"),
    shiftwindow(1).

show_move( state(X,W,G,X), state(Y,W,G,Y) ) :-!,
    shiftwindow(3),clearwindow,
    write("          WEST                    river
      EAST"),nl,
    write(" ----------------------------------------------
      ------------------------ "),nl,
    showside(X,Y,"Farmer "),
    showside(W,W,"Wolf   "),
    showside(G,G,"Goat   "),
    showside(X,Y,"Cabbage"),
    shiftwindow(1).
```

```
showside(east,east,Item):-!,
  write("                          river
  ",Item),nl.

showside(west,west,Item):-!,
  write("      ",Item,"               river
  "),nl.

showside(east,west,Item):-!,
  write("      ",Item,"      <=  <=  <=  ",Item),nl.

showside(west,east,Item):-!,
  write("                          ",Item,"  =>
  =>  =>        ",Item),nl.

delay(0).
delay(N) :- !, NN=N-1, delay(NN).
```

Logic Puzzle Solving

The world can be divided into two groups: those who love logic puzzles and those who don't know what they are. Or something like that.

You know what a logic puzzle is, don't you? It's that aggravating little word puzzle that creeps into your favorite crossword puzzle books from time to time and seems to have little if anything to do with words. Usually, there is a hopelessly incomplete scenario and a demand that you answer not one question, but a whole series of questions.

In this chapter, you look at how one Turbo Prolog programmer solved such a logic puzzle. Then there's a discussion of general programming concepts to solve such puzzles so you can apply them to other scenarios.

Whodunit Problem

The class of problems in this chapter is typified by the exercise on page 30 of the Turbo Prolog programming manual. Borland's writers didn't give a word description of the puzzle. If they had, it would have looked something like this.

> **Puzzle:** Susan has been found murdered with a club. There are four suspects: Allan, a 25-year-old part-time football player and butcher; Barbara, a 22-year-old hairdresser; Bert, a 55-year-old carpenter with a wooden leg; and John, a 25 year old who earns his money "lifting" things from other people's pockets and purses. A preliminary investigation has revealed the following. Shortly after the murder, Bert was seen smeared with blood (as was the victim, who was bludgeoned to death) and Allan was spotted smeared with mud. John owns a pistol. Further probing unveils the sordid affairs John had with both Barbara and the victim. In addition, Barbara had an affair with Bert. Whodunit?

The fact that Bert was smeared with blood was not included in the original list of facts in the manual. It was added later by Borland (see the following discussion) to provide a solution to a puzzle that otherwise had no neat solution.

Although Borland did not supply the solution to the puzzle in a final form in the manual, it did furnish some clues about how to approach the problem. However, on the disk included with the Version 1.1 upgrade, Borland supplies a program titled ANS30.PRO, which is a slight modification of the exercise itself. That program is an example of this type of logic problem and its Turbo Prolog solution. Refer to listing 19-1 at the end of this chapter.

Other than the added fact that Bert was smeared with blood and the declaration of appropriate domains and predicates, the significant change to the program compared to the manual is the killer predicate. If you run the program, you'll find that Bert did it because he was smeared with the same substance as the victim and had a motive— jealousy.

Note that the program has to be told explicitly some things that a human solving the puzzle would not need to be told:

```
operates_identically(wooden_leg,club).
operates_identically(bar,club).
operates_identically(pair_of_scissors,knife).
operates_identically(football_boot,club).

owns_probably(X,football_boot) if
   person(X,_,_,football_player).
owns_probably(X,pair_of_scissors) if
   person(X,_,_,hairdresser).
owns_probably(X,Object) if
   owns(X,Object).
```

For example, you know that a wooden leg, a bar, and a football boot can all be used as a club. Similarly, you know the killer wasn't Susan because it's difficult to club yourself to death. But without such background information, the program would never be able to solve the puzzle. This is a principle you encounter again later in this discussion.

A Complex Puzzle

The Whodunit puzzle with (we hope) one solution is one of the two types of logic puzzles that Prolog can solve given the right information. The other type is a fill-in-the-matrix kind of puzzle. In this type of problem, you are given a series of clues that, together with some common sense and logic, can reveal a great deal of information about a group of people engaged in a single activity.

Here is the problem for the next program in this chapter. This puzzle is from the December 1986 issue of the *Dell Official Pencil Puzzles & Word Games* magazine and is reprinted here with permission.

> **Puzzle:** Paul and three other men got together one Wednesday afternoon for a round of golf at the Tall Pines Country Club. They decided to pair off for a challenge match to see which team could produce the better score. (In golf, the team with the lowest total amount of strokes per round is the winner.) From the following clues, can you determine each man's full name (one surname is Curtis), occupation (one was an editor), and score (one man had a score of 78 strokes)?
>
> 1. John and the lawyer were partners and played against Bentley and his partner, who scored an 83.
> 2. Dave scored a 92, and the doctor scored an 87.
> 3. Stevens is an accountant.
> 4. Bob Howell, who kept score, announced that one pair of golfers shot ten less strokes than the other pair.

Because we want to keep the solution a surprise, we'll reverse the usual order of discussion and analyze the program before running it. (I trust you can handle the suspense.)

Analyzing the Program

The program, downloaded from CompuServe, is shown in listing 19-2 at the end of this chapter. (The author's name remains elusive.) I've removed the opening comment section, which is a restatement of the puzzle and a presentation of the solution.

Telling Prolog the Facts

Turn your attention to the last part of the program, where the facts are represented. This section deals with knowledge representation—how to store information in a way that permits you to read it and the computer to use it. This is a major and often-disputed issue in artificial intelligence programming. The author of the program chose to use Prolog structures—predicates—for the storage of knowledge given or derived from the puzzle.

```
player("Dave",_,_,92).
player(_,_,"Doctor",87).
player("Bob","Howell",_,_).
player(_,"Stevens","Accountant",_).

player("Paul",_,_,_).
player("John",_,_,_).

player(_,"Curtis",_,_).
player(_,"Bentley",_,_).

player(_,_,"Editor",_).
```

```
player(_,_,"Lawyer",_).

player(_,_,_,78).
player(_,_,_,83).
```

The first four facts tell you and the computer that you know Dave fired a 92 (perhaps *fired* is too strong a verb for this score), the doctor (whoever he is) shot an 87, Bob's last name is Howell, and the man with the last name of Stevens is an accountant. Note there is not a one-to-one correspondence of facts. For example, you could find that Dave Stevens is an accountant and is also the player who shot 92. The fact pattern is not mutually exclusive. That's because the unknown sections of knowledge in each fact complement each other: you know the first name and score of Dave, and you know the last name and job of Stevens.

The next two facts tell you there are two players whose first names are Paul and John. The following two record the fact that the only thing you know about two men is their last names—Curtis and Bentley. Two more facts tell you that nothing is known about the editor and lawyer, except that they exist. The remaining two facts tell you that two scores— a 78 and an 83—can't yet be attached to a player.

A final set of two facts begins to describe the teams you are trying to identify:

```
team1(p("John",_,_,_),p(_,_,"Lawyer",_)).
team2(p(_,"Bentley",_,_),p(_,_,_,83)).
```

The first depicts team 1, composed of John and a lawyer. You know nothing else about this team. But you know that team 2 has a player whose last name is Bentley and whose partner shot an 83.

Defining Players and Teams

In the middle of the program listing is a fairly large number of lines that tell the computer some commonsense knowledge we humans would not need to have explicitly presented. The predicates are nearly identical, so analyzing one of them suffices for this discussion.

The first predicate defines potential candidates for player 1 and player 2:

```
f_player(P1_1,P1_2,J1,S1),     /* player 1 */

f_player(P2_1,P2_2,J2,S2),     /* player 2 */
```

In essence, the predicate uses the f_player predicate to locate players who might be player 1 and player 2 by setting some conditions for the search. The first two lines in the clause define player 1 as a person with a first name P1_1, a last name P1_2, a job J1, and a score S1. Player 2 is defined similarly. The next four lines make it clear that player 1 and player 2 can have nothing important in common—not the same first name, last name, job, or score.

You would not need to be told that. But if you don't give the computer this information and it comes up with a solution in which John Jones teams with John Jones and all the criteria fit, then that is a solution as far as Prolog (or any other computer language) is concerned.

The rest of the clauses in this section of the program perform a similar service for the other two players, differentiating them from one another and from player 1 and player 2.

Reference Variables

The most educational aspect of this program is the author's use of the reference domain. This often-overlooked and potentially useful Turbo Prolog tool is easy to misunderstand. (It is not part of other Prologs, which do not need it because of fundamental design differences.) Let's take a closer look to see how it's used in this program.

The declaration appears as follows:

```
domains
  player = reference p(fname,lname,job,integer)
```

Why is a `reference` variable needed here? Simply because its purpose is to permit Turbo Prolog programs to pass subgoals between predicates without all the variables from one subgoal being known before the next subgoal takes over. If you didn't have this facility, you'd run into a large number of Warning 3007 messages indicating that the variable is not bound in this clause during compilation.

When you pass partially known information about one person or object in one predicate to another predicate that may be able to fill in another blank, you use reference domain declarations so that the program can compile without the warning. (For a broader explanation of reference variables, refer to pages 149 through 151 of the Turbo Prolog reference manual.)

In this program, the omission of the reference domain declaration results in a number of warnings during the compilation and execution of the program, but the solution is the same. You must be willing to sit and press the F10 key a few times before the program solves the problem. In some programs, the absence of the reference domain declaration makes the program unusable. This is particularly true with programs like that on page 149 of the Turbo Prolog reference manual, where the name of the reference domain is used in describing the domain. This kind of recursive definition is apt to drive the compiler wild if it doesn't know that it is dealing with a reference domain.

Running the Program

As you have probably guessed, nothing special is involved in running the program. Simply load and run it, and it goes through its paces. A "Working . . ." message is displayed in the window for a few moments.

Then the program provides the solution, as shown in figure 19-1. This is the solution printed in the magazine, so solving the puzzle the program's way works at least as well as the author's way!

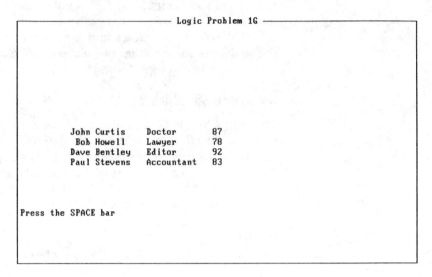

Figure 19-1
Logic puzzle conclusion

Generalizing from the Programs

An important design consideration for programming solutions to logic puzzles emerges from a study of the programs in this chapter.

Principle: The most complete facts available should always be put first in the program.

Failure to do this results in the program "chasing its own tail" a lot of the time, and can even result in the program being unable to find a solution. Thus, in the golf team puzzle, the programmer placed first on the fact list the facts containing two items about a golfer. If there were three pieces of information about any participant, these facts would be first. If you think about how Prolog backtracks and solves such problems, it is not surprising that efficiency and executability increase when you follow this basic principle.

It is necessary to follow Turbo Prolog's requirement that like predicates be grouped together. For instance, in the golf program, suppose three or more facts about one of the teams could be assembled from the information in the puzzle. You still could not place one of the team predicates ahead of the player predicates without moving both of the team predicates up in the listing.

Summary

Solving logic puzzles in Turbo Prolog is a good way to learn programming technique. Puzzles that are candidates for such programming tasks abound.

To solve these problems, you often have to tell the computer commonsense knowledge that you would never tell a human facing the same puzzle. The use of the basic principle of "most complete facts first" and the judicious use of reference domains can make your programs easier to write and more likely to run correctly.

Listing 19-1

```
/*
This is an exercise in domain declarations and
predicate declarations, not a test of your
ability to solve murder mysteries.  Some
modifications are made to the program in the
book to placate those who must have a killer.

Enter the goal
   killer(X).

Bert is guilty because he has a motive and is
smeared in the same stuff as the victim.
(Use trace to follow the resolution of the crime.)
*/

domains
   name, sex, occupation, object, vice, substance =
      symbol

predicates
   person(name,integer, sex, occupation)
   had_affair(name,name)
   killed_with(name,object)
   killed(name)
   killer(name)
   motive(vice)
   smeared_in(name,substance)
   owns(name,object)
   operates_identically(object,object).
   owns_probably(name,object)
   suspect(name)

clauses
   person(bert,55,m,carpenter).
   person(allan,25,m,football_player).
```

Listing 19-1 (cont.)

```
person(allan,25,m,butcher).
person(john,25,m,pickpocket).

had_affair(barbara,john).
had_affair(barbara,bert).
had_affair(susan,john).

killed_with(susan,club).
killed(susan).

motive(money).
motive(jealousy).

smeared_in(bert, blood).
smeared_in(susan, blood).
smeared_in(allan,mud).

owns(bert,wooden_leg).
owns(john,pistol).

/*
Background knowledge
*/

operates_identically(wooden_leg,club).
operates_identically(bar,club).
operates_identically(pair_of_scissors,knife).
operates_identically(football_boot,club).

owns_probably(X,football_boot) if
  person(X,_,_,football_player).
owns_probably(X,pair_of_scissors) if
  person(X,_,_,hairdresser).
owns_probably(X,Object) if
  owns(X,Object).

/*
Suspect all those who own a weapon with which
Susan could have been killed.
*/

suspect(X) if
  killed_with(susan,Weapon) and
  operates_identically(Object,Weapon) and
  owns_probably(X,Object).

/*
```

Suspect men who have had an affair with Susan.
*/

```
suspect(X) if
  motive(jealousy) and
  person(X,_,m,_) and
  had_affair(susan,X).
```

/*
Suspect females who have had an affair with someone
that Susan knew.
*/

```
suspect(X) if
  motive(money) and person(X,_,_,pickpocket).

killer(Killer) :-
  person(Killer,_,_,_),
  killed(Killed),
  Killed <> Killer,   /* We know it is not a suicide */
  suspect(Killer),
  smeared_in(Killer,Goo),
  smeared_in(Killed,Goo).
```

Listing 19-2

```
domains
  fname, lname, job = symbol
  player            = reference p(fname,lname,job,
    integer)
  name              = n(fname,lname)

predicates
  ans(player,player,player,player)
  player(fname,lname,job,integer)
  f_player(fname,lname,job,integer)
  team1(player,player)
  team2(player,player)
  find_score(integer,integer,integer,integer)

goal
  makewindow(1,7,1," Logic Problem 1G ",0,0,25,80),
  cursor(7,10),
  write("Working..."),
  ans(p(P1_1,P1_2,J1,S1),p(P2_1,P2_2,J2,S2),
    p(P3_1,P3_2,J3,S3),p(P4_1,P4_2,J4,S4)),
  clearwindow,
  cursor(10,10),
```

Listing 19-2 (cont.)

```
    writef("%4 %-7    %-10    %",P1_1,P1_2,J1,S1),
    cursor(11,10),
    writef("%4 %-7    %-10    %",P2_1,P2_2,J2,S2),
    cursor(12,10),
    writef("%4 %-7    %-10    %",P3_1,P3_2,J3,S3),
    cursor(13,10),
    writef("%4 %-7    %-10    %",P4_1,P4_2,J4,S4),
    cursor(17,10).    /* for Press Space Bar message */

clauses
    ans(p(P1_1,P1_2,J1,S1),p(P2_1,P2_2,J2,S2),
      p(P3_1,P3_2,J3,S3),p(P4_1,P4_2,J4,S4)) :-

    team1(p(P1_1,P1_2,J1,S1),p(P2_1,P2_2,J2,S2)),
    team2(p(P3_1,P3_2,J3,S3),p(P4_1,P4_2,J4,S4)),

    f_player(P1_1,P1_2,J1,S1),    /* player 1 */

    f_player(P2_1,P2_2,J2,S2),    /* player 2 */

    P1_1 <> P2_1,    /* player 1 <> player 2 */
    P1_2 <> P2_2,
    J1   <> J2,
    S1   <> S2,

    f_player(P3_1,P3_2,J3,S3),    /* player 3 */

    P1_1 <> P3_1,    /* player 1 <> player 3 */
    P1_2 <> P3_2,
    J1   <> J3,
    S1   <> S3,

    P2_1 <> P3_1,    /* player 2 <> player 3 */
    P2_2 <> P3_2,
    J2   <> J3,
    S2   <> S3,

    f_player(P4_1,P4_2,J4,S4),    /* player 4 */

    P1_1 <> P4_1,    /* player 1 <> player 4 */
    P1_2 <> P4_2,
    J1   <> J4,
    S1   <> S4,

    P2_1 <> P4_1,    /* player 2 <> player 4 */
    P2_2 <> P4_2,
    J2   <> J4,
```

```
    S2   <> S4,

    P3_1 <> P4_1,    /* player 3 <> player 4 */
    P3_2 <> P4_2,
    J3   <> J4,
    S3   <> S4,

    find_score(S1,S2,S3,S4).

  f_player(N1,N2,J,S) :- /* finds a potential player */
    player(N1,N2,J,S),
    bound(N1),
    player(N1,N2,J,S),
    bound(N2),
    player(N1,N2,J,S),
    bound(J),
    player(N1,N2,J,S),
    bound(S).

/* put most complete facts first */
  player("Dave",_,_,92).
  player(_,_,"Doctor",87).
  player("Bob","Howell",_,_).
  player(_,"Stevens","Accountant",_).

  player("Paul",_,_,_).
  player("John",_,_,_).

  player(_,"Curtis",_,_).
  player(_,"Bentley",_,_).

  player(_,_,"Editor",_).
  player(_,_,"Lawyer",_).

  player(_,_,_,78).
  player(_,_,_,83).

  find_score(S1,S2,S3,S4) :-
    bound(S1),
    bound(S2),
    bound(S3),
    bound(S4),
    S1 + S2 + 10 = S3 + S4;
    S1 + S2 = S3 + S4 + 10.

/* crucial facts */
  team1(p("John",_,_,_),p(_,_,"Lawyer",_)).
  team2(p(_,"Bentley",_,_),p(_,_,_,83)).
```

Finding Minimum and Maximum Numbers in a List

One of the truths about Prolog you probably learned early is that it is not primarily a number-crunching language. Its calculation abilities are limited, even though it has an impressive range of arithmetic predicates and functions, as you can see in table 20-1.

Table 20-1
Arithmetic Predicates and Functions

Predicate	Function
bitand(X,Y,Z)	logical AND of X and Y
bitnot(X,Z)	logical NOT of X
bitor(X,Y,Z)	logical OR of X and Y
bitleft(X,I,Y)	shift X left I bits
bitright(X,I,Y)	shift X right I bits
random(X)	pseudorandom number between 0 and 1
X mod Y	remainder of X/Y
X div Y	X divided by Y
abs(X)	removes sign; returns value
cos(X)	cosine of angle expressed in radians
sin(X)	sine of angle expressed in radians
tan(X)	tangent of angle expressed in radians
arctan(X)	arctangent of angle expressed in radians
exp(x)	e^x
ln(X)	log X_e
log(X)	log X_{10}
sqrt(X)	square root of X

In chapter 17, you saw how Turbo Prolog can calculate mortgages and loans. In this chapter, you examine a short program that illustrates how Turbo Prolog manipulates a list of numbers. The program accepts as input a list of positive and negative integers and returns the largest and smallest values in that list.

The Problem

At first glance, the program may seem both trivial and somewhat useless. Neither is the case. This program is a classic example of the need for recursive functions, a concept that is one of the most difficult to learn. And program segments that find the minimum and maximum values in a list—called minmax or minimax programs for short—are important components of many kinds of programs, including those that use this tree-searching strategy in game-playing designs.

The statement of the problem is quite simple and straightforward. Given a list of indeterminate size and mix of positive and negative integer values, find the smallest and largest values.

The Program

There are many Turbo Prolog solutions to this problem. None is as clean and easy to follow as the one by Garry J. Vass, which appears at the end of this chapter (listing 20-1).

Running the Program

As the program is set up, Vass has "commented out" the goal statement. To run the program, remove the /* and */ delimiters surrounding the goal statement at the end of the program. If you don't, you'll have to type the goal predicate demonstrate when Turbo Prolog asks for the goal after the program has compiled, as shown in figure 20-1.

The maximum and minimum values are derived from the list, which is hardcoded into the program. This list is named any_list and contains the values −6, −1, −2, −88, −2, 200, −3, −4, and −5.

You can edit the contents of any_list and rerun the program to find the minimum and maximum values in another list. But if you are tempted to type in a new list and ask the program to demonstrate the outcome, it won't work. Why? Because you are thinking procedurally. The value of any_list that you supply first in your goal statement is not equal to the value of any_list in the program, so Turbo Prolog says your goal fails, returning a False result.

We will get to the issue of making the program more general in a few moments. For now, let's look at how the program works.

Analyzing the Program

There are two basic predicates in this Turbo Prolog program: integer_list_maximum and its counterpart, integer_list_minimum. We'll look at the first one; its opposite number is virtually identical in operation and structure.

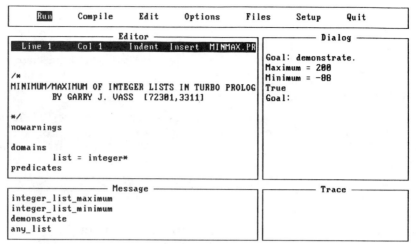

Figure 20-1
Minimax screen after user-typed goal

The `integer_list_maximum` predicate has three clauses. The first is the boundary condition, which must be present in any well-designed recursive routine. If the list is empty when the `integer_list_maximum` routine is called, the maximum value found so far—to which the variable X is instantiated—is the maximum value in the list. The program simply passes that value to the variable M. It then calculates the minimum value in the list in much the same way.

The next possible condition the program can encounter is handled by the second instance of the `integer_list_maximum` predicate. If the current head of the list is larger than the maximum value found so far as represented by X, the head (H) becomes the first argument in the `integer_list_maximum` predicate as it recurses on itself. This is classic recursive programming done right. Other programs I found as I scoured through public domain Prolog libraries for material for this book attempt to do this by assigning the value of H to the variable X when the head is found to be larger than the currently largest value. This is not good programming practice and can lead to many unnecessary complications. Simply putting the newly found larger value in the position of the former largest value when the procedure was invoked the first time is clean recursion.

The only other condition that can arise is if the head of the list is not larger than the largest value found so far in the program. In that event, you ignore the head and compare the current largest value to the tail of the list. That is precisely what the third instance of the `integer_list_maximum` predicate does.

Let's summarize the recursive process. We'll walk through the first part of `any_list`. If you like, follow along with `trace(on)` for the predicate, and you'll see the results in the Trace window on the Turbo

Prolog desktop. Just put the compiler directive trace at the beginning of the program. Turn the trace on with the trace(on) predicate in the demonstrate clause just before integer_list_maximum is called. Then put a trace(off) predicate immediately after that predicate.

Recursion in any_list

When the program first encounters the demonstrate goal, it sets up any_list as given in the program. It then calls integer_list_maximum. The call looks like this:

```
integer_list_maximum(-6,[-6,-1,-2,-88,-2,200,-3,-4,
    -5],_)
```

The first integer_list_maximum clause fails because the list argument—the second in the argument list—is not the empty list. So Turbo Prolog moves to the second instance of the predicate. Because -6>=-6 is true, this clause succeeds and the next call to the predicate looks like this:

```
integer_list_maximum(-6,[-1,-2,-88,-2,200,-3,-4,-5],_)
```

The second argument is still not the empty list, so the first instance of the predicate fails. The next clause tests the truth of the proposition -1>=-6. This is true, so the second clause recurses with the tail of the list:

```
integer_list_maximum(-1,[-2,-88,-2,200,-3,-4,-5],_)
```

For the next three items in the list, -2, -88, and -2, both the first and the second clause fail because the list is not empty and -1 is larger than any of those values. As a result, the third instance of the predicate is invoked. It undertakes a simple tail recursion process.

When the program reaches the call:

```
integer_list_maximum(-1,[200,-3,-4,-5],_)
```

the value of 200 is greater than -1, so 200 becomes the new first argument. The call is:

```
integer_list_maximum(200,[-3,-4,-5],_)
```

It's easy to see how the routine ends with 200 as the maximum value in the list. Through backtracking, it returns the response:

```
integer_list_maximum(200,[-6,-1,-2,-88,-2,200,-3,-4,
    -5],200)
```

The nowarnings **Directive**

There is one final point to make before concluding the discussion of this simple but useful program. At the beginning of the code, Vass has included a nowarnings compiler directive. This prevents the compiler from reporting Error 420, which indicates that a variable is used only once. It is a perfectly permissible way of dealing with the fact that the heads of the lists in some of the predicates are not used later in those predicates.

If you want to compile the program to an .EXE file, however, you will have to resolve all of these warnings. Just remove the nowarnings directive and run the program. Every time the program issues the warning, you'll see that it's pointing to an *H*. Change that *H* to an underscore, representing the anonymous variable.

From that description of the solution, you may wonder why any Turbo Prolog programmer would use the nowarnings compiler directive and permit some variable names to be used only once, instead of substituting the anonymous variable. If the plan is not to compile the code to an executable object code file or to include the program in a Turbo Prolog project, there is no reason not to use this technique. It makes the code more readable, because anonymous variables are difficult to relate to the context of the program.

Generalizing the Program

The program as written is intended not for general use but to demonstrate the recursion and number-handling abilities of Turbo Prolog. To make the routine more useful, add a small user interface in which you prompt the user for integers one at a time, build a list of the responses, and then perform the minimax tests on the list.

Here is one way to do it, though it has the disadvantage of not permitting the user to enter 0 as an integer. (You can get around this by letting the user enter some other arbitrarily high or low value to stop the recursion or by using some other Turbo Prolog input mechanism instead of readint.) You have to add appropriate domain and predicate declarations as needed.

```
build_list(Num_List) if
  write("Give me an integer: "),
  readint(Num),
  Num<>0,
  append(Num,Num_List,New_List),
  build_list(New_List).
```

Summary

This program demonstrates recursion nicely. It proves in another way Turbo Prolog's capability of dealing with numeric values and arithmetic operations. It also provides an example of when to use the `nowarnings` directive in Turbo Prolog code.

Listing 20-1

```
/*
MINIMUM/MAXIMUM OF INTEGER LISTS IN TURBO PROLOG
        BY GARRY J. VASS   [72301,3311]
*/
nowarnings

domains
  list = integer*

predicates
  integer_list_maximum(integer, list,integer)
  integer_list_minimum(integer, list, integer)
  demonstrate
  any_list(list)

clauses
  any_list([-6,-1,-2,-88,-2,200,-3,-4,-5]).

/*  If the list is empty, then the highest value */
/*  found thus far (in X) must be the maximum.    */
/*  Set M to the maximum because X will get       */
/*  reassigned.                                   */

  integer_list_maximum(X, [], M) if M = X.

/*  If the head of the list is greater than       */
/*  the highest value encountered so far,         */
/*  compare the head to the rest of the list.     */

  integer_list_maximum(X, [H|T],M) if
    H >= X and
    integer_list_maximum(H,T,M).

/*  If the above two rules don't work, then       */
/*  continue the tail recursion process.          */

  integer_list_maximum(X,[H|T],M) if
    integer_list_maximum(X,T,M).
```

```
/*    Same logic applies to min predicate         */

   integer_list_minimum(X,[],M) if M = X.

   integer_list_minimum(X, [H¦T],M) if
     H <= X and
     integer_list_minimum(H,T,M).
   integer_list_minimum(X, [H¦T],M) if
     integer_list_minimum(X,T,M).

   demonstrate if
     any_list([H¦T]) and
     integer_list_maximum(H,[H¦T],Maximum) and
     write("Maximum = ",Maximum) and nl and
     integer_list_minimum(H,[H¦T],Minimum) and
     write("Minimum = ",Minimum) and nl.

/* First variable is initialized to head         */
/* of list to avoid hardcoding an initial        */
/* value.                                        */
/*
goal
  demonstrate
*/
```

Part **5**

Useful Utilities

Chapter **21**

List Manipulation

One of the most powerful data structures in Turbo Prolog is the list. Lists are open-ended; you do not need to define or know in advance how many elements they contain. They are also useful for representing different kinds of knowledge. Lists and other complex data structures can even be elements of a list, leading to some very complicated storage mechanisms. In fact, it is difficult to conceive a data storage need that cannot be met by a Prolog list.

In this chapter, you look at fifteen routines for manipulating lists. Some find the length of a list or the identity of an element. Others add new elements to a list in ways different than the more standard append. A group of predicates delete elements from a list. Others change one or more elements or the order of the elements in a list.

The Problems

The predicates in this chapter will be handy in your Turbo Prolog programming. Their utility derives in part from the fact that Turbo Prolog includes no built-in predicates for list manipulation. I should hasten to add that this is not unusual. Many, if not most, Prologs on the market—particularly those for desktop computers—do not include many (if any) list manipulation routines. They are, however, easy to add. In fact, Prolog's extensibility is one of the things that makes it such a popular and usable language.

But Turbo Prolog does present one very special—and particularly irksome—problem in list manipulation. In many other Prologs, a list can consist of elements of any type. Thus, you can have a list that looks like this:

```
["Dee Jones",45000,"L. Mason",28000,"F. Prendergast",
    33655]
```

in which strings are mixed with integers. (This list is typical Prolog list usage. It consists of *object-attribute pairs*. Every nth element is of the same type, which is a convenient way of representing tabular knowledge.)

In Turbo Prolog, lists generally must contain data that is all the same type. If you've done much programming in Turbo Prolog, you've already run into this problem. Lists must be declared as special domains, as in the following program fragment:

```
domains
symlist = symbol*
```

The asterisk is a signal to Turbo Prolog that the domain consists of a list of elements that all have the type symbol. You cannot put any element into such a list unless it is the right type.

Even this problem would be mitigated if Turbo Prolog had a data type broad enough to encompass all types of data you want to work with, and permitted you to convert between data types easily. With the symbol data type, however, you cannot enter numeric values and there are no type conversion predicates available for it. See the Dialog window in figure 21-1.

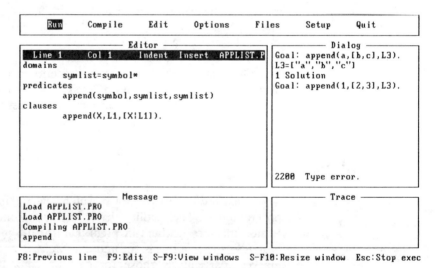

Figure 21-1
Type error when integer is entered for symbol

Strings work quite well for some applications, particularly if the structure of the list is known in advance. Turbo Prolog does provide built-in routines to convert between strings and characters, integers, and reals. And for most purposes, strings and symbols are equivalent.

But because you must know what type of data each relative position in a string contains and because conversion between types is required, strings are inconvenient when designing programs that do a lot of list manipulation. The resulting programs may also run slowly in comparison with other Turbo Prolog programs.

Turbo Prolog does provide a way around the problem, though. It is called the compound list. The concept is described briefly in the Turbo Prolog reference manual. Let's take a closer at the compound list because it is used extensively in the programs in this chapter.

Compound List Structures

A compound list is one that can contain elements of two or more standard data types. A compound list must be declared as a domain in a special way that requires two declaration statements. The first defines a data type. We'll call it an element because we usually talk of lists as being composed of elements. To declare this data type as compound, list the various standard data types that make up the data type, separated by semicolons.

Here are the declarations in the programs in this chapter:

```
domains
  element = c(char) ; i(integer) ; r(real) ; s(symbol)
  mixlist = element*
```

Notice that each data type of which a list of elements can be composed is listed in the same way. First, the name of the data type—in our example, c or i or r or s—is given. Then, in parentheses, the standard data type to which that name is connected in the list is given.

> **Note:** In Prolog, the semicolon means *or.* You can read this data type declaration as: "An element can be either a character, in which case I'll call it a c element, or an integer, in which case I'll flag it with an i. . . . "

Here are a few lists that use this domain declaration and create mixed lists in Turbo Prolog:

```
[s(Dee Jones),i(45000),s(L. Mason),i(28000),s(F.
    Prendergast),i(33655)]
[i(9),c('x'),r(3.14),i(14),i(33),s(test)]
```

To someone experienced in dealing with lists in Prolog, LISP, or other languages with powerful list-handling capabilities, this structure is strange and cumbersome. And it does involve extra typing—three extra keystrokes per list element—compared to "normal" Prolog list structures. But it lets you assemble lists when the types of elements are not known in advance.

You do not need to name the character data type c and the integer data type i. They could have been called *letter* and *number*, but that would have required even more typing.

The Programs

Now it's time to look at fifteen predicates that increase your list manipulation capabilities and make your programs more flexibile. Each program is presented as a separate entity, complete with domain and predicate declarations.

At the end of the chapter, for your use as an include file, is a single program containing all of the predicates in this chapter except bubblesort (which must be handled differently for reasons that are discussed later). You can use listing 21-1 in your Turbo Prolog programs when you need this list-handling power. Simply include it as described in part 1.

Three from the Book

The Turbo Prolog reference manual does contain three predicates for manipulating lists. Two—member and append—appear repeatedly in the other programs in this chapter.

The following program consolidates these three list manipulators. They are modified to accommodate lists of mixed types.

```
domains
  element = c(char) ; i(integer) ; r(real) ; s(symbol)
  mixlist = element*
predicates
  member(element,mixlist)
  append(mixlist,mixlist,mixlist)
  reverse(mixlist,mixlist)
clauses
  member(X,[X|_]).
  member(X,[_|Y]) :-
    member(X,Y).
  append([],L,L).
  append([H1|L1],L2,[H1|L3]) :-
    append(L1,L2,L3).
  reverse([],[]).
  reverse([H|T],L) :-
    reverse(T,L2),
    append(L2,[H],L).
```

Because these three predicates are described in the Turbo Prolog reference manual, you'll only look at them briefly. These predicates form the foundation for much of the rest of the work in this chapter.

The member Predicate

The member predicate takes two arguments. The first is an element, and the second is a list. The predicate then returns True if the element is a member of the list and False if it is not.

Note: If you are familiar with other Prologs, you know that the first argument to the traditional `member` predicate can be a single element or a list. In Turbo Prolog, with its strong typing, implementing this is not straightforward. We have chosen instead to treat the issue of whether a list is part of another list as a question of sublisting rather than membership checking. The `sublist` predicate is discussed later in this chapter.

Because `member` is recursive, the first clause is the boundary condition. If the element for which you are searching is the head of the list, then the predicate is `True`. The second clause embodies the second principle of membership: an element is a member of a list if it is a member of the tail of the list. Each time through this clause, you reduce the size of the list by one by removing the head. Then the first `member` clause is called again to see if the element is equal to the head of the newly formed list. The process continues until membership is determined or the predicate fails.

Note that the element must match an item in the list precisely, including its type. The following dialog demonstrates this:

```
Goal:member(c('a'),[c('x'),i(9),c('a'),r(3.14),
    s(test)]).
True
Goal:member(c('9'),[c('x'),i(9),c('a'),r(3.14),
    s(test)]).
False
Goal:
```

In the second instance, a more traditional, untyped Prolog would find the 9 in the list (unless you surround it with single quotation marks, thereby forcing its type to be a single character rather than an integer digit). But in Turbo Prolog, you must be precise about data types.

The append **Predicate**

The `append` predicate is common to all Prologs. If a Prolog programmer begins working with a new version of the language and the language doesn't have a built-in `append` predicate, it is safe to bet it will be one of the first the programmer creates.

When `append` is called, it must be furnished with three arguments. The first is the list to append, the second is the list to which the first list is appended, and the third is generally an uninstantiated variable to hold the result. Thus the "normal" use of the `append` predicate is as follows:

```
Goal: append([c('a')],[c('b'),c('c')],L3).
L3=[c('a'),c('b'),c('c')]
1 Solution
Goal:
```

The first list is appended to the front of the second list, as you can see. The operation of the append predicate is largely self-evident. It is a typical recursive function, with the first clause providing the boundary condition in which an empty list appended to any list leaves the second list unchanged.

This is a good place to divert, and demonstrate how most Turbo Prolog predicates can be used more than one way. The append predicate has been defined to assemble lists. But it can also be used to decompose lists by leaving its first two arguments uninstantiated and providing a list as the third argument. The result is a list of all possible lists that may be combined to create the third. Here is an example:

```
Goal: append(L1,L2,[i(1),c('a'),s(test)]).
L1=[], L2=[i(1),c('a'),s(test)]
L1=[i(1)], L2=[c('a'),s(test)]
L1=[i(1),c('a')], L2=[s(test)]
L1=[i(1),c('a'),s(test)], L2=[]
4 Solutions
Goal:
```

As you work through other predicates in this chapter, keep this alternate use in mind. There are times when you need a predicate to do something unusual, and you'll spend hours wracking your brain to come up with something when a different use of an existing predicate will do the job.

The reverse **Predicate**

The reverse predicate is of less general use than member and append, but there are times when you want to reverse a list of elements so you can look at the first one or undo the construction effects of backtracking. When you need this capability, the reverse predicate is handy. You give it two lists as arguments, one instantiated to the list to be reversed and the other designed to hold the result. (Will it make any difference whether the first or second argument is instantiated? Try it and find out.)

Getting Information about a List

Now that we have discussed the predicates included in the reference manual, let's examine some new ones created for this book. The first batch we'll describe contains four predicates for obtaining information about or from a list. The first predicate determines the length of a list. The second is the extension of member discussed previously that permits you to find out if one list is a sublist of another. The third predicate pulls the last item from a list, and the fourth, a more generalized extension of that idea, extracts an item from any known position within a list.

The `length` **Predicate**

Sometimes in Turbo Prolog programs, you want to take different actions depending on how many items a list contains. For those occasions, you have the `length` predicate, defined as follows:

```
domains
  element = c(char) ; i(integer) ; r(real) ; s(symbol)
  mixlist = element*
predicates
  length(mixlist,integer)
clauses
  length([],0).
  length([|Tail],ListLength):-
    length(Tail,LL1),
    ListLength=LL+1.
```

There is nothing mysterious or tricky going on here. The program simply recurses through the list, incrementing a value as it recurses, until it comes to the empty list. It then returns the integer value representing the length of the list. If you devise a list that has other lists as one or more elements, those embedded lists are counted as one element, regardless of how many elements they contain.

The `sublist` **Predicate**

As mentioned, the `member` predicate can only be used to find out if a specific element is contained in a list. If the object you are seeking within a list is itself a list, you need a different predicate. That is the role of `sublist`. For a list to be considered a sublist of another, the first list must appear in the second exactly as provided in the predicate call.

Here is the `sublist` predicate:

```
domains
  element = c(char) ; i(integer) ; r(real) ; s(symbol)
  mixlist = element*
predicates
  sublist(mixlist,mixlist)
clauses
  sublist(List1,List2):-
    append(_,List4,List2),
    append(List1,_,List4).
```

This `sublist` approach is, as you can see, nonrecursive. It relies on the following two facts. `List1` is a sublist of `List2` if:

1. You can decompose `List2` into two new lists, `List4` and some other list whose contents are unimportant; and

2. The resulting `List4` can be further decomposed into two lists, S

and some other list whose contents are arbitrary and unimportant.

(I am indebted to Ivan L. Bratko for this information. I have used his book, *Prolog Programming for Artificial Intelligence*, extensively in educating myself about the fine points of Prolog and its implementations.) Because the append predicate can be used to decompose as well as construct lists, it is used here to take lists apart piece by piece, looking for the first list embedded in the second list.

An alternative, but far less elegant and efficient, solution is to recurse through the list looking for the first element of the first list in the second list, then repeat that process for each element in the first list. This would become tricky if the second list contains sublists that are equivalent to the first part of the first list but are not actual sublists.

The last Predicate

The last predicate retrieves the last element in a list. It takes two arguments: an element and a mixed list. In normal use, the element is uninstantiated. If both are instantiated, you can determine if the last element of a list is a specific element.

```
domains
  element = c(char) ; i(integer) ; r(real) ; s(symbol)
  mixlist = element*
predicates
  last(element,mixlist)
clauses
  last(E,[E]).
  last(E,[_|Tail]):-
    last(E,Tail).
```

An element, E, is the last element in a list if it is either the only element in the list (first clause) or the last element in the tail of the list (second clause).

The extract Predicate

A more general case of the last predicate is when you want to extract the nth item in a list. The extract predicate does exactly that:

```
domains
  element = c(char) ; i(integer) ; r(real) ; s(symbol)
  mixlist = element*
predicates
  extract(integer,mixlist,element)
clauses
  extract(1,[H|_],H).
  extract(Position,[_|Tail],E) :-
```

```
        NewPos=Position-1,
        extract(NewPos,Tail,E).
```

This predicate requires three arguments. The first is an integer that represents the position of the element you want to extract. The second is the list from which the extraction is to take place. The last argument, generally uninstantiated, is where the result is returned.

If the integer argument is larger than the length of the list, Turbo Prolog returns No Solution. The following dialog demonstrates the use of the extract predicate:

```
Goal:extract(2,[c('a'),i(9),c('x'),r(3.14),s(test),
    c('b')],E).
E=i(9)
1 Solution
Goal:extract(9,[c('a'),i(9),c('x'),r(3.14),s(test),
    c('b')],E).
No Solution
Goal:
```

Adding New Elements

You have already used append to add a new element to the front of an existing list. Now you'll examine two predicates that add an element to the end of a list and insert one into any arbitrary position in a list.

The add_last Predicate

The add_last predicate is simplicity itself:

```
domains
  element = c(char) ; i(integer) ; r(real) ; s(symbol)
  mixlist = element*
predicates
  add_last(mixlist,mixlist,mixlist)
clauses
  add_last(Add,List,Result):-
    append(List,Add,Result).
```

Like its slightly less flexible counterpart, append, this predicate can only add a list to another list. To add an element, just make it a single-element list.

Here is a sample of the program at work:

```
Goal:add_last([c('y'),c('z')],[c('v'),c('w'),c('x')],
    NewList).
NewList=[c('v'),c('w'),c('x'),c('y'),c('z')]
1 Solution
Goal:
```

The `insert_at` Predicate

You can put a new element or elements at the front of an existing list with `append`; and you can add the new element(s) at the end of the list with `add_last`. But if you want to put a new element into a list at some arbitrary position, you need another predicate. Enter `insert_at`:

```
domains
   element = c(char) ; i(integer) ; r(real) ; s(symbol)
   mixlist = element*
predicates
   insert_at(element,integer,mixlist,mixlist)
clauses
   insert_at(E,1,StartList,[E¦StartList]) :-!.
   insert_at(E,Position,[H¦Tail],[H¦Tail1]) :-
      NewPos=Position-1,
      insert_at(E,NewPos,Tail,Tail1).
```

The first argument to `insert_at` is the element to be inserted into the list. Note that in this example you are processing an element, not a list. The second argument is an integer representing the position in the list that the new element occupies after the insertion. For example, if the integer is 3, the new element is in the third position, not inserted after the old third position but placed ahead of it. The next argument is the present list. The fourth argument is unbound and represents the list in which the return is placed.

Here is `insert_at` at work:

```
Goal:insert_at(i(4),4,[(i(1),i(2),i(3),i(5)],NewList).
NewList=[i(1),i(2),i(3),i(4),i(5)]
1 Solution
Goal:
```

Deleting Elements

In this section, you'll look at four new predicates for removing elements from a list. Each makes a slightly different kind of decision about what to delete.

The `del` Predicate

The simplest of these predicates is `del`. This predicate removes the first occurrence of an element it finds in a list and returns the modified list. The listing looks like this:

```
domains
   element = c(char) ; i(integer) ; r(real) ; s(symbol)
   mixlist = element*
predicates
```

```
   del(element,mixlist,mixlist)
clauses
  del(X,[X|Tail],Tail).
  del(X,[Y|Tail],[Y|Tail1]):-
    del(X,Tail,Tail1).
```

Again, you see the classic recursive model. A boundary condition occurs when the item being deleted is the current head of the list. A recursion on the tails of two lists is the repetitive result as long as that is not the case.

Here is what the program does:

```
Goal:del(s(test),[i(9),c('x'),s(test),s(test2)],
     NewList).
NewList=[i(9),c('x'),s(test2)]
1 Solution
Goal: del(i(43),[i(9),c('x'),s(test),s(test2)],NewList).
No Solution
Goal:
```

The deleteall Predicate

Sometimes you want to expunge all references to a variable from a list. The deleteall predicate does just that. Here's the listing for this predicate:

```
domains
  element = c(char) ; i(integer) ; r(real) ; s(symbol)
  mixlist = element*
predicates
  deleteall(_,[],[]).
    deleteall(E,[E|Tail],Res):-
    !,
    deleteall(E,Tail,Res).
  deleteall(E,[X|Tail1],[X|Tail2]):-
    deleteall(E,Tail1,Tail2).
```

The program deals with three situations. The first is the boundary condition, which arises when the second list is empty. The second takes care of the situation where the program has found an occurrence of the desired element at the head of the list it is now examining. The final handles all other situations.

Here is the program in use:

```
Goal:deleteall(i(9,[i(9),c('a'),i(0),i(9),s(test),i(9)],
     NewList).
NewList=[(c('a'),i(0),s(test)]
1 Solution
Goal:
```

The del_nth Predicate

The next predicate, del_nth, deletes the nth item of a list regardless of its contents, and returns No Solution if n is greater than the length of the list. Here's the del_nth predicate:

```
domains
  element = c(char) ; i(integer) ; r(real) ; s(symbol)
  mixlist = element*
predicates
  del_nth(integer,mixlist,mixlist)
clauses
    del_nth(1,[_|Tail],Tail).
    del_nth(Position,[H|Tail1],[H|Tail2]) :-
    NewPos=Position-1,
    del_nth(NewPos,Tail1,Tail2).
```

The first argument tells the program which numbered item to delete. The second argument is the list from which to make the deletion. The answer is returned in the third, usually uninstantiated, variable.

Here is a sample run of the program:

```
Goal: del_nth(2,[i(1),i(2),i(3),i(4),i(5)],NewList).
NewList=[i(1),i(3),i(4),i(5)]
1 Solution
Goal:
```

The make_unique Predicate

The last deletion routine you'll examine goes through a list and removes any duplicate items, leaving only one of each item in the finished list. The program uses two predicates: make_unique, the predicate you call, and del_dupes, which is called by that predicate:

```
domains
  element = c(char) ; i(integer) ; r(real) ; s(symbol)
  mixlist = element*
predicates
  make_unique(mixlist,mixlist)
  del_dupes(mixlist,mixlist,mixlist)
  member(element,mixlist)
clauses
  make_unique(X,Y) :-
    del_dupes(X,[],Y).
  del_dupes([],L1,L1):-!.
  del_dupes([H|Tail],L1,Result):-
    member(H,L1),
    del_dupes(Tail,L1,Result).
  del_dupes([H|Tail],L1,Result):-
```

```
  del_dupes(Tail,[H¦L1],Result),!.
member(X,[X¦_]).
member(X,[_¦Y]) :-
  member(X,Y).
```

When this program is run, as follows, it removes all duplicates from a list, creating an unordered set of elements.

```
Goal:
make_unique([i(9),i(0),s(test),i(9),s(test),
    c('x'),r(4.09)],NewList).
NewList=[(i(9),i(0),s(test),c('x'),r(4.09)]
1 Solution
Goal:
```

Changing Lists

In this section, we'll demonstrate two predicates that modify lists. The first replaces all instances of one element with another. The other sorts the elements of a list using the well-known bubble sort method.

The replace Predicate

In text processing, search and replace is a necessity. In other programs, the ability to find all occurrences of a specific character or string and replace them with a new character or string is sometimes helpful. The replace predicate handles this task:

```
domains
  element = c(char) ; i(integer) ; r(real) ; s(symbol)
  mixlist = element*
predicates
  replace(element,element,mixlist,mixlist)
clauses
  replace(_,_,[],[]).
  replace(OldE,NewE,[H¦Tail1],[NewE¦Tail2]):-
    !,
    replace(OldE,NewE,Tail1,Tail2).
  replace(OldE,NewE,[H¦Tail1],[H¦Tail2]) :-
    replace(OldE,NewE,Tail1,Tail2).
```

The replace predicate takes four arguments. The first is the element you are searching for, and the second is the element with which it should be replaced. The third argument is the list in which the changes are to take place. The fourth argument, generally uninstantiated, holds the result of the replace function.

Because this is yet another example of recursion with boundary and alternate location conditions, I won't explain in detail how the predicates work. The following sample run shows how the program operates:

```
Goal: replace(i(9),s(nine),[(i(9),c('9'),s(test),i(9),
    i(0)],NewList).
NewList=[s(nine),c('9'),s(test),s(nine),i(0)]
1 Solution
Goal:
```

The bubblesort Predicate

The bubblesort predicate is the only predicate introduced in this chapter that does not use Turbo Prolog's mixed list domain type. Sorting requires that the list consist only of standard types so that comparisons can be made between the values of the elements. This, in turn, requires that the elements all be the same type in Turbo Prolog.

The bubble sort is not the most efficient sort method known. But it is one of the easiest to follow. If you use this predicate on a small list and turn on the trace function, you'll be able to see the sorting process.

```
domains
  symlist = symbol*
predicates
  bubblesort(symlist,symlist)
  swap(symlist,symlist)
clauses
  bubblesort(Start,Sorted):-
    swap(Start,Intermediate),!,
    bubblesort(Intermediate,Sorted).
  bubblesort(Sorted,Sorted).
  swap([E1,E2|Tail],[E2,E1|Tail]):-
    E1>E2.
  swap([E|Tail],[E|Tail1]):-
    swap(Tail,Tail1).
```

The sort itself is pretty straightforward. The program simply goes through the list one element at a time. If it finds that one element is smaller than the next, it swaps their positions. It repeats this process until it makes one entire sweep through the list without finding any number smaller than the number on its right. Then it quits.

Here is the program in operation:

```
Goal: bubblesort([dan,carolyn,sheila,heather,christy,
    mary],NewList).
NewList=(["carolyn","christy","dan","heather","mary",
    "sheila"]).
1 Solution
Goal:
```

Note that Turbo Prolog puts double quotation marks around symbols when it reports them, even though you don't have to use quotation marks when you enter symbols. This anomaly shouldn't confuse you. Strings and symbols are nearly identical in any event.

Summary

I hope you've learned a lot about Turbo Prolog in this chapter. Now when your Prolog purist friends tell you that Turbo Prolog is not a "real" Prolog because of some missing features, you can tell them that many (though not all) such features can be programmed or circumvented.

In the next chapter, you'll look at another "shortcoming" in Turbo Prolog—the apparent inability to call predicates as arguments—and see how one ingenious programmer found an elegant way around the problem.

Listing 21-1

```
domains
element = c(char) ; i(integer); r(real); s(symbol)
mixlist = element*

predicates
member(element,mixlist)
append(mixlist,mixlist,mixlist)
reverse(mixlist,mixlist)
add_last(mixlist,mixlist,mixlist)
del(element,mixlist,mixlist)
del_nth(integer,mixlist,mixlist)
deleteall(element,mixlist,mixlist)
length(mixlist,integer)
insert_at(element,integer,mixlist,mixlist)
last(element,mixlist)
extract(integer,mixlist,element)
sublist(mixlist,mixlist)
replace(element,element,mixlist,mixlist)
make_unique(mixlist,mixlist)
del_dupes(mixlist,mixlist,mixlist)

clauses
member(X,[X¦_]).
member(X,[_¦Y]) if
  member(X,Y).

append([],L,L).
append([H1¦L1],L2,[H1¦L3]) if
  append(L1,L2,L3).
reverse([],[]).
```

Listing 21-1 (cont.)

```
reverse([H¦T],L) if
  reverse(T,L2) and
  append(L2,[H],L).

add_last(Add,List,Result) :-
  append(List,Add,Result).

deleteall(_,[],[]).
deleteall(E,[E¦Tail],Res) :-
  !,
  deleteall(E,Tail,Res).
deleteall(E,[X¦Tail1],[X¦Tail2]) :-
  deleteall(E,Tail1,Tail2).

del(X,[X¦Tail],Tail).
del(X,[Y¦Tail],[Y¦Tail1]) :-
  del(X,Tail,Tail1).

del_nth(1,[_¦Tail],Tail).
del_nth(Position,[H¦Tail1],[H¦Tail2]) :-
  NewPos=Position-1,
  del_nth(NewPos,Tail1,Tail2).

length([],0).
length([_¦Tail],ListLength) :-
  length(Tail,LL1),
  ListLength=LL1+1.

insert_at(E,1,StartList,[E¦StartList]) :-!.
insert_at(E,Position,[H¦Tail],[H¦Tail1]) :-
  NewPos=Position-1,
  insert_at(E,NewPos,Tail,Tail1).

last(E,[E]).
last(E,[_¦Tail]) :-
  last(E,Tail).

extract(1,[H¦_],H).
extract(Position,[_¦Tail],E) :-
  NewPos=Position-1,
  extract(NewPos,Tail,E).

sublist(List1,List2) :-
  append(_,List4,List2),
  append(List1,_,List4).
```

```
replace(_,_,[],[]).
replace(OldE,NewE,[OldE¦Tail1],[NewE¦Tail2]) :-
  !,
  replace(OldE,NewE,Tail1,Tail2).
replace(OldE,NewE,[H¦Tail1],[H¦Tail2]) :-
  replace(OldE,NewE,Tail1,Tail2).

make_unique(X,Y) :-
  del_dupes(X,[],Y).

del_dupes([],L1,L1) :-!.
del_dupes([H¦Tail],L1,Result) :-
  member(H,L1),
  del_dupes(Tail,L1,Result).
del_dupes([H¦Tail],L1,Result) :-
  del_dupes(Tail,[H¦L1],Result),!.
```

Simulating Calls and Predicate Passing

In early 1987, a Turbo Prolog programmer named Tom Morgan suggested the development of standards for naming domains and representing basic Turbo Prolog data structures. While developing his rationale and a demonstration of these standards, Morgan wrote a routine that makes it possible for Turbo Prolog predicates to simulate predicate passing.

In complex applications, you sometimes need to pass a predicate as an argument to another predicate. Most implementations of Prolog make such predicate passing part of their normal syntax. But for complex reasons (involving compiler design strategies beyond the scope of this discussion), such predicate passing is not directly implemented in Turbo Prolog.

In this chapter, you look at predicate passing—a method of calling a predicate with another predicate as an argument—as implemented by Morgan in his early program (listing 22-1). Then you look at a small program (listing 22-2) that uses some of the ideas in listing 22-1 to create highly useful list manipulation routines that are missing from Turbo Prolog and often needed in designing complex applications.

The Problem

Programs that use artificial intelligence concepts are characterized by features that either do not appear or are rarely needed in most other kinds of programs. One of these traits is the ability to treat a computer program itself as if it is a data structure. This ability leads to self-modifying programs (considered bad form in most programming circles but often needed and used in AI research) that appear to learn and modify their behavior based on what they "experience" as they are run.

A simple example of this need occurs when you build a dynamic database in Turbo Prolog. The assert predicates—asserta and assertz—allow the dynamic addition of facts to a database. But they do not take predicates or predicate names as arguments. Thus, you cannot add a new rule to a Turbo Prolog database, despite the fact that this power is one of the key features of most standard Prologs.

Turbo Prolog Manual Sample

Program 63 in the Turbo Prolog manual, called EXAMPL63.PRO on the sample programs disk that comes with the language, provides some insight into how you can make Turbo Prolog interpret its own types of clauses. This issue is at the heart of what you will be looking at in this chapter.

Run EXAMPL63.PRO a few times and read the manual's brief explanation of the program and its key feature: reference domains. Then you will be ready to proceed with the rest of this discussion.

Reference Domains

The use of reference domains was discussed in chapter 19. It is one of the trickiest ideas in Turbo Prolog. But its definition is the essence of simplicity.

> **Definition:** A reference domain tells Turbo Prolog that it will be passing references, or addresses, rather than actual values, when that domain is used in a predicate.

As is often the case with simple definitions, however, this one covers a multitude of sins. In essence, any time you want to call a predicate with one or more unbound arguments so that a subsequent goal can fill in missing information, you need to use a reference domain declaration. In EXAMPL63.PRO, for example, the term domain is declared to be a reference domain. In the predicates section, the unify_term predicate is defined as using, in one of its incarnations, the term domain as two of its arguments.

The unify_term clauses, in turn, are the heart of the program. Their name, incidentally, derives from the Prolog concept of unification, which involves binding values to variables. (See my *Turbo Prolog Primer* for an extended discussion of the unification process.) Essentially, their task is to build responses to the call routines typically contained in goal statements used with the program. The unification process fills empty slots in the argument list until everything that can be satisfied has been completed.

If the term domain in EXAMPL63.PRO was not declared as a reference variable, you would receive a warning message that a variable is unbound in a clause when you tried to run the program.

As you will see when you look at listing 22-1, the use of reference domains permits the definition of a generalized list structure where the combination of types of elements contained in a list is not known when the program is run.

The First Program

The first program—listing 22-1 at the end of this chapter—is a slight modification of Morgan's original code. I have edited some of his comments in the listing to clarify their relationship to the present discussion.

Running the Program

After you type and save the program, or download it, simply run it. The sample goals at the end of the program execute and your display looks like figure 22-1. This ensures that the program has been properly saved and you can safely proceed with the rest of this discussion.

> **Note:** Your program listing will not be identical to that shown in figure 22-1 if you download the code from CompuServe or some other source, because the edited listing (listing 22-1) is not included in any other version of this program.

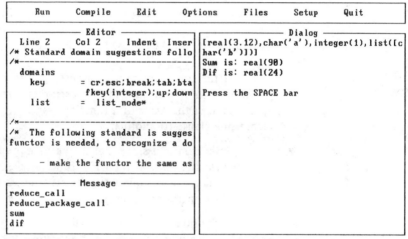

Figure 22-1
Sample run of `call` demonstration

If you want to experiment with the program, try editing the reduce goal statements to provide other mixtures of real and integer numbers, to produce negative results, and so forth.

LISP reduce Function

When Morgan developed his sample program to demonstrate the use of standards for predicate passing in Turbo Prolog, he implemented a LISP function called `reduce`. Without getting into too much LISP, it is important to understand this function so that you can more clearly follow what is happening in the program.

LISP uses a prefix notation in arithmetic operations. For example, to add 5 and 7, you type:

```
(plus 5 7)
```

The LISP interpreter returns the answer, 12, and waits for your next input. (The parentheses are required in LISP instructions and commands, and give rise to the AI joke that LISP stands for "Lots of Irritating Silly Parentheses.")

But the plus function is designed to take two—and only two—arguments. If you want to add three numbers in LISP, you have to do something like this:

```
(plus 5(plus 7 8))
```

You can see how easily and quickly the parentheses become a problem!

The LISP reduce operator reduces the elements of a list to a single result. Given a function (such as plus) and a list of arguments to which the function is applied, the reduce operator applies the function successively to the elements of the list until a single result is obtained. Thus, you can add three numbers as follows using the reduce operator:

```
(reduce 'plus '(5 7 8))
```

In the program we are discussing, the reduce predicate takes a symbol as its first argument and uses this symbol—which turns out in practice to be the name of a function—as a means of passing a predicate from one clause to another.

> **Note:** Do not assume that the reduce predicate in listing 22-1 works the same as the LISP function described previously. It simulates it in some ways, but it is not a precise duplication of its operation. That is not the intent of the program.

In the goal statements in Morgan's sample code, calls to the reduce predicate with two different symbols—sum and dif—as first arguments are the key to understanding the program.

The assumption made by Morgan in designing this sample program was that the sum reduction predicates are furnished with the package as it is developed by a publisher and delivered to an end user, who is also a Turbo Prolog programmer. Then the customer adds the dif reduction predicates. To add them, however, the customer only has to add a reduce_call clause and the four clauses that define the types of subtraction that can take place in the program. The reduce function and the call to the built-in ("packaged") sum predicate, as well as the logic that detects the difference between the two types of calls, are all supplied with the original package.

Package-Supplied Operations

Let's look at how these two different kinds of operations—those supplied by the package and those added by the application—differ operationally.

Change the goal section of listing 22-1 by deleting the first two lines and adding a `trace` function for the first use of the `reduce` predicate. Add the `trace` compiler directive at or near the beginning of the program. The new goal section should look like this (allowing for the possibility that you want to have different values in the list argument passed to the `sum` call):

```
goal
  trace(on),
  reduce(sum,[integer(1),real(33.0),real(56)],
    integer(0),M),
  trace(off),
  write("Sum is: ",M),nl,
  reduce(dif,[integer(1),real(33.0),real(56)],
    integer(0),M),
  write("Dif is: ",D),nl.
```

Now run the program. Your trace will look something like this:

```
CALL:reduce("sum",[integer(1),real(33),real(56)],
    integer(0),_)
FAIL:reduce("sum",[integer(1),real(33),real(56)],
    integer(0),_)
REDO:reduce("sum",[integer(1),real(33),real(56)],
    integer(0),_)
CALL:reduce_package_call("sum",integer(1),
    integer(0),_)
CALL: sum(integer(1),integer(0),_)
FAIL: sum(integer(1),integer(0),_)
REDO: sum(integer(1),integer(0),_)
1=1
RETURN: sum(integer(1),integer(0),integer(1))
RETURN: *reduce_package_call("sum",integer(1),
    integer(0),integer(1))
CALL: reduce("sum",[real(33),real(56)],integer(1),_)
FAIL: reduce("sum",[real(33),real(56)],integer(1),_)
REDO: reduce("sum",[real(33),real(56)],integer(1),_)
CALL: reduce_package_call("sum",real(33),integer(1),_)
CALL: sum(real(33),integer(1),_)
FAIL: sum(real(33),integer(1),_)
REDO: sum(real(33),integer(1),_)
CALL: sum(real(33),integer(1),_)
FAIL: sum(real(33),integer(1),_)
REDO: sum(real(33),integer(1),_)
34=34
RETURN: sum(real(33),integer(1),real(34))
RETURN: reduce_package_call("sum",real(33),integer(1),
    real(34))
```

```
CALL: reduce("sum",[real(56),real(34),_])
FAIL: reduce("sum",[real(56),real(34),_])
REDO: reduce("sum",[real(56),real(34),_])
CALL: reduce_package_call("sum",real(56),real(34),_)
CALL: sum(real(56),real(34),_)
FAIL: sum(real(56),real(34),_)
REDO: sum(real(56),real(34),_)
CALL: sum(real(56),real(34),_)
FAIL: sum(real(56),real(34),_)
REDO: sum(real(56),real(34),_)
CALL: sum(real(56),real(34),_)
90=90
RETURN: sum(real(56),real(34),real(90))
RETURN: *reduce_package_call("sum",real(56),real(34),
    real(90))
CALL: reduce("sum",[],real(90))
RETURN: *reduce("sum",[],real(90),real(90))
RETURN: reduce("sum",[real(56)],real(34),real(90))
RETURN: reduce("sum",[real(33),real(56)],
    integer(1),real(90))
RETURN: reduce("sum",[integer(1),real(33),real(56)],
    integer(0),real(90))
```

This trace shows that the built-in sum routine is accessed through the reduce_package_call routine. Under Morgan's approach, the reduce_package routine is never used when the publisher supplies the routine with the program.

Application-Supplied Operations

When an application-supplied operator is encountered in the goals of the program as designed by Morgan, the reduce_package_call predicate fails on the first pass. The second occurrence of the clause leads to an invocation of the reduce_call predicate, which is the one intended for use by application-added operations.

This can be seen clearly in the trace of the execution when the goal statements are changed to trace the dif calls:

```
goal
  reduce(sum,[integer(1),real(33.0),real(56)],
      integer(0),M),
  write("Sum is: ",M),nl,trace(on),
  reduce(dif,[integer(1),real(33.0),real(56)],
      integer(0),D),
  trace(off),
  write("Dif is: ",D),nl.
```

When this is run, the trace is similar to the following:

```
CALL: reduce("dif",[integer(1),real(33),real(56)],
      integer(0),_)
FAIL: reduce("dif",[integer(1),real(33),real(56)],
      integer(0),_)
REDO: reduce("dif",[integer(1),real(33),real(56)],
      integer(0),_)
CALL: reduce_package_call("dif",integer(1),integer(0),_)
FAIL: reduce_package_call("dif",integer(1),integer(0),_)
REDO: reduce_package_call("dif",integer(1),integer(0),_)
CALL: reduce_call("dif",integer(1),integer(0),_)
CALL: dif(integer(1),integer(0),_)
FAIL: dif(integer(1),integer(0),_)
REDO: dif(integer(1),integer(0),_)
1=1
RETURN: dif(integer(1),integer(0),integer(1))
RETURN: reduce_call("dif",integer(1),integer(0),
      integer(1))
RETURN: reduce_package_call("dif",integer(1),integer(0),
      integer(1))
CALL: reduce("dif",[real(33),real(56)],integer(1),_)
RETURN: reduce_call("dif",integer(1),integer(0),
      integer(1))
RETURN: reduce_package_call("dif",integer(1),integer(0),
      integer(1))
CALL: reduce("dif",[real(33),real(56)],integer(1),_)
FAIL: reduce("dif",[real(33),real(56)],integer(1),_)
REDO: reduce("dif",[real(33),real(56)],integer(1),_)
CALL: reduce_package_call("dif",real(33),integer(1),_)
FAIL: reduce_package_call("dif",real(33),integer(1),_)
REDO: reduce_package_call("dif",real(33),integer(1),_)
CALL: reduce_call("dif",real(33),integer(1),_)
CALL: dif(real(33),integer(1),_)
FAIL: dif(real(33),integer(1),_)
REDO: dif(real(33),integer(1),_)
CALL: dif(real(33),integer(1),_)
REDO: dif(real(33),integer(1),_)
32=32
RETURN: dif(real(33),integer(1),real(32))
RETURN: reduce_call("dif",real(33),integer(1),real(32))
RETURN: reduce_package_call("dif",real(33),integer(1),
      real(32))
CALL: reduce("dif",[real(56)],real(32),_)
FAIL: reduce("dif",[real(56)],real(32),_)
REDO: reduce("dif",[real(56)],real(32),_)
CALL: reduce_package_call("dif",real(56),rel(32),_)
FAIL: reduce_package_call("dif",real(56),rel(32),_)
REDO: reduce_package_call("dif",real(56),rel(32),_)
CALL: reduce_call("dif",real(56),real(32),_)
```

```
CALL: reduce_call("dif",real(56),real(32),_)
CALL: dif(real(56),real(32),_)
RETURN: dif(real(56),real(32),real(24))
RETURN: reduce_call("dif",real(56),real(32),real(24))
RETURN: reduce_package_call("dif",real(56),real(32),
    real(24))
CALL: reduce("dif",[],real(24),_)
RETURN: *reduce("dif",[],real(24),real(24))
RETURN: reduce("dif",[real(56)],real(32),real(24))
RETURN: reduce("dif",[real(33),real(56)],integer(1),
    real(24))
RETURN: reduce("dif",[integer(1),real(33),real(56)],
    integer(0),real(24))
```

As you can see, the reduce_call predicate is used because the dif function is supplied by the application programmer rather than with the original code from the publisher.

Extending the Concept

You can extend the power of this program in at least two ways: development and implementation of standards for predicate-calling approaches to Turbo Prolog program design, and implementation of designs that would not work without the ability to pass a predicate and arguments to another predicate during processing.

Morgan focused on the former issue in developing this program. His work is the first I have seen to suggest standard domains and representations for basic Turbo Prolog data structures.

In his early work—which was continuing as this book was being written—Morgan adopted four heuristics to guide the development and implementation of these standards:

1. If a convention is available in the Turbo Prolog reference manual, use it.

2. Favor conventions that are easy to remember.

3. Include suggestions that allow the coding of generalizable predicates that can operate on a variety of objects. You do this by adding domain alternatives and by incorporating clauses to standardize predicates.

4. Make suggestions for the most general case rather than the narrowly specific needs of an application.

Morgan further suggests that when a functor must recognize a domain name, give the functor the same name as the domain. In the more complex cases in this chapter, involving a second-order predicate (one that naturally takes a predicate as an argument), the approach shown in the program should be used. The rules for this approach are summarized as follows:

1. Define the argument where the passed predicate will be used in the second-order predicate as a symbol. (In the example program, `reduce`, `reduce_call`, and `reduce_package_call` have a symbol as their first argument, which is where the name of the predicate being passed to them is placed.)

2. Define two auxiliary predicates for the second-order predicate, one consisting of the name of the second-order predicate followed by `_package_call` and the other followed by `_call`. You have seen how `reduce_package_call` and `reduce_call` differ in the sample program. The first passes predicates within the publisher's original package of code, and the second passes application-furnished predicates.

A Complete Example

Now let's take a look at a complete example of the use of the simulated `call` function in Turbo Prolog. This program is listing 22-2 (at the end of this chapter).

You will examine Turbo Prolog's missing ability to handle sets and bags of data (terms that will become clearer momentarily) using Morgan's call approach.

The Problem

In searching a database or scanning a dictionary in a natural language processing application, you often want to obtain a list of values that meet certain criteria while eliminating duplicate answers in the process. Turbo Prolog's `findall` built-in predicate solves the first part of this problem, but it returns every valid answer, even if duplicate data is in the database.

A list of guaranteed unique items is technically referred to as a *set*. Most Prologs have the built-in predicate `setof`, which returns a set of answers to a specific search request or query. Our interest in this chapter is in seeing how easily you can design a `setof` function in Turbo Prolog.

Note: This program should not be considered a good reason in and of itself to design a `setof` predicate. The program is simplistic. And, as Morgan pointed out to me when he sent me the program on CompuServe: "In this case, the idea is ridiculous. You would be far better off to simply code the combination of `findall` and `remove_duplicates` inline to your code." That I decided to include this program "as is" is therefore not a reflection of Morgan's feeling about its value. Rather, it indicates that I think such easy-to-follow examples are a far better way to teach advanced techniques than "meaningful" programs, where other issues can cloud the reader's view.

I should note, too, that after you have worked through listing 22-2 and have seen how to implement `setof`, you will be able to use sets in other ways in your Turbo Prolog programs. In the classic Prolog reference work, Clocksin & Mellish's *Programming in Prolog,* the authors provide a number of set-manipulating predicates that presume the ability to start with a true set of unique items.

This program does not fully implement the usual functions of `setof`. It is, however, quite close to that goal. In Edinburgh standard Prolog, there is no definition for `setof`. But most Prolog implementations discriminate between this predicate and another popularly supplied built-in predicate, `bagof`, as follows. The `setof` predicate eliminates duplicates and sorts the items according to the criteria by which they were first selected. The `bagof` predicate, on the other hand, gathers into one list all answers that meet the criteria, but does not eliminate or sort duplicates. This distinction is worth elaborating because it provides Prolog background.

Let's start with a list of student information:

```
student("Tom Johnson","CS104",87).
student("Ann Johnson","CS104",93).
student("Steve Black","CS104",78).
student("Tom Johnson","ENG13",55).
student("Elmer Frosh,"ENG13",88).
student("Ann Johnson","ENG13",93).
```

This list contains the names of students, classes in which they are or have been enrolled, and their numeric grades in those classes. If you want to use `bagoff` to obtain a list of all students in this collection of facts, do so with this predicate call:

```
bagof(X,student(X,_,_),Result).
```

The program returns:

```
Result = ["Tom Johnson","Ann Johnson","Steve Black","Tom
    Johnson","Elmer Frosh","Ann Johnson"]
```

Similarly, to find all the classes listed in the database, use the query:

```
bagof(X,student(_,X,_),Result).
```

As expected, the system returns:

```
Result = ["CS104","CS104","CS104","ENG13","ENG13",
    "ENG13"]
```

Now if you apply setof in a similar way to the same data, the following interaction takes place:

```
setof(X,student(X,_,_),StudentList).
StudentList=["Tom Johnson","Ann Johnson","Steve
    Black","Elmer Frosh"]
setof(X,student(_,X,_),Classes).
Classes=["CS104","ENG13"]
```

I should point out that bagof doesn't exist in Turbo Prolog, but its function is virtually duplicated by findall. In fact, the program in this chapter uses findall to design a setof equivalent.

The Second Program

The demonstration version of Morgan's program—listing 22-2—contains only four pieces of deliberately duplicated data. (Mr. Morgan asked that I be sure to point out that he gave himself a raise for the purpose of this demonstration.) The information is:

```
employee("Tom Morgan",60000).
employee("Ray Eng",45000).
employee("Tom Morgan",60000).
employee("Ray Eng",45000).
```

In listing 22-2, Mr. Morgan uses the dispatcher technique in listing 22-1 to cause set_of_call to invoke set_of. This latter predicate has three arguments. The first is the name of the predicate on which to perform the set_of operations. The second is a list defining the criteria. The third is the name of the variable into which the set results will be returned. Thus, you will see a call that looks like this in the goal portion of the program:

```
set_of(highpaid,[employee(Name,Salary),real(20000),
    real(100000)],Ans1)
```

This simply tells the program to return a set of those employees whose salaries are greater than $20,000 and less than $100,000. The order of the criteria and arguments is dictated by the set_of_call predicate.

Running the Program

With the program's built-in goal statement, running the program is simple. Load the file and choose Run from the menu. The result looks like figure 22-2.

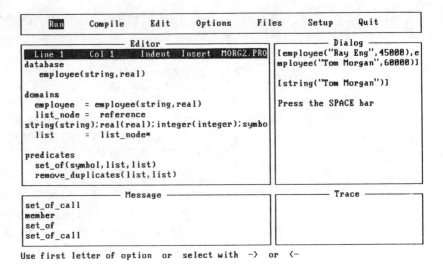

Figure 22-2
Result of running program showing `set_of`

The program has two goal statements. The first asks for a `set_of` employees who make between $20,000 and $100,000 per year, and requests that their name and salary be returned. The second asks only for the names of any employees who earn between $50,000 and $100,000. In both cases, as you can see, the duplicates are eliminated. You can add more people to the list and confirm that the program always returns only one of each valid answer in the return list.

Analyzing the Program

There is not much to analyze in listing 22-2. The program uses the dispatching method described previously to set up the new `set_of` predicate call. Perhaps the most interesting feature is the removal of duplicates from the list, a task handled by the program-defined `delete_dupes`, with assistance from `remove_duplicates_aux`. These routines are quite similar to the `make_unique` predicate described in chapter 21. If you haven't read that chapter, it would be helpful to do so.

Summary

In this chapter, you used one approach to passsing predicates and their arguments as arguments to other predicates in Turbo Prolog. You saw how such an approach can be useful, and you studied the traces of two operations involving Tom Morgan's suggested way of dealing with this problem as part of the need for conventions and standards in Turbo Prolog programming.

You also saw how this novel approach to simulating the `call` predicate for second-order predicate manipulation can be used to program missing predicates in Turbo Prolog. In doing so, you developed a pattern that can be used to design many "normal" Prolog built-in predicates that are not part of Turbo Prolog.

Closing Comments

You have reached the end of your exploration of some of the more powerful aspects of Turbo Prolog. I hope you have learned something and enjoyed the experience.

If you were able to add a trick to your Turbo Prolog programming repertoire or if you found your interest in the language or in artificial intelligence stimulated by what you've read, my efforts will have been well rewarded.

Listing 22-1

```
/* Standard domain suggestions follow */

domains
  key        = cr;esc;break;tab;btab;del;bdel;ins;end;
     home;
     fkey(integer);up;down;left;right;char(CHAR);other
  list       = list_node*

/*                                                   */
/*   I suggest the following standard when a functor
is needed to recognize a domain:
     Make the functor the same as the domain name.
The following is suggested when a second-order
predicate (one that naturally takes a predicate
as an argument) is needed:
     Define the predicate argument as a symbol.
     Define two auxiliary predicates for the second-
     order predicate with the names
          <auxiliary predicate>_package_call
          <auxiliary predicate>_call
     that has as a first argument the symbol and
     clauses to dispatch to predicates with names
     equal to the symbol name.
The first auxiliary predicate is used to dispatch within
the package; the second is used to dispatch to
application provided predicates.
*/

predicates
  append(list,list,list)
  reduce(symbol,list,list_node,list_node)
```

Listing 22-1 (cont.)

```
    reduce_call(symbol,list_node,list_node,list_node)
    reduce_package_call(symbol,list_node,list_node,
      list_node)
    sum(list_node,list_node,list_node)

clauses
  append([],List,List).
  append([X|L1],L2,[X|L3]) :-
  append(L1,L2,L3).
/*                                                      */
/* reduce is a standard LISP function for applying
a function to successive pairs of items from a list.
Here, it is used to show function passing simulated
by a symbol argument.  The example assumes that sum
reduction was provided with the package,
while dif reduction was added by the application. */
/*                                                      */

  reduce(_,[],Answer,Answer).

  reduce(Pred,[X|List],Answer_so_far,Answer) :-
  reduce_package_call(Pred,X,Answer_so_far,
    New_answer_so_far),
  reduce(Pred,List,New_answer_so_far,Answer).

/*                                                      */
/* Predicates delivered with reduce would be
recognized here.  If the Pred symbol was not
recognized, then it would be tried as a user-supplied
predicate. */
/*                                                      */

  reduce_package_call(sum,X,Answer_so_far,
    New_answer_so_far) :-
  sum(X,Answer_so_far,New_answer_so_far).
  reduce_package_call(Pred,X,Answer_so_far,
    New_answer_so_far) :-
  reduce_call(Pred,X,Answer_so_far,New_answer_so_far).
  sum(real(New),real(Previous),real(Next)) :-
    Next = Previous + New,!.
  sum(integer(New),integer(Previous),integer(Next)) :-
    Next = Previous + New,!.
  sum(real(New),integer(Previous),real(Next)) :-
    Next = Previous + New,!.
  sum(integer(New),integer(Previous),real(Next)) :-
    Next = Previous + New,!.
```

```
/*                                              */
/* Code preceding this line represents what was
delivered with the list utility package.  What
follows would be provided by an application using the
list utility package. */
/*   END OF TOY LIST PACKAGE CODE   */
/*                                              */
/* The following declaration would be provided by an
application using list utility predicates.  The domain
definition here provides a fully general definition of
list, given the domains available to this program,
including support for incomplete list structures.
The names used are the suggested standard names.
Applications needing less generality could restrict
the definition of items here.  (Apparently, the only
generality that is costly is the use of reference.) */
/*                                              */

domains
   list_node = reference string(string); real(real);
integer(integer); symbol(symbol); char(char); key(key);
list(list)

predicates
  dif(list_node,list_node,list_node)

clauses
/* Auxiliary predicate for reduce, which maps symbol
arguments to predicates with same name.  An
application would make additions to these clauses to
get other reductions.  The package should provide
"do nothing" clauses, to be copied into the
application code, to serve as patterns.  */

reduce_call(dif,X,Answer_so_far,New_answer_so_far) :-
  dif(X,Answer_so_far,New_answer_so_far).

dif(real(New),real(Previous),real(Next)) :-
  Next = New - Previous,!.
dif(integer(New),integer(Previous),integer(Next)) :-
  Next = New - Previous,!.
dif(real(New),integer(Previous),real(Next)) :-
  Next = New - Previous,!.
dif(integer(New),integer(Previous),real(Next)) :-
  Next = New - Previous,!.

goal
```

Listing 22-1 (cont.)

```
append([real(3.12), char('a'), integer(1)],
  [list([char('b')])],Y),
write(Y),nl,
reduce(sum,[integer(1),real(33.0),real(56)],
     integer(0),M),
write("Sum is: ",M),nl,
reduce(dif,[integer(1),real(33.0),real(56)],
     integer(0),D),
write("Dif is: ",D),nl.
```

Listing 22-2

```
database
  employee(string,real)

domains
  employee  = employee(string,real)
  list_node =  reference
string(string);real(real);integer(integer);
symbol(symbol);list(list);employee(string,real)
  list      =  list_node*

predicates
  set_of(symbol,list,list)
  remove_duplicates(list,list)
  remove_duplicates_aux(list,list,list)
  set_of_call(symbol,list_node,list)
  member(list_node,list)

goal
/**/
/* Get a set of highly paid employees, duplicates
     removed. */
/**/
  set_of(highpaid,[employee(Name,Salary),real(20000),
     real(100000)],Ans1),
  write(Ans1),nl,

/**/
/* Get a set of even higher paid employees, their names
     only, with duplicates removed. */
/**/
  set_of(highpaid,[string(Name1),real(50000),
     real(100000)],Ans2),
  write(Ans2),nl.
```

```
clauses
/**/
/* Mygoal is a symbol, to stand in for a predicate
name.  The missing first argument of the standard
set_of predicate is given as the first argument in
the list of arguments at argument 2.  Set is the
result list.*/
/**/

set_of(Mygoal,Arguments,Set) :-
  findall(Term,set_of_call
(Mygoal,Term,Arguments),Bag),
  remove_duplicates(Bag,Set).


/**/
/* Here are clauses to the dispatch predicate, which
recognizes the symbol that stands in for the predicate
you would like to pass.  The clauses are short here,
so they are coded inline with the dispatcher.
If they had amounted to anything, the dispatcher
would have simply called the desired predicate like:
    set_of_call(highpaid....) :- highpaid(.....).
To use set_of for a new predicate requires adding
clauses here and possibly adding an alternative to the
domain list for list_node. */

set_of_call(highpaid,employee(Name,Salary),
  [employee(Name,Salary),real(Min),real(Max)]) :-
  employee(Name,Salary),
  Salary >= Min,
  Salary <= Max.

set_of_call(highpaid,string(Name),
  [string(Name),real(Min),real(Max)]) :-
  employee(Name,Salary),
  Salary >= Min,
  Salary <= Max.

remove_duplicates(A,B) :-
  remove_duplicates_aux(A,[],B).

remove_duplicates_aux([],Sofar,Sofar) :-!.

remove_duplicates_aux([X|Rest],Sofar,Result) :-
  member(X,Sofar),
  remove_duplicates_aux(Rest,Sofar,Result),!.

remove_duplicates_aux([X|Rest],Sofar,Result) :-
```

Listing 22-2 (cont.)

```
   remove_duplicates_aux(Rest,
[X¦Sofar],Result),!.

member(X,[X¦_]) :-!.

member(X,[_¦Rest]) :-
  member(X,Rest).

/**/
/* Database with some deliberately redundant data. */
/**/

employee("Tom Morgan",60000).
employee("Ray Eng",45000).
employee("Tom Morgan",60000).
employee("Ray Eng",45000).
```

Index